UNIDENTIFIED ANOMALOUS PHENOMENA

A Beginner's Journey into UFOs

Adam Stephen Goldsack

SEKRECY BOOKS

SEKRECY
BOOKS

Cover design by: Art Painter
Library of Congress Control Number: 2018675309
Printed in the United States of America

Dedicted to the UAP researchers and activists who
never gave up in their pursuit of truth.

CONTENTS

FOREWORD

* * *

"There are no experts in Ufology" is a well-worn phrase, one that I have used personally when being interviewed about the subject – and this is true, given the abject lack of understanding that we currently possess about what it represents. We have knowledge built up over decades that includes case reports, photographs, video, official documentation and now footage from cutting-edge military sensor technology, but are we any closer in knowing the truth about just what is going on? If the so-called "Young Guns of Ufology" have anything to do with it, then today's generation may be much closer UFO disclosure than has previously been envisaged. Many of us, myself included, were latecomers to the re-emergence party of Ufology. Adam Goldsack, one of the founders of that "movement", was one of the first Unidentified Aerial Phenomenon (UAP) activists to break cover after The New York Times broke its now legendary story about the Pentagon's secret UFO program, published back in December 2017. As such, he is ideally placed to tell the story of just how interest in Ufology went from being a fringe subject, one reviled in popular media and among the scientific and political communities, to something that soon discarded its "tin foil helmet" image in favour of something much more substantial and appealing – credibility.

With the help of blog and diary entries made in the twelve

months since The New York Times story dropped, Adam's book contains a fascinating look at the rise of Ufology since the end of 2016, charting its highs and lows, heroes and villains, plus the point when the Young Guns finally killed the sacred cow by using the term "UAP" instead of "UFO". The use of "UAP" signified a new broom, one that would sweep away the trappings of the old phrase and all it entailed, in favour of adopting more rigorous investigation and a complete disdain for the lazy "no analysis needed because the answer is 'aliens'" approach that had turned me away from the subject during the 1990s and 2000s. Recent history is charted here, intertwined with the author's motivation in deciding to create meaningful dialogue via the Twitter social media platform without the stigma and lunatic-fringe mentality that pervaded long-established Internet chat groups and forums.

Whilst not a rehashing of old ground, "Anomalous" examines the pre-2017 UFO phenomenon, beginning with the so-called "Battle of Los Angeles" in February 1942 and then the "Foo-Fighters", which is my particular field of research. Adam has also looked at several cases from July 1947 through to the now infamous "Nimitz Encounters" of November 2004, seeking to combine his own conclusions with working hypothesises as to what they represent. Rather than try to prove that "aliens exist", or "there's nothing to this malarkey", Adam charts a much more sensible path, one which retains a healthy dose of scepticism whilst remaining open to other possibilities. No stone is left untouched, however, and Roswell is examined in the same light, as are the official investigations that were undertaken by the United States Air Force. Part of the appeal of "Anomalous" is Adam's unwillingness to be sucked into defending a set narrative. It's clear that he is simply searching for answers, wherever the truth takes him. For me, someone who is following a similar path, that was vitally important in establishing credibility. Adam advocates a sceptical methodology for Ufology, one that seemed to be seriously lacking back in the late 1990s when I tired of the flights of fancy included ad nauseam in UFO magazines, websites and VHS documentaries.

There may be no experts in Ufology, but there are voices that are well worth listening to, even if you don't subscribe to their opinions. Even complete sceptics should find something of value to read here. Adam may not be telling you that aliens are walking among us, but he is laying the groundwork for credible conversations to be had that discuss whether there is anything to the UAP issue. His examination of Ufology's sometimes kicking and screaming change from wacky side-show to informed, intelligent debate only covers the first year of transition from December 2017, and I hope to read further instalments from my friend and colleague on the trials and tribulations that the UAP subject has gone through since then.

Graeme Rendall
Northumberland, England
September 2021

✻ ✻ ✻

We are all searching for the great unknown in our own way. Maybe it's something we don't yet fully understand or perhaps something we simply can never comprehend. My great unknown is the 'anomalous phenomena', the potential for non-human technology and intelligence that show us that there is more to this world than we know. As humans, the search for UFOs/UAP technology and other intelligence(s) represent more than a search for facts, data and quantitative statistics on a soulless android computer system. It represents more than a search for extreme legacy that would see our names etched into the history books as pioneers. The search for truth represents something we all need at the primal level, answers.

We all have our own reasons. Some see UAP technology as the answer to climate change, whereas some see UAP as a potential threat to the national security of Western superpowers. Others see such extreme disclosures as the answer to some of the biggest questions ever asked;

'Who are we?'
'Where did we come from?'
'Why are we here?'
'What is consciousness?'

....and most importantly;

'Are we alone?'

These are important questions that have been at the forefront of scientific and philosophical endeavours for thousands of years. From the telescope of Galileo to the Greek papyrus writings of Homer and Aristotle, the world of humans has sought to understand not only itself, but also its creator God and the great beyond that extends past objective reality.

In the end, the acceptance of the UAP reality could change our world forever and our collective understanding of who we are as a species. It's a brave new world, if we can take it, but we must proceed with scepticism.

Adam Stephen Goldsack
MSc, BSc, Dipl.

✳ ✳ ✳

ॄ

INTRODUCTION

* * *

For decades people have looked up and reported strangely shaped vehicles in the skies that supposedly perform propulsion abilities which cannot be replicated through human technology. The U.S. and U.K. military refer to such obscure 'Tic-Tac' aerial vehicles as 'Unidentified Aerial Phenomena' (UAP). Although historical popular culture better knows them as UFOs – 'Unidentified Flying Objects' – a term developed during the Airforce's study of the phenomena back in the 1950s to replace 'Flying Saucers'. Regardless of the terminology, we are still no further forward in our understanding of these unknowns some 70 years later. Our commonly held scientific understanding of physics allows no credible debate on anomalous phenomena, primarily, as the standard for proof exceeds the standard of evidence. However, this is a ridiculous notion from start to finish as we haven't even begun to openly investigate the phenomena, and yet, we are imposing hypothetical barriers of evidence to dismiss investigating in the first place. Perhaps it opens a conversation that most scientists are not ready to have (particularly astronomers) and perhaps the stigma of a non-human intelligence is mortifying for our collective ego.

Sadly, amateur 'Ufology' research regarding the phenomιa is drowning in a pool of poor discernment, credulity and psychological stigma. Worse still, the entire mainstream perception of unidentified anomalous vehicles has become focused on one solitary, unhelpful concept - that of *extra-ter-restrials*. We need a better strategy. Forget about aliens, forget about the extra-terrestrials from 'planet Zeno' and forget anything you think you know about UFOs. We need to grow up and introduce science, not pseudo-science to a higly complex phenomenom.

The baseline theme throughout this book demands a sceptical and scientific approach to the anomalous phenomena, that holds both 'believers' and 'debunkers' to account for poorly applied research methodologies.

So, you might forgive me for asking the difficult question of UAP, the only question that matters, that weird question, that extremely stigmatised question – *what are UAP?*

In an obscure way I've always been looking for a very specific answer these last few years, although strangely enough, maybe I'm not looking for the existence of life on other planets. Perhaps it's more a question of UAP technology, and the great beyond, other mysterious realities and unseen worlds that one day might free us from our dogmatic pscyhological barriers. After all, we are all confined prisoners of this reality. We follow the laws which direct us, influence us and demand our obedience. To break free from conservative conversation we must be willing to roll the dice and take a chance on what we don't understand, ask difficult questions that haven't been asked before and think differently.

This book sets out to tell the story of the UAP revolution from the early AATIP (Pentagon's UFO program) days in 2017, the role of Tom Delonge and TTSA, the history of how the American government engaged the phenomena, the historical reports, and the radical anomalous technology and possible intelligences. This was my crazy journey into UFOs. A beginner's journey.

Another major theme of this book is human consciousness and the interlinking psychology of the anomalous phenomena – I wanted to examine the how and why. I wanted to know if the two variables are mutually exclusive, or if humans and the anomalous have a symbiotic quantum relationship.

So, in a way, the existence of UAP means more to me than simply looking to the stars and wondering about our place within it, maybe it should mean we wonder about our place without *them.*

TUESDAY
06th of April, 2021
"I don't know."

I initially wrote this introduction for the UAP organisation *UAPMedia* with the intention of looking forward and also of looking backward. Most of my published articles on UAP have come through UAPMedia and I have taken much inspiration from the team of researchers and activists.

This book is based on those blog articles, websites and the diaries I kept in the year 2018 - the first year I researched UAP. For in that timeframe, we did not know what this anomalous phenomenon technology was or where it was from, but we do know what defines it.

'They' are a genuine modern-day mystery for us humans, set in an era of transition that proceeded the Second World War and before hyper advanced artificial intelligence technology would allow us to determine objective reality beyond reproach. The anomalous phenomena are a source of great intrigue and at the same time, a source of great uncertainty, maybe even a projected collective fear. They are a source of impossibility and impracticality whilst also being a possible technological answer to many of our existential issues that threaten our existence as a species on this planet. For less than a hundred years we have been engaged by something anomalous, something that comes and goes at will, something that displays incredible propulsion abilities, that travels through space, time, low atmosphere and the world's oceans without issue, and without any form of resistance. These vehicles can make a 90 degree right angled turn, they engage military personnel, they engage civilians of all background, with race, age, sex and culture being no barrier. It was, and still is a technology that we cannot reproduce in the early 21st century, never mind the mid-to early 20th century when they are said to have first appeared. And yet, the UFO reports came through in their thousands, year after year, decade after decade, and still, we as a species struggle to psychologically accept the objective reality.

We do not know who or what they are, however, we do know what they can do, thanks to a man named Luis. There are currently five acknowledged technological abilities that the UAP display, known as the five 'AATIP' observables (1), which have been reportedly displayed by the 'Tic-Tac' vehicles that engaged the U.S.S. Nimitz in 2004 (2). I would expect other undisclosed abilities to be added in the years to come (The ability to change structural shape during travel – 'Trans-Morphia', etc).

1). Hypersonic Velocity (without signatures)
2). Anti-Gravity
3). Instantaneous Acceleration
4). Low Observability
5). Trans-Medium Travel

These are the core makeup of what anomalous technology can do, as stated by Luis Elizondo - the confirmed former Director of the Pentagon's UAP program, The Advanced Aerospace Threat Identification Program (AATIP) (3), (4), (5). As stated already, a good example of this technology in use would be the 'Tic-Tac' vehicles (plural). As reports state, the vehicles display amazing abilities of hypersonic velocity, anti-gravity, instantaneous acceleration and possibly even *retro-causality* (the ability to know where the fighter jet would be before it was). These abilities disclosed from the 2004 U.S.S. Nimitz incursion case (2), that was reported by The New York Times in 2017. These unique abilities were displayed by a forty-foot white 'Tic-Tac' object that somehow manoeuvred without wings or propellers, rocket thrust or any other means of obvious propulsion.

A technology we didn't have in 2004 (or at time of writing in 2018, and in 2021). Unidentified anomalous vehicles, such as that of the 'Tic-Tac', or the other now famous UAP – the fuzzy looking black and white 'Flying Disc' type shape that was captured in the January 2015 'GIMBAL' video, are historic in the world of UFO/UAP research. These were the first genuine videos of something *unexplainable,* verified by the U.S. military in 2020 and still to this day, remain unexplained and officially classified as 'Unidentified'.

Think about that for a minute.

How can aerial vehicles in today's age of advanced military surveillance, with radar and microscopic camera facilities, be unable to identify an aerial vehicle as it engages nuclear strike groups?

'GIMBAL', not to be confused with the 'Tic-Tac/FLIR1' video, was also confirmed as a genuine Navy video by the Department of Defense (DoD) in April 2020 (6) and was classified as 'Unidentified' by the DoD. It must be said that such technology should be further classified as something *'Unidentifiable'* given the extreme capabilities we simply cannot reproduce.

More appropriately, UAP should transcend the stigmatised unidentified label, and thus be officially referred to as 'Anomalous' – a genuine terminology for potential 'non-human' technology and even intelligences.

The recent military and navy cases that have made front page headlines do not tell the full story of these anomalous objects that out-performed the most sophisticated fighter jets ever built by the U.S. Department of Defense contractors of

Lockheed Martin and Boeing.

Also, the UAP problem didn't start and finish with the three declassified UAP videos. If we look back through the tens-of-thousands of civilian reports spanning the 20th century, we get an idea of the sheer volume of similar encounters. The national UFO reporting centre (7) and the Mutual UFO Network (8) have an estimated 10'000 reports annually. Now that is not to say that this is how many genuine *unidentifiable* anomalous craft are engaging civilians annually, but they do indicate reports of 'Flying Discs', 'Spheres', 'Triangles', 'Cubes', 'Cylinders', 'Pyramids', 'Orbs', and anything else flying at incredible speeds in a way which simply isn't aerodynamic as we understand it. Without question, the reported technology of these anomalous vehicles is beyond what we can replicate today in the early 21st century, unfortunately we have no specific government acknowledgment of these civilian reports, only military cases from recent years. I would advise anyone to take some time and look at the reports that go back to the 1940s. The same objects that are being reported by navy pilots to this very day you will find throughout history in civilian reports, and in the reports of Project Bluebook (the U.S. government program that studied UFOs in the 1950s). For these UFOs have a 70-year history that span back to the 'Foo Fighters' and 'Ghost Rockets' of the World War Two era, and more specifically, to the first nuclear bomb that was detonated in the New Mexico desert on the 16th of July, 1945 - just a few months prior to Hiroshima and Nagasaki in Japan. Almost by direct correlation, the UFO/UAP issue and nuclear age seemed to be intimately correlated with many associated encounters between anomalous technology and nuclear facilities (9), (10).

This is not to say that strange unidentifiable phenomena weren't reported throughout history prior to the 1940s, or that the nuclear connection was the beginning of incursions, but the intensity and dimensions of what was being seen dramatically shifted in the 20th century. The birth of the 'Flying Saucer' age had been discharged into our reality and was instantly associated prematurely as being '*spacemen from another world*'. Additionally, the UFO/UAP issue in early 1950s America became so frequently common that it became part of the pop culture. A space-age mythology that has its routes in fact, not fiction.

Most significantly, it was the July 1952 incursions over Washington D.C. by unknown objects that outran fighter planes (11), (12), and forced the U.S. government to charge the Airforce with taking seriously the phenomenon. Project Bluebook (1952 - 1969) was created on the back of previous investigation programs, Project Sign – originally called Saucer (1947 - 1949) and Project Grudge (1949) whose mandate, it was believed by multiple researchers, was to act as public relation management scheme, rather than a scientific investigative body. When one looks through the case files of Project Bluebook (13), it becomes clear that there was something significant in the skies over America. Whatever they might have been was irrelevant, the fact was, something was there, and that something was being reported over and over. What was certain is that the conclusions of the Airforce didn't match the data that was being reported, and seemingly this was intended as a way to deceive the public. Dismiss, downplay, ridicule and ignore was the policy when it came to 'UFOs' and 'Flying Saucers'. A policy which stretched through the 20th century and right up to the start of AATIP, Elizondo, Mellon and the 'UAP Revolution' from December 2017. Despite the denials and disinformation, pushback and claims of 'conspiracy', it was difficult to know exactly what world governments knew about the phenomenon. With this in mind, it would be foolish of me to discount the argument that some special access programs existed, studying the possibility of exotic materials and other collected data. It would be foolish to consider that this phenomenon exists without someone, somewhere collecting information in secret, under heavy classification, possibly in some dark corner of an Airforce contractor's laboratory or underground bunker. However, simply put, we don't know that, and we certainly can't prove that. We don't know what was done by any government, what they know or what they might have in their possession. And if we can't prove it, basically, it doesn't exist as a concept in the eyes of the public sphere, the mainstream media and the executive branch of a democratic government.

What we can prove is that after Project Bluebook ended in 1969 there was a UFO program that ran from 2007-2012, and that was the Advanced Aerospace Threat Identification Program (AATIP). The AATIP disclosure was the start, quickly proceeded by the AAWSAP revelations in 2018. Disclosed by The New York Times (3) and Politico (4) articles from December 2017, we officially learnt that the United States was still investigating UFOs, although there was now a new terminology, a less stigmatised concept, borrowed from the British – UAP. It was the start of a revolution, the spark we needed, the reframing of a much-needed conversation that allowed people to finally sidestep the fear of being labelled a 'conspiracy theorist' and challenge government to take the issue seriously and openly. It allowed the discussion to take place across the world, in workplaces, pubs and bars, in the gym, amongst friends and family. For the first time since the end of Project Bluebook, the stigma of Unidentified Flying Objects had been partially removed.

That's how it all started, on December 16th, 2017. The AATIP revelation by The New York Times acted as a catalyst, sparking a domino effect that engaged politicians and journalists, researchers and activists. But the problem still remained, at least in part, in the form of stigma. The issue of UFOs had been heavily laden with psychological barriers, stereotypes of tin-foil hat wearing conspiracy theorists who bounced from 'Deep State', 'Flat Earth' to '9-11', 'Fake Moon Landings' and 'Area 51' - it was all the same to the public. It was all unverifiable and unsourced, it was all baseless crazy stories with bullshit Gurus with a seminar retreat to sell and a book to write (irony not lost). Over 70 years the topic had become a self-sustaining multi-million-pound industry with conferences, seminars, retreats, webinars, books, films, apps and a variety of merchandise. Not that I'm saying there is anything wrong with making money in a capitalistic society, but not at the expense of an issue that should be placed within academia and government institutions. There was a huge financial market to exploit the true 'believers', in fact there are hundreds of thousands of people interested in Ufology, UFOs and 'Aliens', but very little interested in objective truth beyond the baseline concept that UFOs equalled extra-terrestrials.

Assumptions of alternative UAP origin were seen by some as counterproductive, muddying the waters to what the UFO field had already worked out.

And that was a problem. Researchers weren't actually researchers; they didn't hold degrees or educational attainment to merit their self-fulfilled status of a Ufologist. Researchers hadn't studied for years and taken qualified seminars on logistical regression, quantitative analysis or even been trained in qualitative interview techniques that searched for truth statements devoid of leading questions. The result was researcher bias. Any missing data was filled with personal expectations rather than objective scientific methodology. And this applied to 'debunkers' as well as 'believers'. Most self-titled 'sceptics' simply didn't have the educational background across the board to ensure the research of debunking UFOs was done professionally. Those that did have a professional background still were prone to biased narrative building, so desperate in their attempts to prove the phenomena wasn't extra-terrestrials. And that was a major problem for me when trying to answer the question in 2017. The data from both sides within Ufology wasn't reliable enough due to the poor methodological approach applied, and consequently, the field needed strong critical evaluation.

* * *

Conclusions

From 2017 to present day, from the research teams at 'UAPinfo' to 'The Unidentified' and most recently 'UAPMedia', I set out not only to ask the UFO/UAP question, but also to change the dynamics of how UAP are considered, to implement UAP terminology, to engage mainstream media, to build a social media network platform which could hold a credible conversation free of conspiracy, poor research methodology, and finally, to create a form of narrative free activism that would push governments and media to take seriously the issue after seventy years. We have spoken with journalists, media organisations, scientists, astronomers, physicists, intelligence agents, directors of national security programs and political figures, all in the hope of trying to answer the one thing that matters above all else. We try to propose hypothetical answers and more importantly hypothetical questions as we ask;

'What are UAP?'

Well, that is a long and complex question to answer, but one that we will try to investigate the best we can within this series of semi-autobiographical research-based books alongside documenting the research and activism efforts.

As a starting point, I will say this.

"...we simply don't know what the phenomena is right now, however, we must seriously consider that UFOs/UAP might not specifically be extra-terrestrial in origin, but they certainly might be alien to us. Not unidentified, but unidentifiable. Anomalous."
-   Adam Goldsack.

References

(1). Daugherty, G. and Sullivan, M. (20th of May, 2019). 'These

Five UFO Traits Captured on Video by Navy Pilots, Defy Explanation.'
History.com.
https://www.history.com/.amp/news/ufo-sightings-speed-appearance-movement

(2). Blumenthal, R., Cooper, H. and Kean, L. (16th of December, 2017). '2 Navy Airmen and an Object That 'Accelerated Like Nothing I've Ever Seen.'
The New York Times.
https://www.nytimes.com/2017/12/16/us/politics/unidentified-flying-object-navy.amp.html

(3). Blumenthal, R., Cooper, H. and Kean, L. (16th of December, 2017). 'Glowing Auras and 'Black Money': The Pentagon's Mysterious U.F.O. Program.'
The New York Times.
https://www.nytimes.com/2017/12/16/us/politics/pentagon-program-ufo-harry-reid.amp.html

(4). Bender, B. (16th of December, 2017). The Pentagon's secret search for UFOs.'
Politico.
https://www.politico.com/magazine/story/2017/12/16/pentagon-ufo-search-harry-reid-216111

(5). McMillan, T. (14th of February, 2020). 'Inside the Pentagon's Secret UFO Program.'
Popular Mechanics.
https://www.popularmechanics.com/military/research/a30916275/government-secret-ufo-program-investigation/

(6). U.S. Department of Defense. (27th of April, 2020). 'Statement by the Department of Defense on the Release of Historical Navy Videos.'
Defense.Gov.

https://www.defense.gov/Newsroom/Releases/Release/Article/2165713/statement-by-the-department-of-defense-on-the-release-of-historical-navy-videos/

(7). The National UFO Reporting Centre.
http://www.nuforc.org/

(8). The Mutual UFO Network (MUFON).
https://www.mufon.com/

(9). Hastings, R. (2008). 'UFOs and Nukes: Extraordinary Encounters at Nuclear Weapons Sites.'
Author House; 1st Edition.
https://www.amazon.com/Nukes-Extraordinary-Encounters-NuclearWeapons/dp/1434398315

(10). CNN. 'Ex-Airforce personnel: UFOs Deactivated Nukes.' (28th of September, 2010).
CBS News.
https://www.cbsnews.com/news/ex-air-force-personnel-ufos-deactivated-nukes/

(11). Holson, M, L. (03rd of August, 2018). 'A Radar Blip, a Flash of Light: How UFOs exploded onto Public View.'
The New York Times.
https://www.nytimes.com/2018/08/03/science/UFO-sightings-USA.amp.html

(12). Maccabee, B. (03rd of August, 2018). 'The Legacy of 1952: Year of the UFO.'
Richard Dolan Press; 1st edition.
https://www.amazon.co.uk/dp/1724594699/ref=cm_sw_r_cp_api_glt_fabc_FBEGQBMVKNQPTHSJCRSG

(13). Fold 3. 'Project Bluebook Files.'
Ancestry.

https://www.fold3.com/search?keywords=Gorman&general.title.id=461:Project+Blue+Book+-+UFO+Investigations

CHAPTER ONE: A CHANGING CLIMATE

* * *

B elieve me, the whole UFO thing is bizarre. At the time, there was absolutely zero intentions of me getting involved with 'UFOs' in 2016. My professional concern was adapting to life in a new hospital and in a new role that brought me to realise just how challenging work in the clinical profession could be. In a way the UAP initiative that was bubbling below the surface was in place long before I arrived on the scene. But like I said, I had no idea of what was coming, or any interest in UFOs, it was all weird fringy stuff that didn't make any sense. Never could anyone have anticipated that within a few short years, *UFOs* would be taken seriously by Presidents, NASA, Directors of National Intelligence, the C.I.A., Senators and bipartisan mainstream media. But it happened all the same, it was real (whatever it was). Unbelievably, the social climate changed around us overnight. We simply weren't prepared, but then how could we ever be?

Right?

***

MONDAY
25th of July, 2016
'*A new start.*'

T he week in which I started my new role at Radcliffe hospital in 2016 was unbearably hot, with temperatures reaching highs of thirty-three degrees on the Northeast coast of England. I arrived unsure of myself and very green on the clinical wards, and despite two years of neuro-rehabilitation under my belt I didn't know my arse from my elbow, obviously. That first Monday I nervously walked through the staff car park that lay adjacent to the old hospital. It didn't take long to weave my way through the parked cars and then through a swarming horde of flying ants that had taken to nest somewhere beyond the large rural grounds. The swarm filled the air around me, never intentionally threatening, but there, unmistakably, just above my head. The janitor would come to tell me that the heat coming from the fields and the sea air that drifted across the small seaside district made for perfect breeding conditions. There was an infestation of bugs as they buzzed and swarmed, it's what they did, programmed to be what they are. But more so it was the conditions that allowed for them to exist.

The surrounding coastal area was predominantly rural, isolated, with large open fields that reached as far as the treeline up towards the north, and beyond that was the chemical works, and then a little further up towards the coast was the nuclear power plant in Hartlepool. The plant was ironically surrounded by a restricted nature reserve, a sanctuary for poisoned wildlife in their innocent decay. Anything noise related coming from the plant could be heard, the sounds of industry carried across the open reserve on the far side of Radcliffe woods. The alarms could be, well, *alarming*, especially when you don't know what they specifically are indicative of. From where I stood in the car park, I could make out the tall flaring stacks that stood adjacent to the nuclear plant. They were big grey towers that reflected bright sunlight as they spurted flaming orange-red-fire hundreds of feet into the air. The grounds to Radcliffe overlooked a large rural area that headed off towards the Guisborough and Eston hills. The scenic beauty was not lost on me despite the looming towers of the industrial facilities.

A beautiful wasteland.

Working within a fallout radius of an active nuclear power plant is surreal, remember Chernobyl? The Tees Valley had historically been labelled as the land of 'Smoggies' due to its historical heavy industries, and understandably it is a less than endearing term stemming back to the early industrial years when the Tees Valley was engulfed in thick grey smog, not unlike old 19th century London or modern-day Beijing. Today, many of the old industrial works still remain, but thankfully due to improving output efficiency, the smog over Teesside has been reduced significantly in toxicity. Despite the beautiful surrounding rural areas, the coastal skyline is a Metropolis relic, a picture of time, frozen as a reminder to the heart of a dying way of life. We lived in the vile produce of a toxic wasteland that was justified in our actions, by our greed and by our reckless ignorance of responsibility. We are not responsible for our planet, and drastic climate change is a consequence of our sins. But there is hope, and things are changing.

As I glanced out towards the nature reserve, it made me wonder if there are hypothetical others who are here on Earth with us. Asking myself a difficult question about a hypothetical 'alien' species isn't easy, but nevertheless, would *they* ensure the survival of life if we cannot?

A question so far without an answer.

As I cautiously walked towards the hospital's main entrance, I was approached by an older man in his late sixties, slim build with an impressive white Santa beard but lacked the overt jolliness of his proceeding stereotype. He introduced himself as Marty, he was the janitor for Radcliffe, a relatively pleasant man who asked if I needed directions. I thanked him but stated I knew the offices where I was to be based. Once inside I was struck by the poetic symmetry of what hung from the four-story ceilings, a row of silver metallic lights, ironically shaped like flying saucers.

This was the start of a new era for me personally and professionally, in many ways, maybe it was fate that the start of the UAP era coincided with my own journey. It was all about to begin, in the humid shadow of the Tees Valley industrial skyline that bordered a protected sanctuary.

It was all about to start for real.

FRIDAY
30th of July, 2016
'Tom's Avalanche.'

By the end of my first working week at Radcliffe, I had settled into my role easier than I first believed I would. My life was as good as it had been in a long, long time. I had a new job working in neuro-rehabilitation for Radcliffe hospital, myself and my wife had a baby girl in the previous year. The bizarre night terrors and headaches I would occasionally suffer from at that time had all but stopped, and equally the weird humming sound I would hear sometimes late at night had thankfully become much less frequent to the point I barely noticed it. You might say the stress of being a new parent in a new job had taken its toll, but as with most things, it didn't last. Life isn't static, it's a dynamic process, full of challenges and unwanted surprises. And then just like that, for me everything was about to change.

You might say, it started with my wife telling me something out of left field as I listen to the morning radio play the song '*Avalanche*' by the rock band '*Bring Me The Horizon*'. It was that one Friday morning before I started work at Radcliffe, my wife randomly told me that Tom Delonge was bringing out a 'conspiracy book'.

"*Right. Who is Tom Delonge again?*" I asked.

"*He was in that band you liked, Blink 182,*" she replied, rolling her eyes.

Ah yes, I knew who he was, and I honestly found it cool he was into UFOs, having had a loose fascination with them myself a few years ago. And yes, I loved Blink 182 songs and had the albums, but never knew any of the guy's names.

4

After a few google searches, my interest started up again in 2016 with the release of Tom Delonge's book 'Sekret Machines' (1). Tom, it seemed, had always been vocal about his interest in the phenomena and now he was making alleged connections in government, relevant to the issue of...*UFOs.*

Ok. So, I semi-believed him, and I certainly didn't discount his claims. However, keep in mind that many people have made similar claims over the years - that they were speaking to people from the intelligence community about UFOs. And also keep in mind that most of these people were lying or delusional, or both.

The claims by Delonge didn't exactly sit well with the better-known career Ufologists either. They didn't like a newcomer rock star claiming to do what they couldn't. To speak with 'insiders' within government about UFOs. It was unheard of.

'Who is this rockstar?' some would ask on social media.

'He wants to call me to find out about real insider UFO info,' mockingly came the cries of others.

However, most people dismissed him flat out, they simply couldn't believe that government agencies investigating UFOs would ever get involved with the guy who would run naked on MTV in the early 2000s. Those who did believe him thought he was being used for disinformation purposes. The weird thing is that Tom Delonge was right, although we didn't know it in 2016, he would be proved correct over the next few years. Truth really is stranger than fiction. Despite this, pushback came early on for Tom Delonge, and all the while not only was he telling the truth, but he was a lot further into the process than people realised. It would turn out that he was talking to people in government about UFOs. Somehow, it was all very real.

Being honest, my reinvested UFO interest came in that hot summer of 2016, mainly because of Tom, something inside me knew he was telling the truth, as unbelievable and unverifiable as it was.

MONDAY
01st of August 2016
'Ufology.'

S uddenly, I was thinking about 'UFOs' again. Something I hadn't done since the disastrous 'Roswell
Slides' of 2015, (2). This was an unfortunate incident that
would shut-off my interest, and like some others, I was completely put-off Ufology by it - like with the Santilli 'alien autopsy' reconstruction video, (3). If I remember rightly, Geordie
celebrities 'Ant and Dec' would make a comedy film based on
the alien autopsy saga in the early 2000s. This summed up the
Ufology field, misinformation and semi-hoaxed events that
became stigmatised comedy within the media. The end result
was always the same. It wasn't good for getting people to take
the phenomena seriously.

It was at this time in 2015 that I had abandoned my
slight interest in anything to do with Ufology and the amateur
study of UFOs, I had stopped listening to the alternative radio
podcasts on YouTube (Steven Greer, Richard Dolan, Grant Cameron and Jimmy Church were always my favourite). Not that
I was ever really into UFOs in a big way, it was always more
of a curious sceptical interest. The amateur field of studying
UFOs was called 'Ufology' - to which I had taken issue with for
various reasons. Despite the good work by some investigative
researchers, the community had become a mismatch of scam
artists, snake oil salesmen and individuals with severe mental
health issues claiming to have travelled to Venus with space
aliens. But for the most part, the field of Ufology was flooded
with CGI hoaxes and faked videos.

A complete disaster.

TUESDAY
30th of August, 2016
"It's time."

By the end of August, Tom Delonge made an iconic appearance on the Fade to Black radio show with host Jimmy Church (4). Probably one of my favourite old interviews to this day about UFOs in a pre-AATIP world, although there was some convoluted information about various details that was stated by a well-meaning and enthusiastic Tom. Essentially, it was difficult to know what was specifically told to him by government 'insiders', what were his own beliefs and what was verifiable as real. To crudely summarise, Tom stated the universe is teaming with life and that it was time for the UFO conversation to happen, his words I believe were, *'it's time.'* How much of this was Tom's personal belief and how much was told to him were a mystery at the time. As the years have passed, some of those mysteries are being answered, slowly.

Towards the end of the interview, Tom stated that he had received a message from one of his government advisors, it read;

'If I say to you one day, that I no longer believe in the metaphysical reality of God, how would I answer a later question asking if I've ever felt the presence of God?'

-         Anonymous, Tom Delonge source, *Fade to Black (2016)*. (4)

Now personally, this statement got me thinking, I still don't fully understand what it is implying, but I think it is referring to both acknowledging and dismissing the effects of a phenomenon which one doesn't even accept as being real. Obviously, you would change your perceptions and experience of the presence of God to coincide with your belief system of whether God existed. As I mentioned earlier that statement allegedly came from one of Tom's advisors in government. And this leads us into another issue. The issue of being able to verify data.

With this in mind, the other point we should touch

upon was with issue with undisclosed government sources, a problem which had plagued the world of UFO research and would continue to be a massive part of disclosure initiatives over the next few years. A frustrating and clever strategy.

In the Fade to Black interview, Tom mentions the universe is teaming with life, that there are conscious beams of light floating through space. This sounds marvellous, but how can we accept and absorb this information? We don't know the source, we don't know how this person formulated this belief or if that person had data, and this is an issue.

For any field of research to progress and attain credibility, the foundations should rest upon solid ground made from open transparency and data which can be peer reviewed and verified. Despite the paradigm and culture of unsourced data and hidden advisors, the climate was indeed about to change on how UFO transparency was approached. It was time, as Tom stated. Something was being planned from within a small dark corner of the United States government - however fate is not without a sense of irony.

MONDAY
10th of October, 2016
"The Wiki-leaking ship."

In the world of political activist groups, Julian Assange and Wikileaks had long been heralded as the saviour of truth in the face of extreme government secrecy. They released the 'Collateral Murder' video (5), taken from Chelsea Manning and released into the public, despite the content being classified and considered an issue of national security by the Pentagon (6). In the aftermath, the U.S. government considered that Wikileaks were a threat and thus demonised in the media, but to the political activists on the left they were heroic, fighting for truth and transparency. The decade of 2010 to 2020 was one of a running battle between classified government data and the free-flowing spread of information via a newly accessible platform of the mobile internet. Almost everyone in the western world and beyond now had instant access to information in their pocket, no longer are the mainstream media bottle necking information. Wikileaks was the alternative option, and whether you agree with them or not for what they have done, the interesting point remains, they were unable to find and disclose the UFO issue during the official AATIP years (2007-2012).

Not only did they fail to uncover any relevant information on UFOs, but they also derailed the first disclosure attempt that was planned for 2016. Ok, so maybe *derailed* is too harsh a word, maybe shifted timelines is a better terminology. Either way, Wikileaks unwittingly played a part in the UFO disclosure process.

The Wikileaks hack into John Podesta's emails (7) in late 2016 did two things (besides effecting they Presidential election process). Firstly, they showed the world that Rockstar Tom Delonge had been talking to major people within the military industrial complex.

It was all true.

Secondly, the leaks torpedoed the formulated UFO disclosure initiative that possibly involved TTSA, whatever that plan was for late 2016 we may now never know. Ironically, Wikileaks, as an organisation that has always promoted the transparency of highly sensitive information, had arguably just ended the biggest push in history to end UFO secrecy. They were completely unaware of the UFO phenomena's significance or reality, seemingly they cared only for destroying John Podesta and Hillary Clinton.

The leaks that were dumped into the mainstream showed a few things that were of importance. For example, John Podesta was talking with Tom Delonge about a UFO project, a documentary in fact. They had arranged for Podesta to meet important people associated with running anomalous 'UAP' programs. The leak showed that Tom Delonge was telling the truth about his connections to high-ranking officials – unfortunately, the general who had helped him set up his advisor team was disclosed and outed to the world (I won't repeat his name here). That was it, the initiative died, sources went dark, and the entire game changed and was pushed back.

Side note, if you are interested in 'Roswell', - the leaks also highlighted that the wreckage was indeed sent to Wright Patterson Airforce Base in Ohio and it would seem an active program operated from that location, but then this is just my own speculation, or was it Tom's?

Getting back to the story, it appeared that Wikileaks did not seem to like Podesta, they did not appear to take kindly to Hillary Clinton and they certainly didn't seem to like (or realised) the genuine importance of UFOs (hence the possible mocking photo of a flying saucer cake they sent him over social media in 2016). UFOs were a distraction or conspiracy from other genuine issues, this was the thinking in the alternative media circles and the importance of the phenomenon was sadly lost on certain truth seekers such as Assange.

Hillary Clinton and others had been turning up the UFO heat, appearances on talk shows always included the topic of transparency, the term unexplained aerial phenomenon was even used. Mrs. Clinton was famously associated with the 'Rockefeller initiative' back in the early 1990s, which attempted to get President Bill Clinton to disclose information on the 1947 Roswell incident. In recent years, she has become the poster woman for the 'deep state' conspiracy theorists. However, despite the unfounded conspiracies, it seems clear the Clinton's did have an interest and did push the Airforce to be transparent on Roswell.

John Podesta was the campaign manager for Hillary Clinton in 2016 and the former chief of staff to Bill Clinton. He was also an advisor to President Obama during office when Tom Delonge was in contact with him. Seemingly an important person within the executive branches of government. Thankfully, he has pushed for UFO transparency since as far back as 2003, stating, that 'they' (the government) should open the UFO files to the public, as it is the law, and people can handle the truth. Famously, Podesta had also tweeted back in 2014 that his biggest failure was not securing the disclosure of the UFO files. He was not joking. You would have thought this would prompt a positive response from the UFO crowd, but it did not. For some strange reason there was some crazy conspiracies created to discredit him, people believed them and arguably the negativity spread, impacting on the 2016 American election. Even more strange is that these conspiracy theorists were alternative right-wing UFO believers, despite the fact he was openly promoting UFO transparency and was working the Tom and his team. It made no difference. The political and conspiracy crowd trumped the UFO disclosure crowd.

Speaking as a non-American with a non-political perspective on the Wikileaks-Clinton-Podesta saga, I can say I was disappointed with how politics impacted UFO transparency, which was unfortunate in timing. A separation was seemingly occurring between alternative 'far-right' Republicans and the Democrats who were in office at the time, with the then President, Barack Obama.

Presidential candidate Donald Trump brought about the ideology of change, a different approach and a challenge to the old foreign interventionist ways. He would make America great again whilst draining the swamp, a chance for America to balance the books. Terrorism and endless economically draining wars in the Middle East spanning 15 years and multiple countries had opened the door to 'America First'. The United States was approaching a climactic point, the relationship between people and government strained to the point of bursting.

Obama was deemed as aiding the old paradigm of creating terrorism with bombs that created economic instability through over-spending on foreign wars. Rinse and repeat. America's dependency on foreign oil and the petrol dollar was coming to a foreseen end. At least, that was the promotion campaign ideology of Trump.

The problem was that Trump on the other hand had no interest in UFOs. He was not part of the initiative running behind the scenes, and possibly wasn't someone who could be trusted to act in a way the establishment deemed responsible. Clinton was viewed as being part of the 'deep state' and believed was read into the initiative. So here we had a very bizarre scenario in which 'UFO disclosure' was overridden by political perspective. The old paradigm of war, terrorism and the deep state was not going to be trusted about revelations regarding UFOs. Too much hatred and anger bubbled beneath the surface, that to some Americans was seemingly more important than accepting official UFO transparency as a genuine goal.

I did wonder, '*why now?*'

Had something occurred which was forcing the hand. Climate change? Ending energy wars? The fear of civilian exploration and UAP discovery in space? We can only but speculate.

Tom Delonge went into shutdown mode following the Wikileaks dump. Any lingering belief about UFO transparency had suddenly transformed to a sceptical mirage of conventionalised normality. The status quo was safe, and UFOs were once again dismissed as they are so easily.

Too easily.

By the November of 2016, a sea of red hats dominated social media. Trump had won the Presidential election over Clinton and the hopes of disclosure went away. Within months of the election, Trump would pull America out of the Paris Climate Change Agreement and the world hurtled headfirst towards a global crisis with no means of stopping, and no means of healing.

All seemed lost around that time-period, the plans for 'UFO disclosure' had just taken a massive hit. I lost the slight re-interest that I briefly gained, stopped monitoring the situation and focused on everyday life. Without an official 'disclosure' plan, I was not interested in the opinions of amateur Ufology. For almost an entire year the UFO subject disappeared again, back into the depths.

It was done.

Disclosure was dead in the water. The world was headed for a global warming disaster, and nothing could stop it. And as for the advanced technology? It remained hidden in plain sight, us as humans, probably too incapable of seeing things for how they really are and what to do about it.

Or, perhaps, I was too quick to conclude with limited data.

* * *

Conclusions

In 2016 the field of Ufology was fixed to position, unable and generally unwilling to progress past the fringe bullshit of tall tales and hoaxed CGI videos. Ufologists *knew* that 'UFOs' were extra-terrestrials coming from another planet, which they might be, but this was not the issue. The issue was 'disclosure' itself, which had been a major theme since Doctor Steven Greer's (2001) press club event through to Stephen Bassett's Citizen Hearing on Disclosure (2013). Consequently, what Ufology wanted was an 'extra-terrestrial disclosure' acknowledgement of what they had already established, they wanted the government to disclose that 'Aliens' in 'Flying Discs' had been recovered and that the phenomenon was real, plus all the other versions of secret space programs, etc. What we didn't know back in 2016, is that there was a plan in place for 'UFO' disclosure, however, it wasn't going to be anything like Ufology expected.

It was never going to be 'extra-terrestrial disclosure.' At least, not in an event form.

References

(1). Hartley, J, A. & Delonge, T. 'Sekret Machines: Chasing

Shadows.' (2016).
To The Stars Media.
https://tothestars.media/

(2). Carpenter, L. (2015). 'Slides uncovered in an Arizona home seemed to unlock the Roswell incident; a riddle that has baffled UFO enthusiasts for years. But was it all too good to be true?'
The Guardian.
https://www.theguardian.com/science/2017/sep/30/alien-photo-roswell-new-mexico-mystery

(3). Largerfeld, N. (24th of June, 2016).' How an Alien Autopsy Hoax Captured the World's Imagination for a Decade.'
Times Magazine.
https://time.com/4376871/alien-autopsy-hoax-history/?amp=true

(4). Fade to Black. (31st of August, 2016). 'Ep. 515, Fade to Black, Jimmy Church with Tom Delonge: Sekret Machines: Live.'
Fade to Black. You Tube.
https://youtu.be/VzLqBx5lN8Y

(5). 'Collateral Murder.' (05th of April, 2010).
Wikileaks.
https://collateralmurder.wikileaks.org/

(6). McGreal, C. (05th of April, 2010). 'Wikileaks reveals video showing US aircrew shooting down Iraqi civilians.'
The Guardian.
https://amp.theguardian.com/world/2010/apr/05/wikileaks-us-army-iraq-attack

(7). Wikileaks. (2016). 'The Podesta Emails.'
Wikileaks.
https://wikileaks.org/podesta-emails/

CHAPTER TWO: TO THE STARS

✳ ✳ ✳

S ome things in life are simply unbelievable, and yet are true. For example, in 2016 Donald Trump became President of the United States in the same year that former Blink 182's Tom Delonge was working with people inside the government to disclose UFO information. The Wikileaks Podesta emails uncovered something stranger than fiction, that Podesta knew the UFO reality was real and was willing to act upon it. What Wikileaks ultimately did, so I was told, was to obliterate the 'Plan A' for UFO disclosure. The planners were down, but not out.

We still don't know who 'they' are but be assured they were a small pocket from inside DoD who wanted to get this information out. What we do know, is that Tom Delonge was again used and became a massive part of 'Plan B'. His company, 'To The Stars Academy' (TTSA) would become a huge part of the UAP revolution in those first few years that started in 2017. The 'insider' TTSA group was a huge catalyst with a distinct ability to reach into the mainstream.

Most people think December 2017 was the start of the UAP revolution, however, the resurgence began a few months earlier in October, on a surreal stage set as a media presentation, only without the media.

The era of TTSA had arrived.

***

WEDNESDAY
16th, October 2017

"A quiet place."

T he crazy story of how I became *involved*, and how the world acknowledged the existence of 'Unidentified Aerial Phenomenon' (UAP) began on a Wednesday no different to any other. It was just before five in the afternoon and if I remember rightly, I was in the kitchen, frozen in a state of superposition, unable to continue with my former life. So, there I was, standing motionless, watching a live stream from a Seattle stage without an audience, with only 16k viewers on Facebook. Tom Delonge (Blink 182, Angels and Airwaves) was on stage, although not singing, but instead with an assortment of suited people I had never laid eyes on before (besides Doctor Hal Puthoff). Interestingly, all of them were sat on stools in front of a night sky background ready to give their own personal live speech about something. The opening video presentation followed Tom Delonge as he introduced a very adventurous project that was to the layperson, bizarre. Then, as if giving a mini lecture, the team got up to speak, one by one.

The theme was UAP.

Tom Delonge confidently stood with one hand on his hip, his shirt slightly untucked as he set about detailing how this new company, To The Stars Academy of Arts and Science (TTSA), was combining Science, Aerospace and Entertainment. The idea was to provide people with an opportunity to invest into the company and build a perpetually funded system that inputs credible UAP technology and information into the world.

The starting problem was their target audience was mainstream Ufology – a rambling cohort of semi-delusional conspiracy theorists who saw the world as either a deep state psychological operation or well-meaning misinformation. Naturally, TTSA struggled to gain traction and the pushback was immensely difficult to watch. But I'm sure they expected such things due to the perceived associated link with the super evil 'deep state'. Although, we can ask if these people on stage with Delonge were bad people?

One of the guys was from the defense contractor Lockheed Martin (Skunkworks), another guy had worked in the Clinton administration, and then, the guy with the white goatee beard looked like he could punch through a brick wall without flinching, well he stepped up to say he worked for the United States government and ran a UFO program, right before claiming that the phenomenon is indeed real. Erm. *What?*

And, then there was Tom Delonge. The multi-album selling Hollywood styled rock star from Blink 182. The guy who was always naked on those music videos from my early teens in the noughties. Was this a joke? Were they all about to take off their pants and jackets on stage?

Thankfully, they didn't.

They were deadly serious, not once did they crack a joke, even when the tall guy from Lockheed said they seriously wanted to build a craft based on what they called 'UAP technology'. Naturally, I was sceptical but curious and pondered about all those conspiracy tales of TR-3B vehicles that supposedly came from Area 51.

Anyways, that was the infamous initial presentation of TTSA, and that is how it all started for me.

Although it took me a while to process the information, which was complex and highly profound in scope and measure. That was one of those times in life you have to see into the future and assess what it's all going to mean.

The following week, I set about researching who exactly these people were. I asked the question.

Who were TTSA?

- Tom Delonge: The Co-founder and CEO, I knew him from the rock band Blink 182 and from my early teens when I would watch him run naked on MTV.

- Luis Elizondo: Fmr. AATIP Director and a Career Intelligence

Officer with U.S. Army, the Department of Defense, the also National Counterintelligence Executive and also the Office of Director of National Intelligence. (1)

- Christopher Mellon: Fmr. Deputy Assistant Secretary of Defense for Intelligence. He served with 20 years in the federal government under Clinton & Bush administrations, additionally he was also a Minority Staff Director of the Senate Select Committee on Intelligence. (1)

- Jim Semivan: Fmr. Operations Officer for the Central Intelligence Agency's Directorate of Operations. (1)

- Justice: From 2012 to 2016 he served as 'Director for Advanced Programs' at Lockheed Martin Aeronautics Company'. (1)

- Doctor Hal Puthoff: Fmr. advisor to NASA, the Department of Defense, and the Intelligence Community. (1)

These were people heavily involved with national security, who influence the highest powers in government and are not conspiracy crackpots. Keep in mind, in the October of 2017 the general opinion of the world was that UFOs didn't exist, that they are on a par with 'Flat Earth' conspiracy theories. So, to see these important names was an eye opener, not just for me, but for some interested eyes in high positions.

Upon checking the official TTSA website (1), I found a few things interesting, firstly was the big unmistakable investment button and the amount raised so far. Honestly, it doesn't help with image when you mix money with disclosure.

I'll be quite up front and say I did keep a close eye on how the investments poured in, wondering if they would have enough to achieve their goals. Secondly, I found the team was made up of more additional members than those on stage at the initial launch. Scientists such as Doctor Garry Nolan, Doctor Norm Kahn and Doctor Paul Rapp to name but a few. To me, the standard of people involved were impressive and intriguing to say the least. When we looked closer, we noticed a few of the employees were from a *semi-Ufological* background, Doctor Hal Puthoff had links going back to Zero-Point energy and even was interviewed by Doctor Steven Greer some years ago, whilst Doctor Nolan was known for his research study of the Atacama humanoid and from the 2013 documentary 'Sirius' (2).

Steve Justice, formerly of Lockheed, discussed how they planned to build a craft based on UAP technology, Christopher Mellon talked about a military case from 2004 that involved the nuclear strike group U.S.S. Nimitz (which would go on to be the most famous UFO case in history), with the very first mention pointing to an online article by Paco Chierici in 2015 (3).

Additionally, I personally found the early strength of TTSA to be their ability to project highly ranked and verified government employees, people who were in the roles to which they claimed and a team which was academically the best in their fields.

Why now? What had made so many credible people from the Department of Defense suddenly claim the reality of unidentified aerial vehicles?

TUESDAY
10ᵗʰ October, 2017
"The end of Skyrim."

It was the day before the TTSA Seattle presentation and I had come home from work to a Huffington Post piece (4) on UFOs, authored by a journalist by the name of Leslie Kean. I guess thinking back, this was the very first time I had become re-interested in the topic following a few years abstinence. It was the very first article in the new 'golden era of UFOs', aka, the UAP revolution. Kean's article revealed to the world glimpses of what was about to drastically unfold. A teaser into a bizarre new world that even I didn't appreciate at the time. Little did we know that the credibility and interest of UFOs was about to surpass the beginning of the modern era that started in 1947.

So, the story goes that Leslie Kean had a connection with Doctor Hal Puthoff, and it was this connection that arguably got the meeting with the newly formed TTSA team. Now, Kean had a credible history of reporting on UFOs, from the Cometa Report to her 2010 book, 'UFOs: Generals, Pilots, and Government Officials go on the Record' (5). It came as little surprise to me when her name was directly above the HuffPost article.

Kean wrote in her article that she met Luis Elizondo, a man who had run a DoD program that studied *anomalous aerial threats* (4).

As far as I can remember from those early few days, the HuffPost article made little impact upon the mainstream media. When you consider the implications, that a start-up company is claiming to be able to build a craft based upon UFO technology and to have so many credible individuals with such high-ranking government backgrounds, yes, that is a big story. Then consider the concept that Luis Elizondo was claiming he had been part of a government UFO program and that he was stating the phenomenon of UFOs was real. How did the media react? Well, they mostly didn't. The few articles that did get around to covering the presentation went with the headline 'Rockstar leaves band to hunt for aliens'. The concept was too much to comprehend, UFOs weren't real in the October of 2017. And therefore, to base a theoretical concept upon something which wasn't even real was simply put, crazy.

In the article Kean refers to Steve Justice, formerly of Lockheed Martin who has the task of creating a vehicle that can display advanced technology. Such a technology would be able to move the vehicle through land, air, oceans and space with ease by manipulating the fabric of space-time continuum (4). If the guy hadn't worked in classified programs for Lockheed, you might consider him a bit out there. But the strength of his credibility and who he was became a selling point.

Regardless, I and others invested, I believed in their cause, as I do now. Something told me this was going to impact the world - as unlikely as it may have seemed to the layperson. Even to the Ufologists, this seemed to invoke outrage, confusion and a hostile reaction like I've never seen before. TTSA in those early days, weeks and months, were hated with a linked distrust to government. Almost immediately the wacky online gimmicky conspiracies started to circulate that TTSA was a CIA limited hangout, Jim Semivan wasn't who he said he was, Chris Mellon was a disinformation agent and Tom Delonge was trying to raise money to clear his debts by conning 'UFO believers'. The egos and fragile mentality were being challenged with claims that Ufology was under attack. And it wasn't just the conspiracy UFO crowd that were in meltdown mode. Believe it or not, thanks to UFOTwitter's @FOIABOI, we know that even Wikileaks founder Julian Assange would attack Hal Puthoff's credibility on twitter (6), due to the tenuous links to John Podesta and the 2016 Wikileaks hacking which ended the initial TTSA disclosure plan.

Thinking back, I do remember watching a YouTube video online about a review of the TTSA opening presentation with the host, whose name I can't quite recall, was very much raging with less than muted anger. He sat behind his desk on camera, tapping his finger and shouting how, *'we (U.S. government) already have the technology'*. It became obvious to us then, that TTSA would have to absorb seventy years of Ufologists frustration and anger, simply because they had ties to the CIA and DIA. When TTSA used a picture of a balloon to illustrate the 'Tic-Tac' UAP, it caused uproar in some Ufology subcultures, and in particular the balloon photo had some UFO radio hosts sharpening their knives. The most disappointing element was the treatment in Ufology of Luis Elizondo, a man who had stepped out of the shadows to bring credibility to the topic of UFOs, risked his classification status and ended his prosperous career to ensure the United States government and its people could have the conversation. He was labelled a disinformation agent, only to be defended in later months by Danny Silva, myself and others from our team (UAPinfo). We defended TTSA and their mission because it was something we thought that could help the world. Imagine that extreme UAP technology and it being the key to ending climate change. But these are just words.

As you'll come to see, it wasn't easy for them or us.

Those first few months were the hardest.

THURSDAY
October 26th, 2017
"Hard to watch."

T hen, a few weeks later, TTSA would be really brought into the spotlight for the first time. Tom Delonge went on the Joe Rogan podcast in what would turn out to be an infamous appearance (7). It was possibly the most difficult segment I've watched on UFOs entering the mainstream, not helped by the fact that Rogan didn't really understanding why Tom couldn't discuss the sensitive elements of what TTSA was doing. The situation was equally not helped by Tom talking about a TR-3B video from the internet, oh, and Atlantis. Again, let's not forget that UFOs were not accepted as real in the October of 2017, they were still pseudoscience, fringe at best. Add into the mix the ridicule factor and you have extreme pushback. When the Paris TR-3B YouTube video was shown, the conversation seemed to take a turn for the worst. The comments famously were negative, and overall, it was a difficult start for TTSA with pushback from pretty much everyone - except for a handful of rag-tag researchers scattered across social media.

Nevertheless, I followed Tom's Instagram account closely and even commented a supportive message on Tom's Instagram about the Joe Rogan podcast and Tom replied to me, saying he understood the situation Joe was in, which was big of him. I suppose Tom didn't need to be disheartened by the attitude of the world at that point, he knew exactly what was about to happen. He knew the path TTSA was on.

Things were about to change.

※ ※ ※

Conclusions

Tom Delonge's company, TTSA, broke the mould for many reasons. An aerospace, science and entertainment company that engaged the United States government with UAP transparency. Whilst Ufology raged and cursed the very idea that the big bad *government* could be trusted, others quietly and effectively rallied around the concept of disinformation. Some career Ufologists even claimed this type of disclosure had been done before and that it was nothing special. The truth is that TTSA were reaching further and wider than anything that had been done before and were about to provide a fatal blow to the secrecy. On the other side of things, the wild claims of TTSA wanting to build a 'spaceship' based on UAP technology sounded as fantastic as the attempts to bring the Pentagon to the point of acknowledgement. However, they were the only game in town. At least, they had the only players who had genuine inroads to congress.

Whether they could do the impossible would remain to be seen. I remained sceptical, but optimistic. The problem was that Ufology wasn't going to help us.

We needed to separate and create something better. Something different.

References

(1). To The Stars Academy Official Website
https://home.tothestarsacademy.com/

(2). Kaleka, A. (2013). 'Sirius.'
Sirius Documentary.
Neverending Light Productions.

(3). Chierici, P. (14th of March, 2015). 'There I was: The X-Files edition.'
SOFREP.
https://sofrep.com/fightersweep/x-files-edition/

(4). Kean, L. (10th of October, 2017). 'Inside Knowledge About Unidentified Aerial Phenomena Could Lead To World-Changing Technology.'
HuffPost.
https://m.huffpost.com/us/entry/us_59d-c1230e4b0b48cd8e0a5c7

(5). Kean, L. (2010). 'UFOs: Generals, Pilots, and Government Officials Go on the Record.'
https://www.amazon.com/UFOs-Generals-Pilots-Government-Officials/dp/0307717089

(6). @FOIABOI, Twitter, (2017 - Original Twitter post 19/12/17 from Julian Assange deleted)
https://mobile.twitter.com/mikeb8637/status/1270149542369996802

(7). Rogan, J. (26th of October, 2017). 'Joe Rogan Podcast with Tom Delonge.' YouTube.
https://youtu.be/5n_3mnJfHzY

CHAPTER THREE: THE ADVANCED AEROSPACE THREAT IDENTIFICATION PROGRAM (AATIP)

* * *

For almost two straight months following the TTSA presentation, the company started by Tom Delonge took the full rage of mainstream Ufology. Conspiracy and disinformation were shouted out from the UFO types who wanted the bodies of extra-terrestrials on stage, not Tom Delonge and his band of government officials. At this point in late 2017, UFOs we're still very much fringe, as was the tin-foil hat wearing reputation of those publicly calling out TTSA. With almost zero media exposure, the world demanded something more than an aerospace company dedicated to entertainment. Thankfully for those UFO enthusiasts and boffins, there was something momentous about to be revealed, something that would change Ufology, forever.

The Advanced Aerospace Threat Identification Program (AATIP) was about to become the biggest revelation in UFO history, even if it wasn't recognised at the time in late 2017. But what was AATIP, *really*? Why was there so much confusion and feet-dragging? What was the strategy?

The complex story of AATIP has always got me thinking. I've been back and forth many times and even the inner conspiracy minded part of my brain considered whether the program was created for the sole purpose of being a vessel for *disclosure.* By that I mean a government program that was designated unclassified (or at least parts of it), allowing the public to acknowledge and absorb the fact that the American government has been studying this anomalous technology. If that wasn't their intention, then maybe it should have been? Who knows? But what better way to bring in the mainstream media than to show that UAP was real via a Department of Defense portfolio that allows a public dialogue.

Regardless, I'm glad that AATIP was disclosed and that the Director himself took the steps he took. A genuine hero with a unique goatee was about to step out from the shadows.

Not something he was comfortable with.

***

SATURDAY
16th December, 2017
"The Golden Age."

T hat first day was wet, cold to the point of freezing and devoid of anything to cherish. My football team 'Boro' had lost *again*, and my hangover from the night before was only just starting to subside. My only solace was holding on to the fact that I knew something big was coming in the weird world of UFOs, thanks mainly to the social media posts of Tom Delonge and the rumblings of researcher Grant Cameron, along with other prominent personalities and UFO researchers who seemed to know something as well. I remember another UFO researcher and political 'ET' activist, Stephen Basset of 'PRG', mentioning on Facebook that something was coming, but no one was saying anything meaningful. But being truthful, I don't believe anyone knew exactly what that was, and certainly no one would have ever predicted what was about to be disclosed that cold Saturday evening. Again, the only real hints, were coming from the Instagram posts of Tom Delonge, and if I remember correctly, he posted a small audio clip of the pilot from what would become known as the 'GIM-BAL' video.

"It's rotating...."

***

It was sometime after five in the afternoon, as I ran the evening's warm bubble bath for my two-year-old daughter, a night unlike any other. The late December darkness had descended upon us quickly, ensuring our house was filled with light as it looked over the distant tree line, casting shadows as they swayed slightly with the chilled breeze. From outside the top floor Victorian window, I thought for the briefest of moments, I could make out snow flutter on the air from the frozen world outside. It certainly was cold enough.

And then, I just happened to momentarily take my attention from the outside world of the upstairs window and glance down to my phone, on Twitter some random account was asking Tom Delonge if the article was what he meant with his 'big revelation', the same one he had been building up to in the weeks prior.

There was a link to an article. Two of them in fact. Two 'UFO' articles.

And there they were, the articles from The New York Times (1) and Politico (2) hit the Internet. Everything stopped in that moment as I scrambled to read as much as I could.

The Advanced Aerospace Threat Identification Program (AATIP) had crash landed into our reality that evening, it would become the start of something that would impact my life in the years ahead, and everyone else's as well. Although it would be years before the world would know the full story.

We had the confirmed acknowledgement of a Pentagon program from the spokespeople that represented the officials within the United States Department of Defense (DoD). But was this what it seemed?

What exactly was happening here? Was this actually a

program that officially investigated 'Unidentified Flying Objects' like those we see in bad Hollywood movies from the 1950s? Was this disinformation?

Was this *'UFO Disclosure'* with a capital 'D'?

No. It was something else, and when you look over the official statements of the Pentagon in December 2017, they never actually claimed to run a 'UFO' program at all, nor did it say *aliens* or anything anomalous. Is that important? *Yes.* The confirmation that AATIP was an 'Unidentified Aerial Phenomenon' (UAP), aka, UFO program, came through the multiple sources of The New York Times and Politico, and through Senator Harry Reid who was confirmed to have created the program, (1), (2), plus Luis Elizondo who was confirmed by DoD (at the time) to be the Director of AATIP and various undisclosed DoD programs. One might argue that the Pentagon (particularly elements within the DIA and OUDSI, et al) were blindsided in a tactical move that saw them admit to the existence of a program which was semi-hidden from them, aka, they didn't know what they were admitting to, and they certainly weren't expecting the Director and Senator who created AATIP to openly say they studied UAP.

That is just a theory I considered which has not been verified, but in all fairness, might have some merit to it.

Could the true nature of AATIP have been shielded to enable an unclassified element to break free? That this would essentially break the tricky barrier of DoD acknowledgement, that UAP have been investigated officially by the Pentagon? I'm relatively sure the Airforce was pissed off.

What we do know for sure, is that whatever AATIP was, it started its unclassified public life on Saturday the 16th of December, 2017. As reported by The New York Times, the program investigated reports of 'unidentified flying objects' for years according to some Department of Defense officials (1).

Initially, Pentagon spokesman Thomas Crosson confirmed to The New York Times in 2017, that the program was dissolved of funding in 2012 by DoD, due to *'higher priority issues that merited funding'* (1). Politico had similar investigation conclusions, with Pentagon spokeswoman Dana White confirming AATIP *'existed and was run by Elizondo,'* (2) however, Politico journalist Bryan Bender went on to source an undisclosed DoD employee that suggested there was seemingly nothing to AATIP besides paperwork. From the opening day we see contradictions within DoD on AATIP, a theme which would continue for years after.

This brought me to consider a few options, the first is that these statements were made by the Pentagon spokespersons and DoD officials in good faith, meaning they genuinely believed AATIP existed but was a program for investigating foreign (terrestrial) enemy craft - which arguably is what AATIP was designed to look like for anyone on the outside looking in. The second option was that the Pentagon spokespersons and DoD officials knew AATIP, and Elizondo was UAP/ UFO in nature, acknowledging only half-truths and in some cases, intentionally downplaying the significance of UAP to dismiss the entire issue. The third option is that AATIP wasn't UAP at all and ended in 2012. Bryan Bender reported in the Politico that AATIP wasn't worthy of tax-payer money, according to his sources. Apparently, there was nothing there to justify its existence (2).

For me, this was a very interesting and telling statement taken from the 2017 Politico article, referring to that of an individual within the DoD who seemed to have direct involvement and knowledge of the program. These statements directly contradicted the AATIP Director, Lue Elizondo who claimed that they found 'a lot'.

At this point, I started to consider a theme of significant and intentional contradiction that was emerging in those early months and years which continued right up until the time of writing in 2021. I guess at that time we didn't consider that such an internal war could ever exist. Maybe we were naïve, full of *Ufological* hope and poor discernment. We hoped AATIP was the first step in government and DoD transparency.

I guess we all felt that way at one point or another.

***

A little after seven at night and after finally putting my little girl down to bed, I took the time to really investigate what was being reported on the front page of major newspapers. It was at this point late evening that I noticed that I had overlooked a second, very significant article in The New York Times. The second article focused on the direct testimony of two navy pilots - Cmdr. David Fravor and Lt. Cmdr. James Slaight. They were disclosing a real navy encounter with a UAP, which was the first time such statements had been made by high-ranking military people. The case sounded familiar; it was the UAP case put forward by Christopher Mellon at the TTSA presentation in October. When you look through the article, you find some very compelling quotes from credible sources. Blumenthal, Cooper and Kean report the U.S.S. Nimitz case from 2004 in which objects appeared at 80'000 feet before dropping to sea level and stopping at around 20'000 feet. Then they disappeared from radar (3). This is impossible technology for humans in the very early 21st century, and yet the reports remained constant.

You might argue a variation of debunking points, but ultimately, there are multiple sensors and witness testimony of these 'Tic-Tac' objects.

What I found amazing was the description of an incursion that occurred back in the early November of 2004. Lt. Cmdr. David Fravor stated that a 40ft long white 'Tic-Tac' object was moving erratically above the ocean and breaking whitewash over a submerged object, big enough to break waves. According to the Navy Pilot the water looked as though it was frothy with foam, as of the ocean water was boiling (3). There have been many theories of what this might have been including Whales, a crashed plane, a submarine and even a whirlpool. Again, no one knows and when the pilots returned to that area, whatever it was had vanished.

As the story hit the mainstream that Saturday night, almost immediately, I shared the British Channel 4 news story to my Facebook feed and argued the case. People joked, ridiculed and mocked me in the comments, *understandably*, the pushback was incredible, almost to the point that they thought I was trying to pull a prank on them and sell them in some 'Flat Earth' themed conspiracy. Stephen Mckeown, a renowned higher-class socialist from by hometown of Middlesbrough, commented on my social media post, saying I had been watching too much X-Files.

But this was all quite real, and people simply couldn't accept it. Even when I quoted the navy pilots involved, the attitude was one that acted as though nothing had changed that late Saturday evening.

But it had changed.

The U.S.S. Nimitz encounter would go on to be the most famous UFO case in history and spearhead the 'UAP revolution' - a paradigm change in world attitudes towards the anomalous phenomena, by which the world was finally starting to become aware. The 'FLIR1' video and the 'GIMBAL' UAP/UFO videos became the first ever government *acknowledged* videos of actual anomalous craft (although wouldn't be officially released by the DoD until April 2020). They were released by an unknown source to Christopher Mellon who brought them to The New York Times - who released them alongside TTSA.

Whilst the videos were eyebrow raising, and the pilot's voices really give them credibility, the leaked videos were still an uninspiring blur of black and white unambiguity. What the videos didn't show was clear cut HD visuals (the clear videos were used to brief congress) nor the undoubted instantaneous acceleration, but I've always thought they were leaked that way for the purpose of strategy, just enough to get people to look up. Awareness without focus.

And it worked.

Suddenly, the world's awareness was raised, bipartisan

media outlets ran stories with everyone wanting to know what was going on. Two genuine videos of UFOs had been declassified and released via The New York Times, 'FLIR1' which was a silent 30 second clip of the 'Tic-Tac' UAP (later confirmed in 2019 to have been taken by airman Chad Underwood), and 'GIMBAL' of which a short 30 second clip that seemingly showed a 'Flying Disc' shaped object (with the pilots involved still undisclosed). There surprised/alarmed voices etched into history.

At the time, I remember Seth Rogan (the actor who played the 'Grey Alien' in the film PAUL) even tweeted,

'And by the way, THERE'S FUCKING ALIENS!!!!!!!!!!!!!!!!!!!',
(4).

SUNDAY

17th of December, 2017
"Cold and frosty morning."

The following day was cold, snow fluttered across the roads as I worked across the Tees Valley, which meant I was driving around the county in minus temperatures. Still obsessed, I drove through the glistening snow and listened to the emergency recorded UFO radio show with long-time researchers Linda Moulten Howe and Grant Cameron. The 'Ufology' community was a buzz with early excitement, hoping for the revelations to build towards the long demanded 'extra-terrestrial disclosures' by the President and the Pentagon. An age old, outdated ideology. Some say this will never happen because there aren't any extra-terrestrials, at least not in the way we understand them.

***

That Sunday morning felt as though we had entered something new, something clean and something that vindicated good people, such as the Marcel family who were famously indicted within the July 1947 Roswell incident. This was the last time a fragmented field would momentarily come together as one in celebration. For the first time in 70 years, they were no longer the crazy people, they had been partially right all along.

The exuberance didn't last.

Over time, mainstream Ufology would lose interest upon releasing that their own ideology about how disclosure would occur wouldn't be realised, mainly due to how the UAP issue is managed in the real world. The UAP revolution wasn't their idea of a revolution. Where was the alien bodies and the crashed saucers? Where was the underground bases and moon bases?

You have hundreds of different, unverifiable extra-terrestrial conspiracies all wanting to be on the front page of The New York Times by their pushers. It was not going to happen, and AATIP was never going to be enough for mainstream Ufology.

Some career Ufologists would come to realise the implications of this new form of global UAP disclosure (even without the specific *alien* aspect), how it was promoting science and evidence-based practices, which wasn't good for business and eventually might absorb their cash cow and their sense of importance. Such Ufologists relied on the unverifiable nature of their claims to make a profit.

Then there was the ego driven Ufology old guard, who didn't want the TTSA Rockstar narrative to destroy their own work.

A revelation such as AATIP and the concept of genuine UFOs brought out the conspiracy type people alongside credible researchers looking for the truth. My focus at that time was gathering as much information as I could to understand what was occurring. Having followed the topic of 'UFOs' since the eye-opening Citizen Heating on Disclosure (2013), I knew that credulity that followed the notion of 'Aliens' and 'Flying Saucers', Ufology in essence is awash with a credibly reported unknown technology and the crazy storylines that try to explain it. People ask how this UAP issue has remained a secret since 1947 – a time when the technology really started to come onto radar - the answer is seemingly that the psychological stigma ensures no serious professional has touched the phenomenon.

Disclaimer: Whilst we can't dismiss the probable concept that some intelligence agencies have actively pursued and enhanced the psychological stigma surrounding the issue, the field of Ufology has also been starved of any credible data, testimony and most importantly, footage of this technology displaying its hypersonic dead-stop abilities.

This all changed over a weekend before Christmas in 2017. This was the start of the process, and it was the U.S.S. Nimitz case (2004) that ran with AATIP which made headlines around the world that weekend, even the usually UFO-shy British press covered the story.

TUESDAY
19th of December, 2017
"Whatever that means…"

W ithin the following week of The New York Times and Politico articles, the mainstream media and social media was lit. Some questioning, whilst others mocked and giggled at the notion. Some journalists went so far as to quote an expert (5) who adamantly stated the *clouds* within the 'GIMBAL' video were faked, and that the objects were misidentified jets. It was surreal to experience. As I would come to find about this topic, it was more about the psychology of how humans manipulate their own reality than the search for objectivise truth. Human psychology really is so important to UAP.

Others, however, with a knowledge of UAP incursions were more optimistic. Investigative journalist for the Nevada I-Team, George Knapp, suggested on social media that the rest of the mainstream was catching up on seventy years' worth of

UFOs. It seemed at that time that we might get what we had all hoped for all these years, *'UFO disclosure'* or a form of it. But it was the former director of AATIP that grabbed all the headlines in the weeks following. Luis Elizondo, the same man who stood up on stage with Tom Delonge and TTSA was now on Fox News and CNN discussing the fact that the United States government had a UFO program. Famously, he even stated on CNN (6) that,

> *"We may not be alone, whatever that means."*

WEDNESDAY
20th of December, 2017
"The first UAP case report."

T he most famous UFO sighting in history is that of the flying 'Tic-Tac(s)' spotted of the west coast of America in the November of 2004. The U.S.S. Nimitz incident is one of the first officially released 'UFO' cases unclassified by the Pentagon. The 'FLIR1' video footage, taken from an F-18, was first released by a German company in 2007 and then to the website forum 'Above Top Secret' (7) in 2007. The comments in the thread were speculative and conspiracy based and lacked any desire to gain further information. The very brief attention it received was dropped from the hidden Ufology internet forums and consequently wouldn't be heard of again for another 8 years until a 2015 article in Fighter Sweep by Paco Chierici. This was the first time we see a credible military based website discuss UAP technology and the extreme abilities. Chierici refers to UAP as AAV (Advanced Anomalous Vehicles) and describes how the AAV are tracked on radar. These objects moved away at high speeds, hovered and completed sharp turn rates with accelerations faster than anything known (8).

The next mention of the 'Tic-Tac' incident would come 2 years later in the October of 2017 as Christopher Mellon would stand on stage at the To The Stars Academy (TTSA) launch and declare that the U.S.S. Nimitz encounter was a very serious military case. TTSA gave the case the worldwide attention and introduced UAP to the world and even interviewed the navy pilot involved.

Then, two months later, in the December of 2017, TTSA (9) and The New York Times would release the same 'FLIR1' video of the Tic-Tac that was leaked in 2007, with the testimony of Cmdr. Dave Fravor and Lt. Cmdr. Jim Slaight.

Over the next few years additional data would come forward with other crewmen and pilots. But initially, it was very basic data in 2017, but enough to get us started.

A DoD contractor report would be released by George Knapp (10) and his team about the event and specific details of what occurred.

This was just the beginning, the war for AATIP had just begun.

* * *

Conclusions

In the December of 2017, the Nimitz (2004) incursion was limited with details. Today we have a lot better understanding of who was involved and the roles they played. Other pilots have since come forward alongside multiple crewmen aboard the strike group ships. Without this one case and its association to AATIP we might never have been able to make a dent on the secrecy. It would come to grow in the subconscious of the public sphere, changing the narrative slowly on UAP acceptance and awareness. The case was also aided significantly by Lue Elizondo and the acknowledged AATIP, which was confirmed as being a UAP program by Elizondo, who had been acknowledged by the Pentagon as being the director.

To me this was a brilliant strategy, *if that's what it was.*

Those in the Pentagon, who didn't want the UAP conversation being public, were blindsided. They unwittingly paid no attention as the little-known Advanced Aerospace Threat Identification Program and Luis Elizondo (as director) who was acknowledged by the office of public affairs to The New York Times and Politico in late 2017. However, they seemingly didn't acknowledge AATIP as a UAP program at that time. The case was built for AATIP being a UAP program came through the acknowledged director, Mr. Elizondo, the creator of AATIP, Senator Harry Reid and anonymous intelligence sources.

This lack of awareness was a problem for some in the Pentagon that they would need to reverse and corrected over time. Which they certainly tried to do in 2019.

Despite the controversy, AATIP was and still is a massive part of history. Keep in mind, the Pentagon are supposed to have stopped studying 'UFOs' in 1969 with the closure of Project Bluebook, and yet, here from 2007-2012 at least, it seems as though an effort was undertaken to assess unidentified anomalous technology. The confirmed director, Luis Elizondo, even stated that AATIP continued past 2012 and through to 2017 until the day he resigned in protest of excessive UAP secrecy and stigma. And contrary to some reports from inside the Pentagon, AATIP did find something extraordinary, in fact they found lots of things anomalous according to Mr. Elizondo.

This upset people within the Pentagon, who unbeknown to us at the time, would start a process to walk back AATIP, Elizondo, or the UAP videos and the mention of anything 'Anomalous.' However, it would be too little, too late, as various congressional oversight committees in 2018 (and previously) were finding out from program directors, navy pilots, DoD physicists and intelligence officials what exactly was occurring in our skies that shouldn't have been there.

Once you know, you can't un-know.

References

(1). Blumenthal, R., Cooper, H. and Kean, L. (16th of December,

2017). 'Glowing Auras and 'Black Money': The Pentagon's Mysterious U.F.O. Program.'
The New York Times.
https://www.nytimes.com/2017/12/16/us/politics/pentagon-program-ufo-harry-reid.amp.html

(2). Bender, B. (16th of December, 2017). The Pentagon's secret search for UFOs.'
Politico.
https://www.politico.com/magazine/story/2017/12/16/pentagon-ufo-search-harry-reid-216111

(3). Blumenthal, R., Cooper, H. & Kean, L. (16th of December, 2017). '2 Navy Airmen and an Object That 'Accelerated Like Nothing I've Ever Seen.'
The New York Times.
https://www.nytimes.com/2017/12/16/us/politics/unidentified-flying-object-navy.amp.html

(4). Rogan, S. (19th of December, 2017).
Twitter.
https://twitter.com/Sethrogen/status/943185352084377600?s=20

(5). Wills, E. (19th of December, 2017). 'Classified US military footage showing Navy pilots tracking UFOs are 'fake', says expert... but former UFO official says, 'we are not alone.'
Evening Standard.
https://www.standard.co.uk/news/world/classified-us-military-footage-showing-navy-pilots-tracking-ufos-are-fake-says-expert-a3723511.html?amp

(6). CNN. 'Ex-UFO program chief: We may not be alone."
YouTube. (19/12/2017)
https://youtu.be/-2b4qSoMnKE

(7). TheFinalTheory. (04th of February, 2007). 'Fighter Jet UFO Footage: The Real Deal.'

Above Top-Secret Website
http://www.abovetopsecret.com/forum/thread265835/pg1

(8). Chierici, P. (14th of March, 2015). 'There I was: The X-Files edition.'
SOFREP.
https://sofrep.com/fightersweep/x-files-edition/

(9). To The Stars Academy. (2017) '2004 USS Nimitz Pilot Report'
https://thevault.tothestarsacademy.com/nimitz-report

(10). Knapp, G. (2018). 'Executive summary of the U.S.S. Nimitz encounter.'
I-Team
https://media.lasvegasnow.com/nxsglobal/lasvegasnow/document_dev/2018/05/18/TIC%20TAC%20UFO%20EXECUTIVE%20RE-PORT_1526682843046_42960218_ver1.0.pdf

CHAPTER FOUR:
UFOTWITTER - ADVANCED
AERIAL TWEETS

* * *

T he interest in 'UAP' or *UFOs* as they were still commonly
known as, had skyrocketed in the weeks following The
New York Times and Politico articles in late 2017. Pockets of
conversations popped up across social media and Twitter in
particular, it was as though a mini awakening had occurred,
but only for a selected few. Until that point, I had never been
interested in talking to anyone else openly about the phenomena, in fact, I had never spoke to anyone on Twitter before
that point. For some reason it felt the right place to gage the
temperature of the public due to the accessibility to the world
via that social media platform. How I became involved in the
whole UAP-thing was a strange and complex story and in no
way did I expect to find myself pushing one of biggest social
media activism efforts in history.

Back in those early AATIP days, the concept of *#UFOTwit-
ter* wasn't even a thing, there was no team, no community,
it really was all random, unconnected people using hashtags
within Ufology subculture groups that had no affiliation to the
mainstream.

But that, was all about to change forever. Spearheaded
by the TTSA crowd of *'Fan-Boys'*, *'Disclozure Kidz'* and most in-
famously the Danny Silva *'Young Guns'*. The issue of 'Unidentified Flying Objects' received a shot in the arm like never before
with new younger blood becoming engaged and passionate

about UFOs. The beginning of the UAP revolution brought new ideas with UAP blogs, podcasts, magazines, artwork, gifs, memes, social media communities that all utilised different research approaches like never before. There was a change in attitude towards government, but it didn't come easy. To get there, we needed to change the old *believer* paradigm, the stigmatised imagine of UFO researchers within the mainstream - and that was going to be very difficult.

With the emerging UAP initiative, it seemed that the age-old Ufology mentality of dogmatic pseudo-believers and snake oil salesmen was about to be shattered by this newly energetic group, a group which wanted science not pseudoscience, who decided that didn't want to suffer the conspiracies of previous decades. No more tabloid rubbishing and money grabbing 'insiders. The 'Young Guns' group was passionate, hungry and took no prisoners. They wanted the mainstream to take the issue seriously from within government. If some old paradigm ideologies got broken and realigned along the way, then so be it.

This was the start of the UAP revolution.

'Fuck Ufology.'

***

TUESDAY
02nd of January, 2018
"The platform of platforms."

I've been asked why did I choose Twitter over other social media outlets to start openly discussing the topic of the phenomenon? Well, I suppose whilst Facebook was generally the platform that housed hundreds of thousands of passionate 'believers' and 'Ufologists', most of whom were confined to private groups, they were ultimately ineffective. What good is hundreds of thousands of believers if they sit passively in a private or public group that the mainstream won't touch? An untapped army lay dormant.

Also, when I looked over most of the content, they involved 'Ufology trash', completely unverifiable and unsourced speculation about men from Venus in the Pentagon and Secret Space Agencies that have fought extra-terrestrials on Mars. Then there were the fake UFO videos, hundreds and hundreds of CGI videos with questionable audio. So, you might say there was a problem with context from the start, and then on top of that there was a problem with scope and reach. Closed Facebook groups do not have the ability to reach billions of people in the same way Twitter does, however, given the conspiracy content of Ufology at the time, this wasn't necessarily a bad thing.

My personal feeling was one of complete disdain towards *Ufology*, and one that can be summed up by very small fragments of truth mixed in closely with inaccuracies and directed misinformation. This all was contained within a large echo chamber on a platform that ensured the genuine aspect of UFOs would never see the light of day. UFOs and Twitter, however had a nice ring to it.

Any hope of genuine activism faced critical issues, even with the credibility coming from the Politico (1), New York Times articles (2), (3). And in the January of 2018, we certainly weren't able to tackle them, a complete overhaul of how UFOs was perceived with would be required. However, despite such a difficult starting point, the future concept of 'UFO' activism was a possibility to me, even back then.

Maybe it was for this reason that I choose to develop the conversation on Twitter. Additionally, I didn't really understand how Reddit or Instagram worked, so, I personally decided to use a platform that reached billions, but more importantly, a platform that reached political figures, scientists, celebrities and journalists.

I envisaged that a small team (even ten to twenty active people) could input credible UAPinfo into mainstream articles using comments, likes, retweets, Gifs, videos. Even by developing a platform in the form of a hashtag - *#UFOTwitter* - could

UNIDENTIFIED ANOMALOUS PHENOMENA

unite such a group under one banner.

As the years progressed, it would prove to be an overall effective decision despite the problems with apathy, the stigma of being labelled an activist, and general engagement by old guard Ufologists. Plus, the problems of our interest and association with TTSA made life very difficult.

The conversation had started, and unofficially the 'Young Guns' of #UFOTwitter was in its early infancy. We created the start of an 'infant Hercules', a unique ideology of momentum that uses credibly sourced UAP data points that could be absorbed by even the hardest of pseudo sceptics and then pushed into the mainstream via social media. Instant access to billions with UAP information that was, believable and stigma-free.

In fact, the sheer believability of the data from the 'Tic-Tac' - U.S.S. Nimitz and the 'Flying Disc' - U.S.S. Roosevelt cases were so powerful that it made the debunkers look like the tin-foil hat wearing conspiracy nut-bags as they tried and failed to use the same old tricks from previous years and decades. Despite the best efforts of our favourite debunker, the conversation came in waves and the mainstream media started to become increasingly interested as more and more military personnel stepped forward.

Debunking a farmer's UFO sighting as crazy is easy, not so easy when a navy pilot makes similar claims and have radar and video footage to back up their claims. Undeterred, the debunkers tried anyways.

***

Taking the lead from Elizondo and TTSA, first point of call was to reframe UFO to UAP and essentially semi-eliminate the highly stigmatised 'aliens' and 'extra-terrestrials' from the conversation. The problem was old guard Ufologists saw this as a 'PSY-OPP' (psychological operation) to deceive the field, which I promise you it very much wasn't. We did this to allows non-UFO people, journalists, scientists and politicians to talk openly without the stigma, and it also allowed them to slowly come to their own conclusions that this may actually be a 'Non-Human' phenomenon. Once UAP was established and the terminology in place across the new UFOTwitter platform, we set about eliminating the 'crazy bullshit' from the parameters, which, was very difficult as most of our proposed target audience were still very much indoctrinated in Ufology and conspiracies.

Our only hope was to get our house in order.

WEDNESDAY
03rd of January, 2018
"The conversation had begun."

It was early January that an individual by the name of Keith created a twitter group, 'Advanced Anomalous Tweets', adding Jason, Sven, Danny, Tim and Christian. It was from here that my own UAP conversation really started. If it hadn't had been for Keith, none of this would have ever happened, and sadly, most people still to this day don't realise how much of the UAP initiative was due to him saying one day in December that he wanted to *'spread the info'.* Keith was a tech genius with a very creative mind, and let's say, passionate about the work that he does. He was one of the original founders of modern day UFOTwitter alongside Danny. Everything in Ufology was discussed from Bob Lazar, George Adamski, Skinny Bob to Roswell and the Dome of the Rock case (2011), it was a time in which people really started to open. And for the first time since 2013, I spoke to other people about UFOs.

For the first time, non-UFO people were taking a serious interest in large numbers.

***

The mainstream media coverage continued like never

before on early 2018, all of which was mapped by OmniTalk Radio Network which is still used as a reference to this day. Giuliano Marinkovic is recognised as running OmniTalk Radio Network and would feature heavily in the disclosure of various UAPdata points from 2017 onwards gaining him appearances on Coast 2 Coast. I always regarded him as a strong voice and a strong rational advocate of UAP disclosure. He was also one of the very first people to interview AATIP director Luis Elizondo post December 16th, who had made appearances on both the Glen Beck show (4) and then Giuliano Marinkovic's OmniRadio (5) in quick succession in the days following December 16th, 2017. In essence, Luis Elizondo reaffirmed the world he had resigned from the Department of Defense in frustration at not being able to get this UAP issue in front of the then Secretary of Defense, James Mattis.

As the concept of AATIP would become the norm, more issues came in January. From the off, the very title of AATIP itself provided a war across the field of UFO researchers. Attacks came in the form of the two videos 'FLIR1' and 'GIMBAL, claims that the audio had been tampered with, 'that's not how pilots talk', and that the UAP on the 'GIMBAL' video was a bug on a windshield, the clouds had been altered, that all the videos had been released before (FLIR1 was the only video that been leaked back in 2007). Basically, we endured some bizarre claims alongside some more genuine considerations.

Was the first 'A' in AATIP 'Aviation' or was it 'Aerospace'? The then confirmed AATIP director, Luis Elizondo and the New York Times both confirmed it as 'Aerospace' (2), whilst Politico stated 'Aviation' (1). After months of debate, it eventually turned out to be indeed 'Aerospace', following documentation from Sen. Harry Reid to William Lynn 111, that would be released by George Knapp in the July of 2018 (6), (7). Additionally, other congressional documentation would also verify 'Aerospace' (8). The on-record statements by Senator Harry Reid, who created the program would also go a long way to explaining AATIP's true nature and at the same time cleared up a lot of manufactured confusion. The conflicting statements didn't stop researchers doing what they do best, researching, in fact it made them more determined to disprove anything related to AATIP or Luis Elizondo.

Without the direct testimony of Senator Harry Reid, the issue of AATIP would have been buried and UAP exposure along with it.

MONDAY
08th of January, 2018
"The freedom of information."

L ong term researcher John Greenewald has been an important part of engaging the United States government on the topic of *UFOs* via freedom of information requests, and in many ways a vital part of the civilian research story into AATIP. He currently hosts one of, if not, the largest collection of government documents on the issue of UFOs. John Greenewald would come to play a massive part in the AATIP story in the years following the December disclosure, I personally would clash with him on various issues on UAP videos, AATIP and Elizondo. I found John to be precise, clinical but always with an opposing viewpoint to my own with regards to TTSA, AATIP and Elizondo, and whilst this back-and-forth conflict approach is ideal for peer reviewed research and finding the truth, it directly clashes with the very Ufology of 'activism'. After all, activism takes established information and exposes it to a wider audience in hope of progressing legislation, research however, is constantly challenging those established facts. Activism and research share both communalities and critical differences.

So, being honest, I never begrudged John with any genuine animosity in that respect, despite the wars over AATIP. However, the UAP activism initiatives never became solidified until the war over AATIP ended. It wasn't until we all agreed on AATIP that the fighting stopped, and the joint working began to hold those persons in DoD accountable for UAP.

What John Greenewald was able to discover over the months and years preceding the AATIP revelations, was that AATIP was a muddied water of official statements. Nothing was clear cut. Initially, it was found that AATIP was not mentioned in the usual government places you might expect to find data on such unclassified programs (6), whether this was a case of AATIP not being FOIA-friendly? Was AATIP just a case of the program being classified to the point it wouldn't allow for data to flow to the public? We had more questions than answers.

Another point made my Greenewald at The Blackvault, was that AATIP didn't appear in Intellipedia (intelligence server), until *after* The New York Times article from 2017. Greenewald states that the author of the information presented to Intellipedia simply based their information from the public news articles (8). To me this suggests that AATIP was very cleverly buried in places where others couldn't access it, and there are plenty of people who want to kill off anything to do with UFOs. Thankfully, the people who managed AATIP pre-2017 disclosure, knew how and where to bury it from daylight. Rumours are that parts were indeed classified, however that has never been clarified by those involved (as far as I know).

Sadly, this brought a lot of pushback from people who are angry with the government for various reasons. Some were the 'deep state conspiracy theorists' and others 'cloud cultists', but they all took the time on social media to attack anything to do with AATIP, Elizondo, TTSA and UAP.

For the next two years the issue of AATIP would be fiercely debated across social media and was highly claimed by research, not activism - UAP activism was not even considered in 2017/2018. It was almost impossible to gather support for something that isn't fully understood and debated within research, and AATIP was a symbol of this problem. The FOIA information wasn't there (by design), to show support for Elizondo in his claims of AATIP.

My own support and objectivity were brought into question as I fought in favour of both Luis Elizondo, TTSA and the UAP program through the very early platform of #UFOT-witter - originally termed *#TwitterUFO* by Danny Silva and Keith Mayoh (9) in 2018.

It's strange, but at no point did I ever even consider the possibility that Lue Elizondo might have been lying. Call it in-tuition, ignorance or naivety, either way my defences were up, and I came out fighting.

In the end it would be proved that I back the right horse.

✳ ✳ ✳

Conclusions

Social media exploded into life in early 2018, the birth of UFOTwitter (although not titled or accepted as such), had occurred. The 'Young Guns' of Ufology, headed by Akam, Aida, Ryan (UFOJesus), Joe Murgia (UFOJoe), 'FOIA Boi' Deep Prasad, Danny Silva, Keith Mayoh, Jamie, and Chris Wolford to name a few, burst onto the scene and ripped up the rule book. The unwritten guidelines of an outdated dogmatic Ufology were ignored by a group who very effectively used social media to engage a new paradigm of approaching the UFO topic.

And so, UAP terminology was created.

It was thanks to Lue Elizondo and AATIP that people started to open up and talk about their own experiences of the phenomena. There was an overwhelming feeling of unity, people who had never spoke to another person about UAP were suddenly able to have the conversation. Talk of the very first UAP (as opposed to UFO) themed website was discussed as a way to reduce the stigma and allow the public to get involved.

Social media research and activism had arrived.

References

(1). Bender, B. (16th of December, 2017). The Pentagon's secret search for UFOs.'
Politico.
https://www.politico.com/magazine/story/2017/12/16/pentagon-ufo-search-harry-reid-216111

(2). Blumenthal, R., Cooper, H. & Kean, L. (16th of December, 2017). 'Glowing Auras and 'Black Money': The Pentagon's Mysterious U.F.O. Program.'
The New York Times.
https://www.nytimes.com/2017/12/16/us/politics/pentagon-program-ufo-harry-reid.amp.html

(3). Blumenthal, R., Cooper, H. & Kean, L. (16th of December, 2017). '2 Navy Airmen and an Object That 'Accelerated Like Nothing I've Ever Seen.'
The New York Times.
https://www.nytimes.com/2017/12/16/us/politics/unidentified-flying-object-navy.amp.html

(4). Beck, G. (20th of December, 2017). 'Former Pentagon Official on the Possibility of Alien life: 'Evidence' is 'Overwhelming'.
GlenBeck.com.
https://www.glennbeck.com/amp/former-pentagon-official-on-the-possibility-of-alien-life-evidence-is-overwhelming-2566584643

(5). Marinkovic, G. (08th of February, 2018). 'Exclusive 60 minutes with Luis Elizondo – Former director of AATIP (UFORadio International #11.'
Omnitalk Radio.
https://youtu.be/zhvClGiBB2c

(6). Knapp, G. (26th of July, 2018). 'I-Team receives key documents related to Pentagon UFO program.'
I-Team.

https://www.8newsnow.com/news/exclusive-i-team-obtains-some-key-documents-related-to-pentagon-ufo-study/1324250087/

(7). Basterfield, K. (30th of June, 2018). 'That 2009 AATIP letter from then US Senator Harry Reid.' Unidentified Aerial Phenomenon- Scientific Research.
https://ufosscientificresearch.blogspot.com/2018/06/?m=1

(8). Greenewald, J. (2018). 'The Advanced Aerospace Threat Identification Program (AATIP), Tom Delonge, Luis Elizondo and the Claims of To The Stars Academy.'
The Blackvault.
https://www.theblackvault.com/casefiles/to-the-stars-academy-of-arts-science-tom-delonge-and-the-secret-dod-ufo-research-program/amp/

(9). Stahl, F, A. (2021). 'UFOTwitter: The small group of UAP activists who are trying to change the world.'
The Unidentified.
https://www.the-unidentified.net/ufotwitter-the-small-group-of-social-media-activists-who-are-trying-to-change-the-world/

CHAPTER FIVE: UNIDENTIFIED AERIAL PHENOMENA INFORMATION (UAPINFO)

* * *

UFOlogy - *the amateur believer and debunker field of UFO research* – sensed something was wrong with the UAP initiative. They after all had dealt with disinformation, honey traps and setups for as long as the field existed, so it was understandable that they were paranoid. When I say something was *wrong*, I mean simply *change*. The threat was there that something drastic could change how Ufology operated. Consider that the field, not really a professional field, was filled with opportunities for those who knew how and where to invest their time and energy. This was evident on both sides of the debunker and believer divide. The payday could be immense, financially, and through status. This was a goldmine, ready to be dug up, with thousands of willing, unwittingly deluded customers at the beckoning, ready to believe and debunk whatever their guru instructed without thought or question. I know that my words will anger a lot of people, just as the UAP initiative angered a lot of people in 2018, but it didn't matter. What mattered is that Ufology changed, that UAP helped replace UFO and that claims of extra-terrestrials were stripped back. To do this, we needed a new platform to carry that change, a social media platform and a home for UAP. Enter *UAPinfo*, the first major longboat vessel that carried the

UAP campaign up the narrow rivers of a disjointed UFO community.

Ufology was about to be raided, and at its helm was a Viking with muddy boots.

***

SATURDAY
17th of February, 2018
"Pushing back."

M y time was spent trying to gage the intentions of TTSA - who they were, and how they had come to be in possession of such delicate UAP information. Also, there was an opinion no at that time that another UAP video was still to be released, although no one would confirm it. And then there was Mr. Elizondo, a career intelligence official of high-ranking status within the United States government who had quit his role in protest of extreme UAP secrecy and stigma. He joined rockstar Tom Delonge and announced, '*the phenomena, is indeed real.*' To me this was a big deal, but to Ufology it wasn't, they had apparently seen this sort of thing over and over. Although, *no,* no they hadn't, this was unprecedented. Even Pentagon whistle-blowers such as Colonel Philip Corso didn't have such an impact.

Credibility of UAPinfo

The day after the New York Times AATIP story broke, a rather obscure oversized man popped up on the internet claiming to be an Area 51 pilot and that he had chased actual aliens. Completely and utterly not credible in the slightest, but the timing was almost too much of a coincidence, almost as if he was planted to discredit the real pilots. Most probably however, he was just a random weirdo whose type pops up often in Ufology.

Around that time, other stories were leaking to the tabloid press trying to discredit Mr. Elizondo, some claiming he had stolen the UAP videos, others attacked his link to Tom Delonge. Scepticism (pseudo debunking in some cases) against Elizondo, TTSA and the UAP concept was rife. Honestly, I only half understood it at the time, most was mindless drivel.

Not only were we dealing with the most audacious claims to come through a mainstream media outlet on the most stigmatised topic in human history, but we also had a prize trophy ready to be claimed by anyone eager to disprove UFOs exist and that The New York Times was full of rubbish. The gauntlet was thrown down to any disgruntled journalist and debunker to prove they could unpick The Times on such a 'silly issue'.

Everyone knows *'UFOs* are *bullshit'*, right?

Never before had so many pseudoscience writers and journalists popped up to debunk and denounce the topic, almost as though their own personal livelihoods depended on UAP not being real. Wave after wave of attacks against the videos, Elizondo, TTSA and AATIP flooded social media, as a desperation took hold. Like antibodies fighting a virus that threatened to infect healthy cells, over and over the shouts became louder and louder, something had to be done to stop this 'UAP nonsense'.

But unfortunately for them, there was no cure.

Mid-level journalists used ridicule and stigma as the main mode of defence, with the age-old narrative that anyone who *witnessed* a 'Flying Disc' must be a nut-job. Extra-terrestrials were pushed by debunkers as a predetermined pseudoscience to dismiss the entire concept. The mainstream thinking is that if an 'alien spacecraft' was here then NASA would know about it (just like in the movies), they would contact the media straight away, the President would announce it within hours and the world could act in unison - Amy Adams would be waiting by the phone at the ready to make inky-extra-terrestrial-giant-hand contact.

This is a naïve, childish view of how national security works in the real world. Unfortunately, the public haven't really considered how much of a national security *threat* such UAP would be considered by DoD and how they would respond. How do you have the conversation that a hyper advanced technology is entering your protected airspace in a post 9/11 world? Credit must be given to the field of Ufologists, despite their shortcomings they knew that this issue was housed within the dark intelligence world, with black money and compartmented classification. They knew NASA and specifically the DoD wouldn't pick up the phone to the media or Amy Adams. Quite the opposite. This created a cultured climate. A situation leading to a very poorly informed public. An atmosphere that aided unhelpful conspiracy over decades and decades.

When the first videos of UAP were released, it fed directly into this situation, and it fed into the pushback. The Department of Defense wasn't all on the same page as the very beginning of the contradictory Pentagon AATIP statements started to unfold. Whilst AATIP was acknowledged as existing, Elizondo was acknowledged as the director and although he himself was very limited on what he said, he did indirectly *infer* the videos came under AATIP. He was, however, very clear that AATIP was a UAP program, that is, the program specifically focused on anomalous hyper advanced technology.

The problem came through a lack of definitive answers from DoD, they didn't link the videos to AATIP and hadn't even acknowledged that AATIP was a UAP program – remember at that point in 2018 they had only acknowledged the existence of AATIP and Elizondo as director – the formal acknowledgment of AATIP as a UAP program wouldn't come until summer 2019 (prior to the start of the very real coordinated pushback).

Journalist Sarah Scoles asked these very same questions (1), quoting Pentagon spokesperson Audricia Harris saying the Department of Defense did not release those videos. Which was true, the three videos were not officially released, they were leaked out in 2017/18 and wouldn't be acknowledged or formally released by DoD until April 2020. Scoles also went on to question whether the testimony of Cmdr. David Fravor in the To The Stars Academy website (2) is referring to the same videos presented by The New York Times. Additionally, she questions if the fleet of objects off camera aren't from Finland.

They weren't as it would turn out. They would be classified as 'Unidentified'.

And that was just the start as the truth slowly made its way out to the world.

FRIDAY
09th of March, 2018
"A failure of intelligence."

Almost an entire month had passed with very little happening. Ufology was obsessed with claims of disinformation and the 'Tic-Tac' balloon picture used in the TTSA presentation - which they had got from the 2015 SOFREP fighter sweep article. I instead, became obsessed with what TTSA was trying to accomplish, despite their links to former government employees. I guess it helps that I'm not American and not influenced by what the CIA does or doesn't do, I also don't care for conspiracies. If these connected TTSA individuals knew about how UAP technology might work, or how quantum consciousness is involved in the UAP mystery, then I was all in.

And just in time.

The moment arrived. The third and final declassified UAP video 'GO FAST' had arrived via a Washington Post article, written by Christopher Mellon of TTSA. Firstly, as I watched it in my bathroom (where I seem to watch all unclassified UAP videos), the video struck me as incredibly underwhelming, another grainy gun camera footage in which some unverifiable object flew over the ocean. Keith from UAPinfo caught my frustrations.

'Well, that video won't change the world.'

The one main benefit was the reaction of the pilot's voices (incidentally, one of the pilots sounded very similar to the pilot of the 'GIMBAL' video). Of all the leaked three videos, it would be the 'GO FAST' video which would receive the most *debunking* from sceptics. Trigonometry would be 'proven' to show that the object was going slower than assumed due to the parallax effect. However, without further radar data it would be highly disingenuous to suggest conclusively what the object was, or how fast it was traveling. Of course, the debunkers made no attempt to request more data from government and concluded on a short blurry video regardless. Christopher Mellon would write in the Washington Post that the videos along with pilot's testimony provide evidence for the existence of superior aircraft (3).

Christopher Mellon had access to the relevant data and would liaise directly with the Senate Select Committee for Intelligence over those years. Through his interactions with congress and military personnel, he became adamant the objects showed something anomalous and would go on to help draft UAP legislation for navy pilots the following year.

Mellon would be revealed in later years, thanks to a James Foxx documentary (2020), as the individual who sourced the three videos from an unknown DoD insider in a shadowy Pentagon car park scene straight from an X-Files plot line. From there, they were distributed to The New York Times and the company To The Stars Academy. Mellon would then himself write an article for the Washington Post about the significant intelligence failure regarding UAP.

He additionally released the third video 'GO FAST.' Filmed in the January of 2015, the 'GO FAST' video is gun camera footage which shows a small object travel across the ocean, the pilots involved are excited as they exclaim '*whooaa, got it,*' as they lock on. At the time of writing, we still do not know what the object is, however, some claims suggest it is a sphere, others it is a 'Cube within a Sphere', whereas the debunkers tried to explain the object away as a simple balloon, that somehow the military weren't able to identify. These are some of the worst pieces of debunking you can expect to see ever on the topic, and sadly, this didn't stop other claims that 'GO FAST' was a duck, or a goose and that the most sophisticated nuclear powered defense technology in the world couldn't identify mundane, slow-moving objects.

Why does Russia spend billions on anti-ballistic rockets when you can simply send in rogue balloons or an errand duck?

As a genuine sceptic, you would argue for more data that included the pilot testimony, but as stated the '*sceptics*' or should they be called, *debunkers*, showed very little interest in pushing government for more data even months after the release. Strange how often that happened across 'GO FAST', 'GIMBAL', and 'FLIR1', almost as if debunkers don't want more data for some reason. This would prove to be a deeper problem from within Ufology, which we will discuss later in the book.

SATURDAY
10th of March, 2018
'UAPinfo arrives.'

B y the time March roared into season, I had been asked to both consult and write for a new startup website by the name of 'UAPinfo', which involved the same people from the 'Anomalous Aerial Tweets' group, (Danny, Keith, Jason, Sven, Tim and Christian. Later joined by 'Dregs'). The website was incredibly professional and set apart from the usual amateur UFO websites. Created by tech-wizard Keith Mayoh to promote everything and anything to do with Ufology, Unidentified Aerial Phenomenon (UAP) and AATIP.

My starting point was based in case reports and creating new qualitative methodology to analyse UAP but soon I would go on to write about pretty much everything from consciousness to ultra-terrestrials. The first few months of UAPinfo were exciting, riding the December 2017 wave into the future, a future in which anything was possible, maybe even *disclosure*.

We liaised with TTSA members, writing a positive article on the Atacama humanoid whilst taking a lot of aggression and threats from disgruntled Ufologists in the process. Incidentally, it was around this time that some individuals believing themselves to be genuine 'Aliens' from space (spoiler alert, they were human), started asking who we are, where we lived, to which I questioned how they didn't already know that if they were allegedly 'Aliens'. It was due to these unpleasant interactions over Twitter that I decided to use an alias, and with that, myself and UAPinfo member Sven (from Germany) created, Andreas Freeman Stahl – social engineer of disclosure and Duke of UFOTwitter.

We ran into other issues. Our assumed support and association with TTSA and AATIP rang the conspiracy dinner bell, this occurred in a time by which distrust of both AATIP, and Elizondo was at its highest. Our group, UAPinfo was accused as being part of a AATIP PSY-OP, and the gun camera videos were apparently 'CGI' (4).

None of this was true.

No offence intended to the gentleman quoted, I'm sure he was well meaning but we weren't what he claimed. Keep in mind those early months following December 2017, Ufology was still rife with the 'old guard' Ufologists who believed that if something wasn't a government, deep state conspiracy, then it should be. This was also at a time when President Trump had taken office and Q-Anon (a political conspiracy group) was emerging. As you can imagine, this time in history was drowning in the unverifiable conspiracy claims. 'Fake News' was on the rise which didn't help our emerging small group who requested science over pseudoscience.

UAPinfo was the first blogging website that broke free from mainstream Ufology and instinctual conspiracy. We dared to accept that the secrecy surrounding UAP was acceptable and even *necessary* in some cases. We wanted to know the truth about AATIP and TTSA and so when young gun Danny Silva phoned into Fade to Black radio to state that Luis Elizondo was not a *'disinfo' (disinformation)* agent. The gloves were off as Danny announced himself and UAPinfo to a bewildered Ufology.

'This wasn't part of the Ufology script?'

This made us public enemy number one with the old guard, it made people angry. Our coincidental timing couldn't have been better, nor worse, as we went public on the same day that Christopher Mellon wrote in the Washington Post, releasing the third UAP video.

A *potentially* genuine craft of anomalous origin?

'GO FAST'.

TUESDAY
13th of March, 2018
"Those lights over Phoenix?"

W ithin a few days of the 'GO FAST' UAP video release (leak), the community was buzzing once again. This was the third (and sadly, the final), leaked videos from TTSA, it again followed the pattern of 'GIMBAL' and 'FLIR1', in that nothing concrete could be taken from the video, other than the pilots extreme reaction.

After writing up the case report my attention turned to a big case from history. March 13th is a famous date on the UFO calendar. I remember that I wrote a UAPinfo case report for the Phoenix Lights (see later in this book for case report), possibly the most important mass sighting event in modern day history and certainly in my mind an important point in historical UFO research. The Phoenix Lights incident is arguably the largest and most documented UFO case in the history of Ufology. It occurred on a March early evening with an estimated 10'000 witnesses across several hours. Over 700 witnesses went on to report the event which consisted of a 'mile wide triangle/boomerang' craft slowly and silently flying over the city of

Phoenix, Arizona.

Consider the sheer size of such an aerial vehicle would destroy anything underneath it, given the incredible thrust it would need to propel itself in the air. That is, given the massive craft wasn't lighter than air helium or not using conventional propeller type of propulsion. Should this vehicle not have been a mass hallucination, it would need to display some of the AATIP 5 observable technology in a big way.

Some individuals had even suggested that such mass-sighting cases would present huge coverage in today's modern-day age of camera phones, and that it was a shame it happened 21 years ago. Other researchers suggested that if the Phoenix Lights incident had occurred today in 2018, we might have had a form of forced government disclosure. But who knows for sure? Mass sightings are not that common, especially ones in which a massive craft estimated to be a mile wide, slowly travels across the state of Arizona and most notably across the city of Phoenix itself. The craft(s) were witnessed by thousands of people across the state and civilian reports/complaints were made in their hundreds. The incident has become one of the major cases within Ufology, and even has its own documentary, based on the book by Lynn Kitei (5), who should be credited for her efforts.

According to some witnesses, one of the craft was a silent 'V' shape with two lights on either wing and one in the middle. Reports state that the craft was completely silent and blocked out stars as it passed overhead. Others saw varying orbs and lights. Some witnesses reported seven lights in a Christmas tree formation.

Fife Symington, the governor of Arizona at the time, was one witness to this incident. As governor he originally ridiculed the idea of alien origin, calling a press conference and then unmasked his chief of staff dressed up as an alien. Despite the laughter on the press room, the joke didn't go down well with those that saw the massive UAP craft.

However, several years later whilst being filmed for a

James Fox documentary (Out of the Blue), he apologised and called the lights he personally saw "otherworldly" after admitting he saw a huge 'V' shaped craft.

There were allegedly two distinct events involved in the incident: a triangular formation of lights seen to pass over the state, and a series of stationary lights seen in the Phoenix area. The United States Air Force later made efforts to identify the second group of lights as flares, dropped by A-10 Warthog aircraft that were on training exercises at the Barry Goldwater Range in southwest Arizona. However, reports from the multiple witnesses stated that what they saw wasn't flares.

From reviewing the case myself, I have never believed that 'military flares' accounted for the multiple witness testimony. It is simply not what the people reported seeing, at all. As I wrote up the UAPinfo case report I wondered about the conditions for such a massive event.

Ask yourself, where exactly did this gigantic craft disappear to? Where did it come from? Something so big would have surely been spotted by astronomers and others for days. It didn't make sense.

WEDNESDAY
14th of March, 2018
"New kidz on the block."

The next day was my day off work. After finishing and publishing the Phoenix Lights case online to UAPinfo (see chapter on case reports), I remember noting just how little 'likes' and 'retweets' the report gained on a sparse social media platform. At that time, there was less than a handful in the 'UAP community' or the 'TTSA community', what would become 'TwitterUFO' and eventually 'UFOTwitter.' The support wasn't there for us, and the idea behind what we wanted to achieve was a struggle to get off the ground. Ufology was its own monster, hardened behind the insatiable support for the leaders of the field.

You might imagine that coming new into an established *field* comes with established boundaries. Fit in or fuck off was the attitude. We were limited by what we could say, what we couldn't say, who we were allowed to believe is telling the truth and who wasn't. Oh, and what you mustn't do, ever, under any circumstances, is to write an article that backs research that the Atacama Humanoid is human.

It went down like a led balloon.

What made things even more difficult was the lack of transparency from any established form government body. Denials came from the Navy that any records existed regarding AATIP. FOIA responses gained via The Blackvault stated that there was *'not a single photograph, video, report, letter, or memo existed within the Navy's possession'* (6). As you might imagine, this caused further division over AATIP and Elizondo, and by extension we feared the worst over UAP disclosure. Keep in mind, we were up against old guard Ufology, debunkers and trolls, all of whom wanted to shut down the initiative and ourselves for the Atacama support.

It very nearly worked. If it hadn't of been for Sven (UAPinfo) telling me to change my name to something else, I personally wouldn't have continued.

FRIDAY
16th of March, 2018
"Don't put the blame on me."

One week after launch of UAPinfo and it had been quite the week. Keith had contacted a contractor within TTSA, securing a press release for a piece of work on the Atacama Humanoid. Keith and I jointly wrote up the report. It would prove to put an early nail in our coffin with the usual conspiracy types from mainstream Ufology. The Atacama creature, despite having genetic anomalies, would prove to be human, much to the anger of various people who had invested much time and effort into the little being. Unfortunately, as we were the first to release the article and data at 5pm on the Friday we became the target.

But the early days were good. We had our new organisation and a new UFO video (GO FAST) to absorb and evaluate. The scene was exciting in those days, and we pressed forward. In UAPinfo we all had our own roles. Mine was case reports, I wrote dozens of hot and cold case reports in those first few months, looking back, it was one of my favourite times about the whole experience. I was a genuine UAP researcher, looking into cold and hot cases as they appeared, making important emails to witnesses and pushing and collaborating with researchers for further data. In short, those first few months at UAPinfo were thrilling. We were making our own waves and it seemed like nothing could stop us.

We couldn't wait to find out what was coming next.

SUNDAY
18th of March, 2018
'Don't conclude on limited data.'

One of the big parts of our research group UAPinfo, was creating boundaries for ourselves. We as a team needed to think about who we were, and what we wanted to achieve. Did we want to be another 'UFO' group who hated the government and claimed that space aliens had taken over the world and controlled the militaries of the world? Or did we want to emulate TTSA and approach UAP methodologically?

My own personal ideology was one that wasn't compatible with conspiracies, mainly due to the stigma of adopting the big evil cabal government narrative. Even though I knew that *'some'* government contractors most probably had some working knowledge of UAP and maybe things behind the hanger door, I couldn't prove it in a court of law – which is an important and yet frustrating point.

Adopting 'UAP terminology' as I called it, meant adapting a new format of assigning classification to unexplained cases. Whereas most UFO websites across Ufology and Facebook groups would slap an extra-terrestrial bumper sticker on most cases no matter how mundane and easily explainable, we wanted to stop that from happening. Not that we had any intention of controlling Ufology, we knew that was an impossible task. What we needed to do was to create a new platform, something that was unique in the field of Ufology, and that might require a completely new way of rebranding UFO as UAP.

After all, what the point in doing something that's already been done a thousand times? As the great Stanton Friedman once said in 2013 at the Citizen Hearing on Disclosure to a panel of retired congresspersons. *'Change comes from doing things differently, the future is not an extrapolation of the past.'*

✳ ✳ ✳

Conclusions

The importance of early social media campaigns in 2018 cannot be overstated. UAPinfo symbolised the beginning of the UAP revolution. Following in the footsteps of TTSA, the rebranding of Ufology and UFOs into something the public could accept was an absolute necessity. However, we naively thought that with the release of 'GO FAST' the floodgates would open, and the government would declassify whatever they had. No, that didn't happen and instead they clamped down hard.

The other surprise was the weird and wonderful explanations that Ufologists (believers and debunkers) created and imposed on the three UAP videos. Balloons, birds, planes and super classified military technology from Area 51 and Lockheed flooded the internet. Different sides of the extra-terrestrial argument, same methodology applied. Only a handful of researchers held back on conclusions and instead requested more data from their government.

References

(1). Scoles, S. (17th of February, 2018). 'What's up with those UFO videos.'
WIRED.
https://www.wired.com/story/what-is-up-with-those-pentagon-ufo-videos/amp

(2). To The Stars Academy Official Website
https://home.tothestarsacademy.com/

(3). Mellon, C. (03rd of September, 2018). 'The military keeps encountering UFOs. Why doesn't the Pentagon care?'.
Washington Post.
https://www.washingtonpost.com/outlook/the-military-keeps-encountering-ufos-why-doesnt-the-pentagon-care/2018/03/09/242c125c-22ee-11e8-94da-ebf9d112159c_story.html?outputType=amp

(4). Zeke. 'Unidentified Aerial Phenomenon Info.' (26th of June, 2018).
AlienExpanse.com.
http://alienexpanse.com/index.php?threads/unidentified-aerial-phenomena-info.2246/

(5). Kitei, L. M.D. 'The Phoenix Lights: A Sceptics Discovery that we are not Alone. 20th anniversary edition.' (07th of February, 2017).
Waterfront digital press.

(6). Greenewald, J. (24th of August, 2020). "Evidence of U.S. Navy Involvement in UFO Program May Have Been Destroyed.'
The Blackvault.
https://www.theblackvault.com/documentarchive/evidence-of-u-s-navy-involvement-in-ufo-program-may-have-been-destroyed/amp/

CHAPTER SIX: THE ADVANCED AEROSPACE WEAPONS SYSTEM APPLICATION PROGRAM (AAWSAP)

It was always difficult for us to accept at the time, but the role of the FOIA researcher and the quantitative data collection types was incredibly important to the progression of UAP truth. The problem, as we saw it, was that the Department of Defense (DoD) wasn't exactly being truthful about UAP or various aspects of AATIP. The data that was coming forward was through leaks and bits of information via the FOIA process, a quantitative process that ignored testimony. As you might imagine, this caused immense frustration and a clash between those who supported TTSA/Elizondo, and those who didn't realise the government was manipulating the narrative. In 2018, the Advanced Aerospace Weapons System Application Program (AAWSAP) would be no different as time progressed. As far as we could make out, AAWSAP was also a UAP program but more focused on the paranormal. AAWSAP was the big sister program of AATIP and held a contractor Bigelow Aerospace Advanced Space Studies 'BAASS' who investigated a location in northern Utah following the departure of the National Institute for Discovery Science (NIDS) sometime earlier. Both BAASS and NIDS were owned by Robert Bigelow, an important name in the field of UFOs.

Without him, this wouldn't have happened as it did.

***

FRIDAY
13th of April, 2018
"One man's disinformation..."

It had now been almost a month since the 'GO FAST' video was released. Depressingly, it was becoming more and more obvious that we weren't going to get any more needlessly blurry UFO/UAP videos anytime soon. The notion that we would have open access to DoD footage of actual UFOs died quickly within the first quarter. It was depressing and certainly wasn't 'disclosure'. Keep in mind, back in 2018 we were all still trying to figure out what exactly was going on. Our hypothetical position was that the Pentagon program AATIP was possibly part of an official government disclosure initiative to tell the world that extra-terrestrials were the occupants of UAP. Not exactly accurate in hindsight.

The opposite argument was that the AATIP revelations were part of a disinformation campaign, which didn't make much sense considering UAP or 'UFOs' were as un-credible as they could possibly be anyways. This was an outlandish theory and didn't hold water. Then as time progressed, it would be shown that the legislation and executive branches of government didn't know what was happening with UAP and more importantly, the higher executives of the Department of Defense were seemingly unaware that AATIP was a UAP program. Pushback would be rolled out in the form of limiting what data would be released to the public, no official details were provided on the U.S.S. Nimitz case from 2004 (FLIR1 video) and no additional data provided on the 'GIMBAL' or the 'GO FAST' object. We didn't have the names of the pilots or the battle group, or pretty much, *anything*.

Why hadn't TTSA provided those details? Was it because they were using the data as strategy? Or was that data still classified? We had more questions than answers.

And still we waited in our ignorance, hoping this was disclosure with a capitol 'D'. We would have accepted anything, maybe a new video or a new Elizondo figure to step forward. It didn't happen.

We started to consider all possibilities.

MONDAY
30th of April, 2018
"Another UFO program?"

By late April, The Blackvault and John Greenewald reached out to Maj. Audricia Harris (Pentagon spokesperson) to get further clarification on AATIP (1). She stated that the program ended in 2012 which was already known thanks to The New York Times (2). Also, she stated that the three 'UFO' videos were not released by the DoD in relation to AATIP (that was new information, and a whole other convoluted story which contradicted the statements of Luis Elizondo). And finally, it was stated that the aim of the program was to investigate *'far-term foreign advanced aerospace threats'*, again, no mention of anything genuinely extra-terrestrial and no mention of Unidentified Aerial Phenomena (UAP).

***

A new UAP program

Researcher Paul Dean made an intriguing claim in the later days of April of 2018. He stated that he had been in contact with a senior DoD program leader back in March who had confirmed something regarding a new program (3). Apparently, according to Dean's anonymous source, was that the true name of the overall program was the *'Advanced Aerospace Weapons Systems Application Program,'* (AAWSAP). investigative journalist George Knapp and his team also confirmed the program as genuine.

I found this interesting to say the least, however the

lack of an officially named source causes problems whenever trying to verify such data. Having said that, the person in the *'senior Defense leadership role'* did have prior knowledge of AAWSAP's existence, a very niche and delicate piece of information that very few had knowledge or access to in early 2018. It did raise questions for me over the true sense of AAWSAP as a government program. The revelation also brought more uncertainty over AATIP's relationship and slightly muddied the waters - consider that in early 2018 we only knew about AATIP and its link to Luis Elizondo, he nor anybody else within The New York Times had even mentioned this mother program.

Things didn't improve, it caused fractures within the new emerging research community. It seemed like researching came with egos and agendas, *my data is better than your data.*

Honestly, I was put off on investigating the newfound UAP program (AAWSAP), primarily because when it was revealed the focus was negatively attributed towards Elizondo and AATIP. Famously, George Knapp would joke at the time that *'dogs start barking at the caravans as they passed'*, which meant negativistic people shouted loud when they heard something they didn't like. The main cries were, *'the real name of AATIP wasn't AATIP'*, and *'why didn't Elizondo tell us.'* As it would turn out, AAWSAP were linked but not the same program, and Elizondo would later state that it wasn't for him to out a program he wasn't directly apart of. Either way, the second UAP program got the same treatment as the first – criticism, denials and anger from debunkers and believers within Ufology.

In my career of working across various professional disciplines, I've never come across anything like what I witnessed in Ufology, at least not to that extent. Researchers, various debunkers, Ufologists and mostly internet trolls, treat any new information with such disdain that you might think their livelihoods depended on it. Well, in some cases, that was true. Ufology is nice little cash cow for some, although not all cases.

Despite the UAP data causing problems and infighting,

I had always said from the start I appreciated the work of the FOIA researcher who gathered the information from government spokespeople. I won't pretend that we didn't wage war with various people, particularly those who had questions over the legitimacy of Luis Elizondo and AATIP. Considering the mixed messages from the Pentagon at that time, our focus should have been on bringing them to account. Thankfully over time it would be shown that some within the Pentagon were lying about both AATIP and AAWSAP.

THURSDAY
03rd of May, 2018
"Sisters of aerospace."

W ithin a few days, the Advanced Aerospace Weapons System Application Program (AAWSAP) revelations had not resolved any remaining confusion, in fact they had increased. Like AATIP, the new program's definition again was another highly sensitive issue for researchers to uncover. There was a lot of confusing and controversial statements made by the Pentagon.

Was AAWSAP a possible sister program to AATIP, or was it born from it, or was AAWSAP the bigger program, or was it just a contract to AATIP? The answer was dependent on who you chose to believe. The truth has been that muddied in contradiction that it is almost impossible to know for certain (although I tend to believe Luis Elizondo's account). The problem is that the various elements of the Pentagon and DoD weren't being accurate with information. For example, The NSA gave *'no records'* to John Greenewald of The Blackvault after he filed a request on the 02nd of May, 2018 for all records on AAWSAP, and yet we have acknowledgment from other government sources that both programs existed.

The link between the two programs would provide further bewilderment from Pentagon spokesperson Maj. Harris, who stated to researchers in April of 2018 that AATIP and

AAWSAP were the same program, but just a different name (4). Glassel would also get Pentagon spokeswoman Maj. Harris to acknowledge AATIP's mandate was to access, *'far-term foreign advanced aerospace threats the United States'*, and that included *'anomalous'* events *'such as sightings of aerodynamic vehicles engaged in extreme manoeuvres, with unique phenomenology'*, (4). Major Harris would also clarify to Glassel in 2018 that AATIP was terminated in 2012 due to concerns over a lack of progress and the program's validity. And yet in direct contrast, the Director of the program, the Senator who created it and the head physicist were all saying that AATIP studied UAP, and it founded significant results.

Very important point here as Roger Glassel gets Pentagon spokesperson Maj. Harris to confirm that AATIP investigated *anomalous events* such as those reported by the navy with *'unique phenomenology'*. This is the first time we see this sort of acknowledgement from the Pentagon and would be one of the very few occasions they did so. As a rule, in those early years 2017-2019, the Pentagon made it their policy to downplay and dismiss anything that was UAP or AATIP related.

Not to be deterred, John Greenewald was again being stonewalled with AATIP and AAWSAP.

Not everyone in the DoD was playing ball.

FRIDAY
May the Fourth, 2018.
'BAASS'

As with most things *UAP* in 2018, much credit went to George Knapp for being the medium between the public sphere and those involved in DoD programs. It was his 'I-Team' which first released documents that included the AATIP DIRDS (5).

It was his book on Skinwalker, that I would later read in 2018, which opened my eyes to how paranormal encounters were studied by government contractors. Although it's difficult to grasp, the United States government did in fact study such things in the early 21st century. Although, I don't believe everything documented in the book 'Hunt for the Skinwalker', I do believe that there is something there which needs investigation.

And I'm not alone in thinking that.

The Advanced Aerospace Weapons System Application Program (AAWSAP) was what started it all. It was created prior to AATIP, and setup to investigate the events of a strange farming ranch in northern Utah. According to researcher Joe Murgia, the story features a DIA scientist who had an anomalous experience on that rural property (6).

The DIA scientist and Fmr. Director of AAWSAP (wishes to remain anonymous) would both help create AAWSAP and then go onto manage the program. Apparently - as Murgia reports - after only 15 minutes there, he had his experience - a multi-coloured 'pretzel' shaped anomaly, that changed to a 'Möbius Loop/strip' that was visible only to him from the angle he was sat.

From there, the gentleman went back to Senator Harry Reid and had a conversation about officially starting up a program to investigate, that program became AAWSAP. Whereas AATIP was concerned with military UAP cases, AAWSAP was concerned with the broader range of paranormal encounters - which are said to be linked strongly to UAP.

* * *

Conclusions

To summarise the good work of George Knapp, Joe Murgia and the FOIA researchers, both AATIP and AAWSAP were shown to be connected officially with DoD comments going as far as to confirm anomalous events with unique phenomenology. Something I'm guessing they didn't want to say at the time.

But they did say it.

Interesting to note that the NSA would give a no records response to the program (1), which again draws more curiosity as to what data was being accessed and by whom within the spokesperson department. A division which would come to define the whole AAWSAP/AATIP story in those early years. My personal feeling was that AATIP was born of AAWSAP, the decision to split was probably taken to focus specifically on UAP, rather than the paranormal, thus ensuring credibility and stop funding being taken away. After all, if congress finds you studying ghosts and Bigfoot you are running a risk of having your program taken away, but, if you focus on aerial threats, you can argue that national security is at stake. Then should you wish to go public one day, the mainstream will more likely accept aerial threats as a genuine reason to spend taxpayer money.

References

(1). Greenewald, J. (2018). 'The Advanced Aerospace Threat Identification Program (AATIP), Tom Delonge, Luis Elizondo and the Claims of To The Stars Academy.'
The Blackvault.
https://www.theblackvault.com/casefiles/to-the-stars-academy-of-arts-science-tom-delonge-and-the-secret-dod-ufo-research-program/amp/

(2). Blumenthal, R., Cooper, H. and Kean, L. (16th of December, 2017). 'Glowing Auras and 'Black Money': The Pentagon's Mysterious U.F.O. Program'.
The New York Times.
https://www.nytimes.com/2017/12/16/us/politics/pentagon-program-ufo-harry-reid.amp.html

(3). Dean, P. (30th of April, 2018). The "Advanced Aerospace Weapons Systems Application Program." UFOs: Documenting

the Evidence.
https://ufos-documenting-the-evidence.blog-
spot.com/2018/04/the-advanced-aerospace-weapons-sys-
tems_30.html?m=1

(4). Glassel, R. (03rd of May, 2018). 'Pentagon Confirmation:
AATIP = Advanced Aerospace Weapon System Applications
Program.'
Blue Blurry Lines.
https://www.blueblurrylines.com/2018/05/pentagon-con-
firmation-aatip-advanced.html?m=1

(5). Knapp, G., and Adams, M. (04th of May, 2018). 'I-Team:
Documents prove secret UFO study based in Nevada.'
8NewsNow.
https://www.8newsnow.com/news/i-team-documents-
prove-secret-ufo-study-based-in-nevada/amp/

(6). Murgia, J. (25th of November, 2019). 'What Did The DIA
Scientist See At Skinwalker That Caused Him To Push For
AAWSAP?'
UFOJOE.net
https://www.ufojoe.net/what-dia-scientist-see-at-skinwalker

CHAPTER SEVEN:
ANOMALOUS TECHNOLOGY
IN THE SECOND WORLD
WAR (1939-1945)

* * *

O ne thing I always found interesting, is how human society is impacted by its own psychological barriers, and equally how society is generally unaware that such a process is even happening. Major existential issues such as 'Terrorism', 'Climate Change', 'War' and 'UAP' become embroiled in conspiracies and political dogma that prevent meaningful progression. A Social psychologist might argue it is very much a process that occurs at the collective subconscious level, forging decisions that might not necessarily be agreed upon openly and in a way that allows society to accept difficult realities. One theory is that the dilution of such problematic issues is a way of human culture allowing itself the time to adapt and respond in ways which might be difficult to accept at a conscious level. However, to be critical of this approach, not all decision made have been in everyone's interest.

We apply subliminal, unwitting barriers and control measures based on our experience and knowledge, ensuring our beliefs and behaviours are guided in specific directions.

As a collective mind, we are influenced by external factors that force our societal decisions as a people through the *democratic* process (see whatever latest drama is on the front pages of national newspapers). And this has been no different when we have engaged the anomalous phenomena. Essentially, we might argue that we collectively all made the 'secrecy decision' regarding the UAP issue. Maybe on some level, we all know that the phenomena are very real, but subconsciously choose to ignore it.

Maybe, we weren't ready to face the possibilities of 'aliens' in the early 1940s, as we proceeded through the deadliest war in history. Despite the reports coming in through various credible pilots and military men, we simply rejected that data, unable to process it, unable to even accept that we might be dealing with something else entirely. What it says to me is that we humans are still very limited in our own self-reflection. It says we don't really understand how we think beyond our focused conscious mind. We as a people have displayed the same dismissive thinking, attitudes and behaviours towards the anomalous since the beginning of the modern era of UFOs that started with Kenneth Arnold in June, 1947 and beyond. My early research found that the anomalous technology didn't start with the pop-culture 1950s or even Roswell in 1947. No, this specific type of reported *technology* started being reported during the Second World War with fighter planes. Most interesting of all, is that in the collective minds of humans, this technology represents a potential ability to annihilate us.

Coincidentally, much the same as nuclear weapons.

***

WEDNESDAY
05th of May, 2018
'War-Time.'

As the warm May sunlight shone through the upper library windows, I sat as far back into the leather-bound chair as I could go. The top floor of the central library in Middlesbrough was always empty on a weekday, just how I like it, quiet and without distraction. With my laptop back and notepad I was ready to make notes from the more obscure text, not always available from the internet. The old leather-bound books at the back of the large dimly lit room filled the wooden shelving. It was here I found what I was looking for - a complete history of the Second World War. In my research, I found that it is not enough to simply look at case reports from a specific time, one must also evaluate the psychology of a socio-economic, cultural timeframe and understand that era. As we will come to find out, the implications of understanding human society and subculture are very relevant to the behaviours of the anomalous phenomena.

However, whether the socio-psycho-economic-cultural mindset of localised population impacts the behavioural patterns of UAP is a question for the ages and one we can only scratch the surface of in the year 2018.

SUNDAY
07th of December, 1941
'Failure of Intelligence.'

War had arrived at the doorstep of the United States in the December of 1941. Devastating scenes, as early morning air-raid attacks on strategic military bases over the course of seven hours was coordinated by the Japanese. Horrific attacks on the U.S. base of Pearl Harbour killed over 2000 and sunk four navy vessels across various locations (1). It was a day which would live in infamy. It was a measured ploy by the Japanese, and ultimately, one which would bring the U.S. into the Second World War and forever change the future of our world.

The fight in Europe had raged since 1939, with some estimated 75 million people losing their lives by the end of the war, but it wasn't until 1941 that the United States was drawn into the conflict. In every historical book I have read, they all agree on one factor, that Pearl Harbour was an intelligence failure like no other. It allowed for a devastating strategic surprise that devastated America's most Western military outpost. A decision that would prove fateful for the Japanese in the long-term.

Up until now, America had been relatively happy to sit back and send aid across to the United Kingdom and its allies, after all, the U.S. was recovering from the combined devastation of the 'dust bowl', and the Great Depression which occurred in 1929 following the Wall Street crash. But now they had no choice, public support backed the congress who made the decision to go to war. As you might imagine, the following days, weeks and months were at the height of suspense, dread, and tensions about the very real threat from Asia as it loomed over the U.S. West coast in the 1940s. You might even understand some of the extreme classification actions taken in those years by a military struggling to cope with a new bloodied war and the potential emergence of one of the biggest hypothetical weapons to ever be created by man.

'Loose lips sink ships.'

As many writers and historians have suggested, the Second World War was a battle for the direction of mankind. The various human ruling ideologies of Fascism, Communism, Capitalism, Democracy and Socialism became convoluted with religious culture and race as they fought for global supremacy. Wars, I have found, are never about land grab at their core, they are about ensuring your own genetical gene pool dominates with your political and religious ideologies and they are by inherent nature, racist, against all other cultures who are different. Arguably, from an objective subconscious perspective, the 1939-1945 global conflicts were about which set of ideologies should come out on top, sparked by a devastating global depression and limited resources resulting from the First World War amongst other things. Sparked by individual countries reacting to economic survival problems, struggling to fill the basic needs of their people. My research found one main pattern; human war happens through the deprived conditions which nurture them.

In that timeframe, our human race was undergoing a

drastic psychological change from who we were, to who we were going to become. A question of what we are willing to do to ensure our continuation.

For me, this is genetic, a code within our nature to do such horrid things, we do it to ensure the survival of our species. We are designed to kill ourselves to save ourselves, no different to how a wildflower chokes and curves upwards toward the sun, gathering the sunlight for itself above all other plants. A simple design of all observed life on Earth, *survival of the fittest.*

Then, at this incredibly sensitive time in history, add into the mix, something very much unexpected, a technological phenomenon that started appearing almost as an unverified direct correlation to the harnessed atomic power within the Manhattan Project, 1942-1946 (2).

Something was here.

And it was technologically superior to the allies or axis powers, something that might be beyond us, something else entirely, something that might not need to have worry about threats of wildflowers as they blow harmlessly in the light breeze.

And yet their actions and behaviours suggested otherwise?

Seemingly, the Anomalous had arrived, and arrived in vast numbers as they swarmed and buzzed the human aerial vehicles of war. But how much of this is true? How much can we verify to the point of confidently concluding?

FRIDAY
25th of February, 1942
'Battle of L.A.'

B ombs were dropped as lives were lost in a bloodied war that devastated people on both sides of the divide. Our collective human psyche was fractured as we came to terms with the horrific implications of war and famine. This was an unprecedented time in history.

The start of the decade saw an influx of unusual sightings across Europe and America. Soldiers were on high alert with increasing threats over the expanding world war, one which had at last arrived at their feet. In 1942, the sleepy Hollywood town was a mixture of immigrants and prosperous movie stars looking to make their names on the silver screen. However, with the war It was also a growing military metropolis and unfortunately lost its original open mindedness, specifically towards Japanese civilians.

It was on a cold winter night of 1942, that unknown objects flew over downtown Los Angeles and were engaged by heavy artillery. The case became known as the 'Battle of L.A.' (3), (4). As Historian Richard Dolan writes in his book *'UFOs and the National Security State,'* the night of February 25th saw Los Angeles residents awoken to air raid sirens at around 2.25am, and as the military fired 1430 antiaircraft shells into the dark sky to bring down the *'Japanese planes'* they were left unsuccessful.

Fear gripped the people.

The incident claimed the lives of 5 people, with 2 heart attacks and 3 road accidents, others dashed around and suffered injuries in the panic. This was wartime and people genuinely believed they were under attack from the Japanese. Obviously, they weren't under attack and the Secretary of Navy would go onto blame 'war-nerves' and that there weren't any actual enemy aircraft that night. Later they would change their story to say the objects were civilian planes flown by 'enemy pilots', then finally, they settled on a series of 'weather balloons' that had fooled people into thinking it was a foreign invasion (4).

This is one of the first times we see weather balloons used by the military to explain something that they had no answer for.

For me it's important to consider the 'Battle of L.A.' case as something unknown, which is not to say that these objects weren't something trivial that couldn't be identified for lack of information. Certainly, we should avoid mentioning any extra-terrestrial in this case. The objects in question do not apply any of the AATIP 'five observables' that classify and distinguish such a case as UAP by DoD standards. However, the case should be given the right context. The 'Battle of L.A.' object wasn't a one-off, it was essentially one of many unidentified cases that began around the 1942 mark. For this was the start of the '*Foo-Fighter*'.

Significantly, this was seemingly the start of this specific type of technology.

Foo Fighters

The world war brought a significant number of 'unknown' reports prior to them even being classified as such in terminology. There literally were no unidentified flying objects (UFOs), or definite 'Flying Saucers' in the early 1940s that would be recognised as such, but there were objects of unknown origin that were beginning to be reported with increasing numbers. The much known 'Foo Fighters' would become the given label at that time. British researcher Graeme Rendall (UAPMedia) found that the Royal Air Force had been experiencing strangely moving lights, varying luminous objects, and rather big *'aeroforms'* within Germany's skies since the March of 1942 (5). *Rendall reamins the go to person for the 'Foo-Fighter' cases.

Original World War Two fighter pilot reports (6) were made about *'strange balls of fire'* that changed colour from red to orange to white to black, and that had no wings or even a fuselage. These vehicles had no exhaust plumes, or rotors or anything to suggest these were conventional aircraft.

The strange unidentified objects would follow B-24 liberators whilst flying missions over Japan. Again, the thinking from the military was that the strange objects were Japanese technology, however, no kamikaze attack occurred as the objects tailed the plane in a curious non-threatening way. To me the pilot reports suggested that these unknown vehicles were acting with genuine curiosity, like a bee that hovers around a picnic table without any deliberate conscious intention.

Other reports come present a similar picture, but this time over Germany. Lt. Ringwald, Lt. Schlueter and Lt. Meier were part of the 415th night fighter squadron that flew above the Rhine on a routine mission, they all witnessed 8-10 fiery orbs travelling at high speed before disappearing.

Another case involving the 415th squadron was from the skies near Hagenau, Germany. On the 22nd – 23rd of December 1944, two orange lights travelled up fast to an Allied aircraft and then tailed their aircraft for two minutes before turning away and flying under *'perfect control'* – as originally reported in 1945 by the American Legion Magazine (6).

Other war-time reports were made by the Eighth Air Force bomber crews, who reported bizarre incursions of *'silver-coloured spheres'* (6). The sheer volume of reports that involved strange orbs was widespread, almost to the point of being widespread, a swarm within the wartime skies. Time and time again, similar (but not exactly the same each time) objects were spotted by pilots.

On the 17th of February, 1945, other pilots reported 'orange-red' lights in the skies near the Italian port town of La Spezia as well as further inland, reports Lindell in 2009, (10). No communication contact was made with these objects as they were also reported across Belgium and France.

On the 03rd of April, 1945, a report stated that 'balls of fire' were spotted by multiple pilots over southern England (10).

One of the interesting things which struck me as I researched the early 'Foo Fighter', phenomenon, was the sheer volume of reports made by pilots and airmen of that time. The distinct pattern became another interesting point. The reports were mostly of small, light-infused, orb-like objects, of different colour that often had a fiery appearance. They were almost always reported to be under intelligent control as they toyed with crewmen on missions, outperforming their planes and taking off at high speeds.

There is a distinct pattern in the data when we consider the technology involved.

The Ghost Lights

A quick internet search shows that other global, historical reports of orbs of light have been reported. For instance, various strange light phenomena have been reported in rural Australia, there is a 'Min' phenomenon or 'Ghost Light' that is associated with the outback. In Australian Aboriginal folklore, there are stories about strange light orbs that act unconventionally and are unexplainable (15). The strange phenomenon is said to interact with truck drivers in the wilderness of dark deserted roads, and some suggest they have encountered the intelligently controlled orbs of light (16).

However, some researchers, such as John Pettigrew, have conducted experiments to show how some of the 'Min-Min' light aberrations might be a 'Fata Morgana' – an optical illusion created through refraction and temperature inversions (17), (18). Could this be what the pilots of World War Two were witnessing?

In the South American countries Argentina, Chile and Uruguay there is a phenomenon known as 'Luz Mala' which literally translates to 'Bad Light.' It is reported that the lights appear at night and then float above the ground, hover and move at speed (19). Stories populate the internet, unverified tales within South American mythology tell of orbs that engage isolated individuals on long lonely trips in the dead of night. In Mendoza, Argentina, it is reported that truck drivers claim to have seen it during their high mountain journeys, between Uspallata, Puente del Inca and Las Cuevas (20).

The problem is that for the most part, these are all just glorified campfire stories that are recorded onto the internet without credible assessment. There is no additional data, there is no witness testimony to evaluate or means to check the persons credibility/mental health. Often, we have no supportive photos, videos or external sensory data on such orbs as they occur. And this is a major problem, we do not have the means to verify the phenomenon in such cases, and we certainly can't correlate cases to the same phenomena. Despite similar testimony of appearance, behaviour or abilities, we can't conclude that any historical orb of light can be linked to any other groups of historical orbs of light. And we can go further and state that we can't link any historical case to the 'Foo Fighter' phenomenon. To do so, would be to apply assumption onto a correlative link which simply isn't backed up by appropriate data.

The problem is that this could be very real, and we simply can't prove it.

THURSDAY
06th of May, 2018.
'Are there patterns in the data?'

My second day in the central library was spent looking - *and not finding information* - on the 'Foo-Fighter' phenomena. So unsurprisingly, I found nothing in a pre-Rendall world. For this topic, isn't mainstream, it's fringe and certainly not worthy of hard backed books from renowned professionals in academic settings. Instead, I was limited to internet searches on the phenomena that Thursday morning.

For some reason I have always felt my research into the Second World War was significantly correlated to the anomalous phenomena in various ways, but such things are incredibly difficult to prove. Is it a coincidence that the early UAP appear during this timeframe? Or is it that we are just seeing and reporting the phenomena due to more planes being in the sky? Or is it that new neurological factors were emerging, making us see tricks of the light?

Questions without answers.

We might consider a sceptical approach regarding the 'Foo Fighters'. Yes, we must look at rational explanations, however, if we cannot conclude because of a lack of supporting data, we must acknowledge that fact, and not attempt to debunk through childish need and psychological dissonance. Applying a 'terrestrial' explanation that doesn't fit the case data is just as dishonest as exclaiming such a phenomenon is extra-terrestrial. For me, the truth is probably that we will never know what the origins of 'Foo Fighters' are, as we do not have accompanied radar data or additional testimony. But does this not mean we can fill in the blanks?

Many scientists at the time attempted to debunk the unknown WW2 lights as 'St Elmo's Fire' (7), which is a form of electric discharge and an historical phenomenon, sometimes seen during thunderstorms and above the masts of sea vessels. Generally, it was thought to be a form of *plasma* and stays close to a charged object such as a wing tip or a mast. However, the 'Foo Fighters' reported by airmen during WW2 displayed controlled movements, which isn't consistent with the concept of 'St. Elmo's Fire'.

There is another possibility, something known as 'Ball Lightning' which is similar in appearance and controlled movements. Like St. Elmo's Fire, the 'Ball Lightning' phenomenon is historical, with multiple cases that span back centuries. For me, one issue with the theory of 'Ball Lightning', is that it isn't really understood, and arguably has been difficult to explain and replicate under controlled circumstances.

Could we consider the other potential explanation that the 'Foo Fighter' objects have been around for centuries and themselves mistaken for 'Ball Lightning' and even in some circumstances 'St. Elmo's Fire'? We might consider that our lack of historical data has left us wondering rather than concluding. After all, mysteries aren't really that mysterious when the relevant data is accessible. Realistically, we still cannot associate or correlate any historical cases without rigorous data, and that data will not be made available, it has been too long.

Regardless, the same problem remains and can be applied - we don't know what this 'Foo Fighter' phenomenon is, we couldn't capture its true essence in the 1940s and to this day we struggle to formulate an appropriate hypothesis. It is intellectually lazy to say it is *aliens* or misidentified terrestrial objects. We instead need to consider that this is something yet to be discovered or explained appropriately. Acknowledging that we don't have the understanding, knowledge and ability to go back historically and thoroughly evaluate is the first step towards a grounded position.

There have been other claimants about the technology of the 1940s, and as bizarre as this may seem, some have concluded that the anomalous technology was from the axis powers. There are some conspiracy theories that Hitler and the Nazis had developed UAP technology and the 'Flying Saucers' of the 40s and 50s were simply German craft. Others (11) have implied that the Nazis had 'Die Glocke' which translates as 'The Bell', a technologically advanced weapon that would be a decisive factor in winning the war. Obviously, it didn't occur and is mainly considered pseudoscience, even in fringe groups. The researcher Nathan Hendrickson told me once that the Germans didn't possess this technology, and certainly didn't build anti-gravity craft a few years after the first manned flight was flown.

Consider it this way. We don't have UAP technology in today's civilian world, we don't have any vehicles that perform the five AATIP observables (12), we don't have hover boards or flying cars, nor do we have anything from science fiction films and books. We haven't mastered the technology of 'warping space-time' that some scientists from AATIP (13) potentially theorised about - that these UAP vehicles are operating under an Alcubierre warp drive (14).

To me, it is almost unthinkable to insist that this highly advanced, and still theoretical concept, was developed in the 1930s and 1940s. Technology we still cannot replicate some

80 years later. Whatever this potential phenomenon is or isn't, almost becomes irrelevant as the persisting problem remains that we still cannot officially identify it due to our limited observation techniques and the elusiveness of the phenomena. As you might imagine, the incursions into wartime skies above Europe by unknown objects of shape, manoeuvring and origin was beyond them in those years. The sudden introduction of such a concept came at a pivotal time, a time when the people of the world were on the brink, a time which might have seen Nazi Germany close to harnessing the power of the Atom. Arguably, this was the most important time in recorded human history, and amongst it all, was something else.

An aberration of thought.

*　*　*

Conclusions

For the first time we see military pilots report strange aerial phenomena to the extent of conscious societal awareness. Media of the 1940s reported on the aerial phenomena and the mystery of the unknowns. The 'Foo-Fighters' have similar types of behavioural and appearance reports that go back through history, however I'm reluctant to associate similar historical phenomena due to a lack of hard, tangible data. Having said that, I believe there is a good possibility that such phenomena are indeed linked. I also fail to believe that UAP appeared for the first time in 1942.

References

(1). Hermon, G. (1957). 'Royal Australian Navy 1939–1942. Australia in the War of 1939–1945.'
Australian War Memorial, Canberra, 1968., 1968
https://www.awm.gov.au/collection/RCDIG1070207

(2). 'The Manhattan Project.' (12th of May, 2017).

The Atomic Heritage Foundation.
https://www.atomicheritage.org/history/manhattan-project

(3). Dolan, R. (2001). 'UFOs and the National Security State.'
Keyhole Publishing Company.

(4). Harrison, S. (23rd of February, 2017). 'From the Archives: The 1942 Battle of L.A.'
Lost Angeles Times.
https://www.latimes.com/visuals/framework/la-me-fw-archives-1942-battle-la-20170221-story.html?_amp=true

(5). Rendall, G. (15th of April, 2021). 'THE FOO FIGHTERS: TODAY'S PILOTS ENCOUNTERS WITH UAP ARE NOTHING NEW: World War II Pilots were among the first to have unusual aerial Encounters.'
The Debrief
https://thedebrief.org/the-foo-fighters-todays-pilots-encounters-with-uap-are-nothing-new/

(6). Chamberlain, J. (December, 1945). 'The Foo Fighter Mystery.'
The American Legion Magazine.
https://archive.legion.org/bitstream/handle/20.500.12203/3811/americanlegionma396amer_0.pdf?sequence=1&isAllowed=y

(7). Scientific America. 'What causes the strange glow known as St. Elmo's Fire? Is this phenomenon related to ball lightning?'
https://www.scientificamerican.com/article/quotwhat-causes-the-stran/

(8). Timothy, G. (2007). 'Need to Know: UFOs, the Military, and Intelligence'
Pegasus Books.

(9). 'The Real Foo Fighters - A Historical and Physiological Perspective on a World War II Aviation Mystery.'

Skeptic Magazine, vol. 17, n. 2 (pp. 38-43)

(10). Lindell, J. (26th of July, 2009). 'A Historical and Physiological Perspective of the Foo-Fighters of World War Two.'
https://web.archive.org/web/20090726103921/http://jeff.lindell.home.comcast.net/~jeff.lindell/The%20Sparticani.htm

(11). Witkowski, I. (2013). 'Prawda o Wunderwaffe.'
RVP Press
https://www.amazon.co.uk/Truth-About-Wunderwaffe-Igor-Witkowski/dp/1618613383

(12). Daugherty, G., & Sullivan, M. (20th of May, 2019). 'These Five UFO Traits Captured on Video
by Navy Pilots, Defy Explanation.' History.com.
https://www.history.com/.amp/news/ufo-sightings-speed-appearance-movement

(13). Aftergood, S. DIA-FOIA. (15th of August, 2018). '38 DIRDS of AATIP.'
Fas.Org
https://fas.org/irp/dia/aatip-list.pdf

(14). Williams, M. (20th of January, 2017). 'What is the Alcubierre Warp Drive?'
Universe Today.
https://phys.org/news/2017-01-alcubierre-warp.amp

(15). Kozicka, M.G. (1994). 'The Mystery of the Min Light. Cairns.'
Bolton Imprint

(16). Bevege, A. (18th of August, 2019). 'Like a star on the ground': Railway worker tells of strange encounter with the mysterious outback Min lights - and orb appeared to be conscious.'
Daily Mail.com
https://www.dailymail.co.uk/news/article-7321317/amp/

Like-star-ground-Railway-worker-tells-strange-encounter-Min-Min-lights.html

(17). Pettigrew, J. (2003). 'The Min light and the Fata Morgana An optical account of a mysterious Australian phenomenon.' Clinical and Experimental Optometry, 86:2,109-120. https://www.tandfonline.com/doi/abs/10.1111/j.1444-0938.2003.tb03069.x

(18). Salleh, A. (28th of March, 2003). 'Mystery of the Min lights explained.' News in Science. Australian Broadcasting Corporation.

(19). 'The Bad Light and the Horrifying Fires.' (15th of September, 2015).
The Country Uruguay.
https://web.archive.org/web/20180915231200/http://viajes.elpais.com.uy/2013/09/05/la-luz-mala-y-los-fuegos-horripilantes/

(20). Nacevich, E. (17th of November, 2020). 'The Legend of Bad Light.'
Ser Argentine.
https://www.serargentino.com/en/people/urban-legends/the-legend-of-the-bad-light/amp

CHAPTER EIGHT: EARLY CASE REPORTS (1947-1952)

✳ ✳ ✳

T he beginning of the Cold War era was extremely volatile. The world took breath as it stepped back from a second catastrophic war in less than a century, one that had resulted in the creation and deployment of the most dangerous weapon of mass destruction ever created. This wasn't a time for spilling the technological secrets of national security, this was a time to ensure the United States and her allies didn't face annihilation through nuclear winter. You might understand why this UAP technology would be classified under the circumstances. What was most interesting is that when you start researching UAP, you don't simply stop at case reports, you find yourself diving headfirst into everything else from that period. In a way that approach makes sense. In order to understand how we as people handled the UAP issue, we must also understand ourselves as a society in that timeframe. Maybe to understand the post war anomalous phenomena we must understand the conditions that nurtured it? We must consider ourselves, our social psychology and our changing culture.

***

THURSDAY
06th of May, 2018
'The end of the war.'

H aving found my search for the 'Foo-Fighters' come up fruitless in the main central library, I took the liberty of using the computers and the internet. Maybe a search for anything loosely associated with that timeframe might help us understand UAP. The one thing I did find, is that anything *Ufological* wasn't in mainstream textbooks, literature and books, it was in private UFO research books and on the less than reliable internet blog posts and sketchy 90s themed websites. Although, if you dig deep enough you can verify some correlating data. You might argue, this part of history had been buried by our collective subconscious, preventing any distracting correlation and examination. After all America and Europe had a world to rebuild.

For example, strange unknowns didn't just appear during the Second World War, the reports stem back throughout history in various patterns and phenomena. Their definitive distinction and origin however have been critically debated, and rightly so due to a lack of supporting information, as we already suggested. However, what is important is that the *reports* of this anomalous technology increased dramatically during the end of the war. Whether this was the phenomena *changing* its very appearance to match human culture (as some have suggested) or whether this was the start of something completely new and 'alien' to us, is still the biggest mystery behind UAP. We still do not know the answers.

What we can state, almost certainly, is that the anomalous phenomena reacted to human beings, our adoption of atomic energy and to our weapons of mass destruction. It has led many to suggest that the appearance of UAP was no coincidence, that possibly, they came as a reactionary effect of human's newfound ability to self-annihilate Earth in a nuclear winter.

To fully understand the phenomenon's behaviour, it was important to look back at what was occurring in those important years. What are we missing? What could have triggered such a wave of activity during the war and then dramatically increased it after as well? What could the data tell us? What happened in that timeframe?

After the war had ended in 1945, the world was in transition. Hitler was dead, Nazi Germany had been defeated, their taken land returned to the people, their armies dismantled, and their technology and scientific minds extracted to the West and secretly placed into classified programs. Wernher von Braun's infamous long-range missile, the V2 rocket, that devastated London and other European targets during the blitz, was the prized advanced weaponry that would be interjected deep within classified military programs. It is rumoured that the Department of Energy (DoE) was involved due to their oversight over the Manhattan Project. The captured missile technology was tested over at the White Sands testing range from 1946-1951 and would even lead to the creation of the Apollo rockets that would take the United States to the moon in 1969. The development of atomic energy alongside the attainment, absorption and application of the advanced Nazi technology propelled the United States into becoming the world's first superpower.

In a way, you could argue that America's rise to power came through capture, development and 'reverse-engineering' of advanced foreign technologies.

There was a formula, and it worked.

SATURDAY
08th of May, 2018
'The early cases'

By the weekend I was ready to start writing for UAPinfo about the very first recognised UAP wave which came in the years following the end of the war. Encouraged by the credible pilot and witness testimony regarding small spherical objects of light (Foo-Fighters), I wondered how the following UAP waves of sightings would differ from the

'Foo-Fighters'.

My own case reports, data collection and analysis research for UAPinfo showed little difference in the old reports and generally followed the mass historical data pattern presented by the standard UFO-researcher.

The first major American wave of 'Flying Disc' anomalous activity occurred primarily in 1947, the data is there from the Airforce's Project Bluebook to clarify this, although 'disc-cases' in the literature go back to 1946 and 1945. There is other 'flap areas' or waves that go back further, but here I focus on the modern era 'Flying Disc' waves.

***

What I didn't understand is the specific conditions that create an 'anomalous wave' - why is there seemingly an influx of reports over a certain period (June to July in the years 1947 and 1952 for example), in a certain global geographical area, with certain types of UAP (although not all exactly similar), but then also, not in other areas (countries, states of the U.S.) and not at other times?

Why did UAP waves occur in certain years with such intensity? What were the contributing conditions for this?

As I sat at my attic desk, and turn to my right, I can look out of my window and confidently assume there won't be a 'Flying Saucer' watching me. Also, I can go home after a day at work and read the paper to find there won't be a rash of sightings over Teesside. That leads me to consider that there are indeed *conditions* by which the reports will be made of sightings. The Anomalous follow a snapshot pattern, they show very distinct behavioural appearance traits, they might seemingly be bound by possible attraction, needs or even intentions (all of which I investigate further within this book).

However, for the time being it was important to investigate the circumstances of the time + geographical area by which the reports were being made and correlate any patterns without concluding. We can evaluate a theory without subscribing to it and must always assume we don't have a complete picture.

***

What I found bizarre, is that the cases of UAP really started to increase within America at the time of the nuclear age – a common theme in Ufology.

Various shaped vehicles were reported by multiple people from all walks of life. The most common shape, however, was the 'Flying Saucer,' or the 'Flying Disc,' and for whatever reason that specific type of 'vehicle' started popping up in reports across the country in those early Cold War years. The data from project Bluebook shows an embarrassment of cases in which witnesses reported 'Flying Saucers/Discs' with various patterns - patterns which didn't make any sense to me at first glance. There are many questions about the Anomalous' psychology, their thought process, attitudes and intentions which lead into behaviours.

For example, a case taken from Project Bluebook reported that on the 18th of October of 1948 a series of silver 'Flying Discs' were reported (1) by an unnamed Major and his wife, and their 8yr old daughter at his home in Honolulu. The objects travelled in a north-eastern direction at approximately 10'000 feet and made no noise, and displayed no signatures (exhaust, flames, etc).

Another case taken from a 1967 report (2) that examined UAP encounters from the year 1947, cited case number 237 (taken from Project Bluebook). On Friday, 04th of July, not far from Twin Falls in the state of Idaho, a man by the name of A.E. Mitchel was one of seven witnesses to report a group of 'disc-like' objects flying west in a V-formation overhead at around 14:50 hours. The unidentified objects were reported to be flying at high speed across the sky. Then, ten minutes later another nine to ten objects were reported as flying overhead, these objects gained altitude quickly but unlike the first wave, were not in a '*well-defined formation*' whilst climbing.

Another case (3) is from the 28th of April, 1949 in which a civilian and his family witnessed six objects in the sky, then after a few more minutes another four objects traveling in the same direction. The individual then writes that he would be available for contact about the flying discs/saucers, and he would provide more details.

An interesting encounter report cites a mass sighting, case - 734. On the 08th of July, 1947, a few hundred witnesses on Catalina Island (off Long Beach, west coast of America) witnessed six disc-shaped objects travel overhead (2) various military men including Army Air Corps veterans Bob Jung, Kenneth Johnson and Alvio Russo.

Bob Jung, an early 1947 witness whose testimony is included in Project Bluebook, stated that the formation of 'Flying Discs' were in formation, '*two elements, of three each*'. He reports that the formation '*came in from the northeast and then completely disappeared over the hills to the south of Avalon Bay.*'

There are hundreds and thousands of these types of cases, all of which were compacted into geographical areas, all specifically compacted into timeframes from 1947-1952. Same 'Saucer-type' vehicles, same behaviours, same advanced abilities. Never did they attack people like in the movies, never did they land on the White House Lawn and demand to see our leader. They, whatever '*they*' are, simply flew from place to place as if they had some goal to achieve, some mission to complete, almost as if they have what we humans know as *intentions*. Sometimes they pretend like we aren't even here, sometimes they take notice of us and our aircraft and semi-engage, even follow for a moment, much like a wasp might fly over to us and buzz around us before leaving. Ultimately, *they* seemingly aren't really interested in us. We and them, are on different levels of existence.

Whilst looking through the old reports, one of the things I found most interesting was the quantitative report presented by Bloecher, T. (1967) 'Report on the UFO wave of 1947,' (2), showed sighting reports taken from June 15th – July 15th 1947. The Bloecher report is a brilliant piece of quantitative data that examines the 1947 wave. A statistical graph used within, shows a steady incline of reports that climaxes around the 6-7th of July with well over 100 reports from each of those days. This was also the timeframe that the alleged Roswell crashes were reported to have happened.

Now imagine, 100 reports per day of 'Flying Discs.'

A swarm.

SATURDAY
09th of May, 2018
'The Modern UFO era'

U fology classes the start of the modern UFO era (1947-2017) as beginning over mount Rainer, Washington on the 24th of June, 1947. Obviously, this case wasn't the start of UFOs being present in the skies, but it was the first time the phenomena had seriously come into public awareness.

Whilst flying, pilot Kenneth Arnold was reported to have witnessed nine bright, flying *saucer-like* objects flying at incredible speeds at 10 thousand feet. Arnold would describe them *moving* like 'Saucers' skipping on a pond. The shape of the crafts that Arnold saw was not the typical 'Flying Saucer' shape we know from movies and books, instead they were almost like a 'crescent-moon' type of shape. However, the term 'Flying Saucer' stuck from that point onwards as a description for the anomalous craft people started seeing. For me the interesting takeaway of the Arnold sighting, was that for the very first time the public started to accept the concept of UFOs like at no other point previously. Even the 'Foo-Fighter' cases hadn't become common knowledge. The other point I found noteworthy, was that the nine objects flew erratically (skipping like saucers) and that they flew in formation – a behavioural theme would come to be associated with many of the early sightings from within Project Bluebook. What we can also be aware of is patterns, which are there in such cases, and that is why we need to look at UAP case reports closely to fully understand behaviour and maybe intention. What they do or don't do can tell us information about the psychology of anomalous phenomena.

What can we take from the early cases?

Arguably, the early cases are key to this mystery, but one which we might not be able to fully unlock. They are at a time in history when people were happy to report what they saw, without the stigma, without the hoaxes or debunking which would eventually follow in later years. The cases (1947-1952) are raw, a snapshot into a genuine anomalous wave that can tell us things about the behaviour patterns and abilities of the anomalous phenomena.

Let's look at the patterns.

Flying Discs/Saucers would be reported in multiple numbers across that period and observed in groups flying at high-speed overhead in specific directions. They are reported to be shaped in a way that is not aerodynamic – they have no tails, wings, exhausts. They are a silver/grey colour – a colour we humans associate with metal.

The 1967 Bloecher report (2) that intervened in case reports made between June 15th and July 15th is important, it shows that there is a peak in the activity of an anomalous wave. We have thousands of 'differently similar' reports, with hundreds and sometimes thousands of variations of a specific shape and type. Case after case in which strange, oddly shaped vehicles that can defy the current understanding of physics, somehow appear as if from nowhere and then disappear off someplace just as mysteriously. And they come in waves.

'*Waves.*'

What does that mean? It means that UAP build up to a

certain point and then recedes, much like the Doppler effect or even an infection. It suggests to me that whatever this anomalous phenomenon is, it follows a pattern, something about it or some external force dictates its behaviour.

What's the point of it?

Does it have a mission? To fly around in groups during a wave, always heading off to a certain place but never seemingly getting there.

There are occasional reports that 'it' lands in a remote location, often somewhere not populated by human consciousness. Sometimes it encounters one maybe two people, but not for a long period of time or to allow people to gather good evidence of it. The phenomenon hides on the edge of our consciousness, it flies at low/high altitude and never hovers over a shopping mall for a few hours. It always evades our civilian efforts to identify it as *unidentifiable*. We are instead left with not enough information to prove to the world that this is something else, and consequently, we are left with major questions.

Do UAP have consciousness the way we understand it?

Why are there thousands of different types of similar objects?

Was there a link between a concentrated 'wave' of UFO/UAP activity and possible crashes? And if so, why did the potential activity reduce (Doppler effect) after the alleged climatic crashes, such as in Roswell?

We simply do not know enough to understand the UAP psychology, and we don't know why there are so many types of UAP. No other link beside a coincidental one can be drawn at this point. Yes, there was a spike in activity that climaxed within the same period of a 'Flying Disc' that crash landed in the New Mexico desert in the summer of 1947. We must question the quality of data received and not assume it's accuracy. We simply don't know if this was the spike, and if there were other cases that weren't reported that change the climax of the 'wave' to another timeframe. And obviously, we can't assume the crash retrieval case of Roswell was a UAP, despite the good multiple testimony that would suggest it was.

The theoretical concepts are interesting if nothing more.

In '*Trojan Horse*', Keel emphasises the different types of 'UFOs' from 'Flying Cubes', 'Discs', and 'Triangles' to 'multi-coloured cigars' and 'transparent flying jellyfish,' (5). The variations of multiple UAP are beyond strange. For me, the multiple variations of the classic 'Flying Disc' are the most interesting. As Keel states from his research, there are some with wheels, wings, antennas, pointed domes and flat domes.

It is this variation which is a unique part of this mystery.

But what are the explanations for this?

Does human misconceptions and faulty memory account for all the very different and specific case details?

Additionally, how are all these UAP seemingly able to deploy some format of the same technology? (the AATIP five observables). Keel documents another ability, that of '*Temporary Transmogrification*,' which we referred earlier to as a 'trans-morphic' technological ability. That these anomalously unidentified aerial phenomena have control of reality at the quantum level, and can change shape, size, colour at will, whilst moving through our skies.

Are they shapeshifters?

If the anomalous can change or create their physical appearance at will, does that explain the multiple variations of unidentified vehicles? Or are there hundreds and hundreds of different objects coming from multiple origin sources.?

We still must be sceptical, as essentially, we don't have good data to verify this UAP ability, yet.

✳ ✳ ✳

Conclusions

The very early 'UFO' cases tell us that 'Flying Discs' existed in concentrated waves, almost as though a doorway was opened for them to pass freely back and forward between worlds/universes/dimensions. Could this 'wave' theory be an adequate explanation for the 'Many Worlds' theory – that many different things are coming from the multi-verse and that explains why there is so much variation of UAP within the given waves. Or does the UAP case data show us that the phenomenon is *one-thing*, one intelligence, and that this thing can change itself into many variations of whatever it desires. The early case data gives us clues as to the patterns of UAP origin, however, we are hindered by the reliability of data and missing information which might take us in a completely different direction.

Now we are starting to ask some real questions at last.

References

(1). Project Bluebook. (20th October, 1948). 'Case Report: Honolulu Flying Disc.'
Ancestry.
https://www.fold3.com/image/6387918

(2). Bloecher, T. (1967). 'Report on the UFO wave of 1947.'
University of Arizona.
https://static1.squarespace.com/
static/5c0fe5673c3a5343f2f06538/t/5e5ba4a2b-
cd48e5c8c442c21/1583064258132/Report_on_the_UFO_
wave_1947.pdf

(3). Project Bluebook. (28th of April, 1949). 'Case Report: Flying Discs.'
Ancestry.
https://www.fold3.com/image/6309694?terms=saucer

(4). Project Bluebook. (01st of October, 1948). 'Case Report: Flying Discs.'

Ancestry.
https://www.fold3.com/image/6388148i

(5). Keel, J. (1970). 'Operation Trojan Horse: The Classic Break-through Study of UFOs.'
Anomalist Books.

CHAPTER NINE: UAPINFO
CASE REPORT FILES

* * *

C ase reports of Unidentified Aerial Phenomena (UAP) have been the backbone of Ufology research over the past 70 plus years. Without the documented cases from military and civilian encounters, we simply wouldn't have the understanding and progression we have today about the anomalous. The value of such professionally wrote case reports featured within Projects Bluebook, Grudge and Sign should be seen as a benchmark for anyone who wants to investigate the phenomena seriously. Even the civilian initiatives of the Mutual UFO Network (MUFON) (1), and the National UFO Reporting Centre (NUFORC) (2), hold a massive database of cases that span 50 years. And it was from here that I drew my own inspiration. The UAP case reports that I wrote in 2018 are what got me started in UAP research. The following cases below are the reports that I wrote whilst at *UAPinfo* and *The Unidentified*. I tried to investigate the historical UFO cases, rather than simply focusing on UAP cases (UAP meaning the recent military incursions). The cases are broken down into the following sections: Location, Date (time), Incident, Possible Explanations, Analysis, Conclusion and Working Hypothesis.

Through this methodology, we can evaluate the case data holistically. With that in mind, I found that it is important to step back from *wanting* to find a specific conclusion, to avoid researcher bias, and consequently allow the case reports to show a holistic objective approach. Unfortunately, many believers and debunkers in the field of UFOs tend to set out with a predetermined narrative which goes against how science is supposed to work. Science doesn't care what the outcome is, and neither should we in the search for objective truth.

***

Case Report: #GLP001

The 'Kansas Flying Disc' is a lesser-known case from history and can be found in the Project Bluebook files online (3). This is an important case to include within the UAPinfo files, due to the fact the unknown aerial object was a reported 'disc' shape and appeared during the height of the 1947 wave (June-July, 1947). The 1947, 'Flying Disc/Saucer' wave incidentally and interestingly climaxed with the infamous Roswell crashes in the New Mexico desert in early July of that year. Intriguing that the 'Kansas Disc' appeared within days of the Roswell incident.

Case Report: The Kansas Flying Disc
Case ID: #GLP001
Date: 06/07/1947, (time 13.45, EST).
Location: 10-11'000ft, 100 miles west of Kansas City.

Incident:
A United States Airforce pilot (unnamed) reported a very bright and low object to his left (approximately 10 miles away), traveling at approximately 210MPH. After the pilot changed his aerial position, he considered that the unknown object was like the *'top of a water tank'*. When the pilot flew closer in his plane (unspecified type), he observed that the unknown object was approximately thirty to fifty feet in diameter. The 'Disc' was round and silvery in colour. The pilot estimated that the disc shaped object was roughly 1000 feet above his aircraft at 11'000 feet. It then appeared around one or two miles from his left wing. As the pilot turned towards the 'unknown', it completely disappeared. However, no additional details on how that occurred are available.

Possible explanations:
We might consider neurological or psychological explanations, or the possibility of a hoax. We might consider misidentifications of airspeed, maneuverers, shape, size and distance of the 'Flying Disc'. We also would need to consider an anomalous (non-human) technology, however, should be careful over assigning origin (ultra-terrestrials, extra-terrestrials, etc) with limited case data available.

Analysis:
The case was reported in Project Bluebook and its credibility is gained through the Airforce pilot's testimony, despite the pilot not being named or the type of aircraft involved. The single source witness is not backed by additional on-record testimony and no other evidence is presented. The large silver metallic disc is historically a typically reported shape, however without further video or witness testimony the case is hindered. Additionally, we must also consider neurological/psychological issues in single witness cases where the pilot is unnamed and can't be reached for verification. The final issue is that this is a 'cold case' from 70 years ago with no potential for additional forthcoming information.

Despite the disadvantages, the case portrays a close, highly detailed example of a pilot witnessing a traditional 'Flying Disc'. The question of anomalous technology is important here, and although we don't have data to suggest origin or destination, we do have enough to consider the potential reality of a 'Flying Disc.' No evidence of a hoax was found.

Overall, this is an official government case report from within the USAF's Project Bluebook of a genuine 'unidentified' vehicle of unknown origin that shouldn't be discounted.

Conclusion:
1). AATIP classification: The UAP displayed 'anti-gravity,' however none of the other 'five AATIP observables' were reportedly displayed by the UAP.

2). Despite the limited additionally data reported in this Blue-book case, the detailed account of a reported 'Flying Disc' by a trained military pilot is presented via an official government document.

3). More data is needed to conclude with a high degree of confidence.

Working Hypothesis: Unexplained -Anomalous Phenomena (Flying Disc), Psychological/Neurological effects, Other.

***

Case Report: #GLP002

The 'Gorman Dogfight' (4), (5), was an important historical case that essentially should be listed under the 'Foo-Fighters' classification. A small ball/orb of light that has the reported abilities of 'instantaneous acceleration' and 'anti-gravity' was reported by a military pilot and seen by other witnesses. This case was premiered on the first episode of the 2019 TV series 'Project Bluebook,' and is lent credibility through the USAF pilot who reported the incursion. For me, this was an important addition to the UAPinfo case report files.

Case Report: Gorman Dogfight
Case ID: #GLP002
Date: 01/10/1948 (time, 21:00, EST)
Location: Fargo, North Dakota, United States of America

Incident:
A fighter pilot by the name of George Gorman, encountered a bright ball of light during a flight in his P51 Mustang. The strange object was reportedly able to technologically out-perform his plane to the point that he was completely out-matched and outmanoeuvred in every possible way. Gorman had become witness to a strange unknown object that as he flew his P51 Mustang in the early evening above Fargo, North

Dakota in 1948. Gorman was in contact with the tower, he told them that he was going to pursue the unidentified object to record its identification markings. It was at this point that Gorman accelerated the Mustang's speed to its maximum capacity (roughly between 350 MPH and 400 MPH) in an attempt to try and close the distance between himself and the 'orb of light', however on each occasion the unknown object was travelling much too fast for him to get near.

According to the USAF Bluebook report, Gorman then attempted to intercept the object by manoeuvring with decisively acute turns that would then allow him to get closer.

Gorman forced his aircraft to make a swift right-angled turn and approached the object head-on at around 5,000 feet in altitude. At this point the unknown 'orb of light' quickly passed over his Mustang plane at an estimated close distance of only 500 feet.

In official debriefings and a report, the description given in the USAF report was that the object as a *'Flying Disc'*, however further description would also report the object as a *'white flying light'* that was round and relatively small (estimated 6inches in diameter) (5a) – not too dissimilar of the 'Foo-Fighter' objects of World War Two.

Gorman also reported that when the unknown object instantly accelerated its speed, the orb would stop *blinking* and then the illuminated vehicle would grow brighter.

After his near-collision, Gorman reported that he lost visuals on the unknown object. When he made visual contact once again, the object appeared to have made a 180-degree turn and was approaching his Mustang again. It was at this point that the object made a sudden rapid, vertical climb into the sky above him. Gorman attempted to again engage the unidentified object in his own climb, however, at approximately 14,000 feet the Mustang's engine stalled.

The object was still above him at around 2,000 feet. After regaining control, Gorman made two final attempts to get closer to the unknown object, however with no success.

The orb of light then swung around, making another head-on pass at him, before diverting off. It was at this point that the object had moved over the skies of Fargo Airport and was seen by the control tower and the air traffic controller. L.D. Jensen was on shift that night and viewed the object through binoculars but was unable to identify any detailed form or shape around the 'ball of light'. Jensen was later joined by Doctor Cannon and his passenger (unnamed) from the Piper Cub after they had landed from their flight at around 21:00. They then walked over to the control tower and tried to get a better view of the reported object (4).

At the same time, the pilot (George Gorman) continued to pursue the object until he was approximately 25 miles southwest of Fargo, North Dakota. Gorman reported that at roughly 14,000 feet he observed the light below him at 11,000 feet. Gorman then acted and dived his Mustang down towards the object at full power. However, again the object made a swift evading move, taking a very quick, steep vertical climb. Gorman again, tried to pursue, but was unable to get close and ultimately, the object passed out of visual range. At this point he stopped his pursuit; the time was now 21:27. Gorman then flew back to Fargo's Hector Airport and proceeded to report the incident.

In pilot George Gorman's statements from the time in 1948, he describes the object as a 'ball of light' and was convinced that there was *'definite thought behind its manoeuvres'* (4). He states that the object's acceleration was rapid, and it was able to turn sharp angles with considerable speeds, completely outmatching the abilities of his aircraft.

Possible Explanations:
A weather balloon has been proposed as a possible explanation for the unknown object and would come to be the official USAF version of events. The 'Air Weather Service' disclosed that on the 01st of October, 1948, they had released a weather balloon from Fargo, North Dakota at an approximate time of 20:50.

In theory, the explanation would be that by about 21:00 a weather balloon could potentially have been in the general area where both Gorman and the Piper Cub passengers would have first saw the unknown orb of light.

Investigators from 'Project Sign' stated that the reported movements of the unknown object could be due to Gorman's own manoeuvres in his Mustang as he chased the light. The theory is that the object's extreme manoeuvres were simply an illusion - a trick of what we might understand to be a parallax effect. The investigators from Sign also stated that, as the 'weather balloon' flew out of sight, Gorman had come to think that the planet Jupiter was the object, and therefore Gorman had been chasing the planet as he flew south of Fargo before giving up and returning to land. By early 1949 the Gorman case was labelled by 'Project Sign' and its successors, 'Project Grudge' and 'Project Bluebook', as being caused by a lighted weather balloon.

Additionally, we could consider potential psychological and/or neurological factors of all witnesses involved, although it's highly improbable.

Given the reported 'light orb' appearance and advanced propulsion capabilities of the UAP, we should also consider anomalous technology.

Analysis:

The UAP was able to display 'instantaneous acceleration,' with sharp rates of lateral and vertical climbs, 'anti-gravity,' with an un-aerodynamic shape and no signatures. Although the UAP reportedly travelled faster than the Mustang P-51, which had a top speed of 400MPH, to classify as hypersonic velocity the objects need to reach or exceed 3000MPH (Mach 5). Also, the UAP does not meet the other AATIP criteria of 'trans-medium travel', or 'low-observability,' based on what was reported - which is not to say the UAP doesn't have these other abilities, just that they weren't observed.

Multiple witnesses confirmed the physical aspect to the

object which would seemingly rule out psychological/neuro-logical explanations. No video or photos could be found of the object in question. One primary witness to the event was a fighter pilot with experience of aerial phenomena and who was a decorated World War Two pilot and was held in high regard. The concept that an experienced pilot is unable to identify a slow-moving weather balloon is difficult to pass as an explanation. The report of a *high propulsion, ball of white light* does not match the description of a slow almost static weather balloon which has no means of instant acceleration, vertical climb or otherwise. The idea that Jupiter became the weather balloon is highly speculative and although should be considered as an explanation, it should in no way be concluded as such, given the lack of supportive data. The other issue with such theories, are that they infer that the pilot is an inadequate pilot, who can't identify a static weather balloon for over 20 minutes.

The unknown light was witnessed by multiple persons on the ground, alongside the credibility of pilot George Gor-man. The object was not however caught on camera, nor has any radar data been made public. The alternative explan-ations (balloon, Jupiter, inadequate pilot assessment) lacked substantial supporting evidence, however, were still promoted as most likely by official Bluebook investigations. These case conclusions unfortunately discredited the scientific process by concluding on limited, speculative data.

Conclusion:
1). AATIP classification: The UAP displayed 'instantaneous ac-celeration' and 'anti-gravity' propulsion abilities.

2). The incursion has very similar traits to the 'Foo-Fighter' cases from 1942 onwards.

3). The USAF (Project Sign) conclusions were based upon a flawed, speculative methodology.

4). More data is needed to conclude with a high degree of

confidence.

Working Hypothesis: Unexplained – Anomalous Phenomena (Foo-Fighter), Weather Balloon, Celestial Body (asteroid, meteor, star, planet), Other.

***

Case Report: #GLP003

The 'Lubbock Lights' (7), (8), is a famous UAP case from history that fits the continued pattern of 'light formations' that are reported to travel across the sky. The case received attention from Captain Edward Ruppelt (6) of Project Bluebook. I chose to include this case as it provides a good example of how the early cases were investigated.

Case Report: The Lubbock Lights
Case ID: #GLP003
Date: 25/08/1951
Location: Lubbock, Texas, United States of America

Incident:
At roughly 21:00, on the 25th of August 1951, multiple 'Unidentified Aerial Phenomena' were witnessed over the Texan town of Lubbock in America. Specifically, and most notably, three professors from 'Texas Technological University', Doctor A.G. Oberg, chemical engineer, Doctor W.L. Ducker who was a department head, and Doctor W.I. Robinson who was a geologist – were sitting in the backyard of one of the Professor's homes when they observed the formation of lights' travel quickly overhead. They reported a total of around twenty to thirty lights, allegedly as bright as the stars but apparently much larger in size. They all stated that the lights flew over the yard at very fast speeds, in a reported *'matter of seconds'*. The professors immediately ruled out meteors due to lack of tails, the sequence, and shape of each, alongside the absence of any noise. It is reported that as they discussed their sighting a second, but similar formation of lights flew overhead. The

three men then reported their sighting to the local newspaper, the Lubbock Avalanche-Journal.

Other reports were made around the same time. For example, three women in the Lubbock area are supposed to have reported that they had witnessed their own sighing of 'flashing lights' in the sky on the same night of the three professor's sightings. Additionally, on the same night of the 25th, a Doctor by the name of Carl Hemminger, who was a professor of German at Texas Tech also reported seeing the lights.

Among other witnesses was a Lubbock woman (unnamed), who reported that in the August of 1951 she had witnessed a *'massive, soundless flying wing that passed directly over her house'*.

Another sighting occurred at a later date on the 05th of September 1951 that involved all of the three original men – Ducker, Robinson and Oberg, along with two other professors from Texas Tech, were sitting in Doctor Robinson's front yard when unknown lights flew overhead.

Doctor Grayson Mead would describe them as small, possibly the size of a 'dinner plate', and were greenish-blue and fluorescent in colour, flying in formation of twelve to fifteen. The objects were said to be 'circular' and smaller than the full moon (6), which was visible at the time.

The group of five professors witnessed one distinct patterned formation of lights flying at an estimated 2,000 feet. The group claimed to be able to calculate that the formation of lights were traveling at over 600 miles per hour. Mead claimed that the lights could not possibly have been simply 'birds', mainly due to their fast speed, amongst other things. The groups credibility was praised by Captain Ruppelt who stated they were qualified to observe a UFO (7).

Lubbock photos

On the 30th of August, 1951, a university freshman at Texas Tech by the name of Carl Hart claimed to witness a group of eighteen to twenty lights in a 'V' formation as they flew over his house. Carl took his camera to the backyard to see if the unknown lights would return.

Hart would report two more fleets of lights passing over his house as he watched from below. Hart was able to take a total of five photos before the objects eventually disappeared. Hart took the developed photos to the offices of the Avalanche-Journal in Lubbock.

Carl Hart's photographs were printed in the local and then also the national newspapers. They were even printed in LIFE magazine, who had taken an interest in the phenomena at that time.

Wright-Patterson Airforce Base in Ohio offered to analyse the photographs in their laboratory after they made headlines. After an investigation of the photos, Captain Ruppelt of Project Bluebook, wrote a statement saying that the Carl Hart photos might never be proven to be *hoaxed*, however, he also stated that they could not be taken as genuine either.

Hart consistently stated that the photos he captured are not hoaxed, despite various criticisms of claims of fraud.

The Texas Tech group of professors were shown the Carl Hart photos, they claimed that the photos did not represent what they had witnessed. Specifically, the professor's objects had flown in an apparent 'U' formation as opposed to the 'V' formation in Carl Hart's photos. Also, Hart's objects were of *'white lights'* whilst the professor's objects were described as *'blueish green lights'*.

Possible Explanations:

One of the main conventional explanations put forward at the time was a flock of birds. Captain Edward Ruppelt interviewed the primary witnesses to the Lubbock Lights when compiling his report for the USAF. At the time of the report, he concluded that a new type of streetlight was so powerful that it had reflected off the birds as they flew information above the town, specifically, a type of bird called a plover. The plovers were supposedly migrating over Lubbock at the time which caused the misidentified sightings.

In support of this conclusion, some local witnesses had claimed to have seen birds as they flew over Lubbock at the same time and had reflected lights. For example, a local farmer called Mr. Snider had stated that on the 31st of August, he had been witness to a flock of birds flying over a movie drive-through, he also claimed that the birds seemingly matched the description given by the professors.

Another local man by the name of Mr. Bryant and his wife claimed that on the 25th of August, (same night as original sighting of professors), he and his wife had allegedly witnessed a group of lights fly overhead, and then two other flights just the same as the professors had, however with closer inspection these were simply a flock of birds.

The potential for anomalous technology should also be considered based on the reported propulsion abilities. Silent lights that travelled quickly across the sky, without obvious signatures, indicated the potential for some of the five AATIP observables.

Analysis:
Various formations of lights were witnessed by credible people on different occasions, however only five photos officially exist of one sighting - Carl Hart's sighting. It is unclear if the lights were separate independent objects or connected to one large object. Should the UAP be anomalous phenomena, the un-aerodynamic shape of the smaller reported lights and/or the complete silence of a 'larger object' would both indicate 'anti-gravity' technology was deployed. However, the lack of noise would depend on various factors including other background noise and distance from the aerial vehicle to observer.

The estimated speed of 600MPH does not indicate 'hypersonic velocity', and the reported UAP case(s) do not meet the other AATIP criteria of 'trans-medium travel', 'instantaneous acceleration,' or 'low-observability.'

UNIDENTIFIED ANOMALOUS PHENOMENA

There are no official photos or videos of the three professors' sightings or any other witnesses' sightings. The descriptions vary from case to case, Hart described white lights, the group of professors stated they saw blueish-green lights. The speed of the objects has been said to be very fast, in one instance, at estimated 600 MPH.

The bird hypothesis is mostly probable for the individuals (Bryant, Snider, etc) who claim to have seen birds with reflected streetlamps. However, to imply that birds are responsible for all sightings is negligent of other witness statements.

Several attempts were taken to replicate the plover bird theory by taking photos of actual plovers over the streetlights in question, however the images were apparently too dim to be developed. Additionally, the migration patterns of plovers were ruled out by Doctor Cross, a biologist at Texas Tech.

Captain Ruppelt oh Bluebook would eventually state that the sightings probably could not have been caused by plovers - due to their slow speed in relation to reports and a tendency to fly in groups much smaller than the number of objects reported by eyewitnesses. Doctor Mead, one of the professors who had witnessed the lights, strongly disputed the plover explanation, stating that the objects he observed were *'too large'* and *'too fast'* to be birds (6).

With regards to the 'Flying Wing' explanation, Captain Ruppelt had suggested the U.S. Airforce did have a *'Flying Wing'* jet bomber and on that basis stated that at some of the potential sightings had been caused by the bomber, should it have been in operation at that time. However, according to the witnesses, the object (flying wing), made no sound as it flew overhead, which is problematic due to the incredibly loud engine sound such craft produced in low atmosphere. The 'Flying Wing' claim also has no photographic evidence to support the statements, or data to suggest they were operating in the area at that time.

Conclusion:

1). AATIP classification: The reported UAP displayed 'anti-gravity,' and none of the other 'five AATIP observables'.

2). The series of reported UAP across the late August to early September week cannot be correlated as the same phenomenon due to a lack of data.

3). There is not enough supportive evidence to make any conclusive hypothesis in this case. A satisfactory explanation has not been presented in this case to determine origin within a high degree of confidence.

Working Hypothesis: Unexplained - Anomalous Phenomena, Flock of Birds, Military Aircraft, Other.

***

Case Report: #GLP004

The most famous case of the 1950s was in the July of 1952. The 'Washington incursions' have been researched within Ufology more than most other cases (6), (9), (10), (11), (12), (14). The political and military engagement sparked a revolution in UAP acknowledgement that spanned into science and pop culture which lasted decades. Arguably, most of what we know about how historical UFO cases were handled within government occurred because of the media frenzy that accompanied the case. The case, like with the 1947 wave, spiked in the hot July of 52 with a significant increase in public awareness.

Case Report: The Washington D.C. incursions
Case ID: #GLP004
Date: 19/07/1952 + 26/07/1952
Location: Washington D.C.

Incident:

Saturday, 11.40pm, 19th of July, 1952

The night of Saturday the 19th, eight unidentified radar tracks instantly appeared on the tracking screens at Washington National Airport. The unknowns were confirmed by Edward Nugent - the air traffic controller on duty that night. The same radar tracks would later be confirmed by both Andrews and Bolling Air Force bases (NOU), (9). The objects were positioned south and then east of Andrews Airforce base and were also spotted by several airliners and towers at the time.

Captain Edward Ruppelt of Project Bluebook wrote that they weren't planes due to the instantaneous acceleration displayed (6). The objects were tracked on radar traveling in formation, between speeds of 100MPH to 130MPH. Reportedly, a couple would instantly accelerate to speeds of 7'000MPH.

Further airline pilots are said to have spotted bright lights hovering in the position of the radar tracks, with one pilot spotting a 'bright light' just after midnight. Another six hovering lights were identified over the next fifteen minutes by the same Capital American pilot - who is unnamed by Ruppelt in his 1956 book (6) but would later be confirmed as Casey Pierman.

Harry G. Barnes, a senior controller at Washington National Airport, recalled that the erratic movements of the unknown lights were radical in comparison to those of any ordinary aircraft he was used to dealing with. He stated that they moved so quickly that radar struggled to track them (13), (14). Barnes then called the National Airport's radar-equipped control tower to report the incident and get clarification.

That night, the controllers there, were Howard Cocklin and Joe Zacko. They both confirmed that they also had unknown tracks on their radar screen and had personally seen a hovering 'bright light' in the night sky, which they stated had departed with 'incredible speed'.

The unknown lights hovered and travelled through highly restricted airspace, looming above the American capitol, and reportedly passed near to the White House and the Capital Building itself.

The immediate response from the military was to send up 'F-94 interceptors' to engage the unknowns. However, according to those operators observing from the radar rooms, such as USAF press spokesperson Albert Chop, the unknown lights disappeared as the jets approached. It is unclear whether they accelerated at high speed or fell off radar. No visual contact was made by the pilots on this night as they approached the merge plot (that we know about).

Saturday, 08:15pm, 26th of July, 1952

One week on from the first incursions, a commercial plane was flying over the D.C. area and coming to land in Washington. Above them were reported 'unknown lights' as they flew with seemingly intelligence. There were once again blips on radar above the American Capital. Radar data was showing identified 'unknowns' in the skies and struggled to adjust for the extreme manoeuvres of the objects.

At 11.30 p.m., the Airforce scrambled two F-94 interceptor fighter jets that flew from New Castle Airforce base in Delaware.

Whilst Captain John McHugo was unable to locate the unknown objects, his wing-man pilot, Lieutenant Willian Patterson, engaged the radar blips head on. Patterson described the unknowns as *'four white glows'*, (13), (15), and proceeded to chase them, however, he was unable to catch them due to their advanced speed. Airforce spokesman Albert Chop, who was present in the radar room at the time, describes the UFOs as disappearing whenever the fighter jets came too close. Chop stated that '.... *the minute they (fighter jets) left, the UFOs came back.*' (15). Seemingly, the unknowns were reacting to the fighter jets presence.

An Airforce information officer by the name of Lt. Col. Moncel Monts had made a following statement to the press that the pilots *'had been under orders to investigate unidentified objects to shoot them down if they can't be talked down'*.

Tuesday, 29th of July, 1952

The aftermath saw an increased focus and attention on the phenomena, with mainstream newspaper articles across the United States headlining, 'Saucers Swarm Over Capital,' and 'Jets Chase D.C. Sky Ghosts.' This would prove to be the high point of publicity for the 'UFOs'. Then, on Tuesday, 29th of July, the biggest press conference since World War Two was held.

On *UFOs*.

Researchers such as Michael Swords have gone into detail about the press conference (16), that occurred after the second incursion. Military men were talking openly and freely, but not everyone wanted this policy to remain in place.

General Sanford, a Pentagon Major General, would hold a press conference following on from the Washington incursions in an to attempt to explain how the USAF was trying to resolve sightings that they perceived as a 'menace' to the United States. The conclusion was that yet again, 'temperature inversions' had fooled radar operators and other witnesses.

Scientific details about how such radar temperature inversions could trick experienced operators were not discussed, neither was the contradictory statements made from such operators who were able to recognise such inversions when they occurred.

Possible explanations:

We can consider 'temperature inversions', as a potential explanation for the radar tracks on both weekends. We can consider 'light refractions' for the objects viewed by the USAF pilot Patterson. Additionally, we might also consider psychological or neurological explanations of those multiple witnesses. With regards to the pilot, would any potential decompression sickness (the bends) or hypoxia cause vivid hallucinations, etc. Possibly we might also consider that the pilot was potentially chasing 'light refractions' from some external source, which would again come under a category of misidentifications. Also, we might look towards misidentifications such as streetlights, car lights, spotlights, meteors and stars.

We must consider something anomalous also occurred, given the potential technology that was able to evade interceptors.

Analysis:

The Washington National Incursions can be taken with a certain degree of accuracy due to the fact the case report data comes primarily from Project Bluebook's Captain Edward Ruppelt who was briefed with Colonel Bower in Major Fournet's office by the intelligence officer from Bolling Airforce base. From this we can assign a higher level of accuracy to what is being reported across the two weekends. Project Bluebook (and the USAF) would conclude that the D.C. sightings were nothing more than 'temperature inversions' and the witness visual sightings were nothing more than misidentified meteors, stars, and city lights. Without confirmed and verified photographic evidence we simply do not have enough to really conclude in these instances. I have chosen not to include a detailed analysis of the well-known photo of the 'lights over the Capitol Building', due to the insufficient supporting data that included the un-holistic Ufology conclusions of possible lights reflecting onto clouds. We should avoid conclusively stating any concrete affirmation on the basis of that particular unverifiable photo. Also, we might consider that any genuine in-depth analysis would reveal an inconclusive outcome.

From an analytical perspective, we can focus on data that we do have, and that is witness testimony from various individuals such as Fmr. radar controller Howard Cocklin. Cocklin told the Washington Post in 2002 that he saw an unidentified light hovering and stating that he personally saw the unknowns on radar and from the window over Washington National Airport (9). Cocklin gives us a significant claim and bolsters the theory that *something* was there, and not temperature inversions that effected the radar.

The claims that the lights were a result of 'mass hysteria' were quickly criticised with high confidence by psychologists at the time and still would be today. Hysteria doesn't induce hallucinations at an individual level (without prior mental health issues such as schizophrenia) or at the group level.

Some claims have theorised that a genuine incursion over the capital of America, would in theory, result in more than two fighter jets being sent up by the Airforce to protect the nation. Arguably however, any such hypothetically undisclosed pilots who might have flown are simply not on record, or not permitted to be on record - even just to say they didn't encounter anything. Therefore, we must be careful to speculate over data we simply don't have access to.

A question can be raised over whether the on-record pilot (Lt. Patterson) did actually encounter unknowns and had a visual on the *'light objects'* – potentially we might consider psychological or neurological issues under a category of pilot misidentifications. However, again this would be speculation considering an absence of data on the pilot's mental health history, or various potential conditions that might create neurological issues during this flight. Would the potential decompression sickness (the bends) or hypoxia cause vivid hallucinations, etc.

Possibly we might also consider that the pilot was potentially chasing 'light refractions' from some external source, which would again come under a category of misidentifications.

And finally, we might consider that more sensitive information was held back by the Airforce under high levels of classification, and that the pilots were placed under strict nondisclosure orders by the Airforce. It is not uncommon for the military to hold back classified information in the interests of national security.

However, this is speculation and without verifying data, it will remain as such.

Conclusion:

1). AATIP classification: The reported UAP displayed, 'instantaneous acceleration', 'hypersonic velocity', 'low observability' and 'anti-gravity'.

2). The series of reported UAP across the July week cannot be correlated as the same phenomenon due to a lack of cross-section data.

3). Seemingly, the USAF explanation of 'temperature inversions' doesn't fit the multiple visual sightings reported by multiple persons over those two July weekends.

4). This case remains unexplained, more data is needed to conclude with a high degree of confidence.

Working Hypothesis: Unexplained - Anomalous Phenomena, Weather/Temperature Inversions, Mass Hysteria, Psychological and/or Neurological issues, Other.

***

Case Report: #GLP005

I choose to include this strange case due to the fact it highlights some of the more bizarre elements to the UAP/ UFO phenomena. The 'paranormal' case of the 'Flatwoods Monster' (17), (18), and links to 'high strangeness' are often dismissed by mainstream Ufologists, however, should not be overlooked without further investigation. The Flatwoods case is a prime example of the more extreme phenomena.

Case Report: Flatwoods Monster
Case ID: #GLP005
Date: 02/09/1952
Location: Flatwoods, Braxton County, West Virginia, United States of America

Incident:

At around 7:15 p.m. on the 12th of September, 1952, an incident occurred in Flatwoods, West Virginia. Two young brothers – Edward May, aged 13, and Fred May aged 12, along with their younger friend Tommy Hyer, aged 10, witnessed an unusual object on the sky as it fell. They all claimed to have seen a *'bright reddish-orange object'* moving across the evening sky, which then come down past the property of a local farmer, a one Mr. G. Bailey Fisher. Together, the boys decided to head home where their mother Kathleen May was and inform her of what they had just seen in the sky moments ago. The three boys told her the story of the strange light in the sky and how it seemed to have crashed not too far away from them on the farmer's property. Kathleen May, then proceeded to accompany the three boys along with local children Neil Nunley, aged 14, and Ronnie Shaver, aged 10. The group was also joined by the West Virginia Guardsman Eugene Lemon, aged 17. The group then went onto the Fisher farm property to locate whatever it was that the boys said they had seen.

As the group reached the top of the hill, one of the boys, Neil Nunley, stated he saw something, a pulsing red-light ahead of them. The oldest boy, Eugene Lemon said that he aimed a flashlight in the direction of the light and then momentarily saw a tall *"...man-like figure with a round, red face surrounded by a pointed, hood-like shape"*. At this point, Engine Lemon was said to have screamed and fell backwards in terror of what he had seen (18).

Descriptions of the *monster* varied. In an article for 'Fate Magazine' and based on his tape-recorded interviews with witnesses, UFO researcher Gary Barker described the figure as approximately 10 feet tall, with a round blood-red face, a large pointed *"hood-like shape"* around the monster's face with eye-like shapes which emitted a *'greenish-orange light'*, and a dark black or possibly green body. Kathleen May, described the monster as having *"small, claw-like hands"*, and clothing-like folds, and also,

'...a head that resembled the ace of spades'.

According to other versions of the story, when the monster made a hissing sound and *"glided toward the group"*, Eugene Lemon then screamed and dropped his flashlight, causing the group to instantly run away. The group consensus was they had smelled a *"pungent mist"* and some later said they were also nauseated.

At the time, the local sheriff and his deputy had even been investigating unverified reports of a crashed aircraft in the rural area, although it is not confirmed of the two incidents are linked. Having searched the alleged area by which the monster was seen, they claimed to not have seen, heard, or smelled anything.

Possible Explanations:
After investigating the Flatwoods case thoroughly in 2000 (17), Joe Nickell of the Committee for Sceptical Inquiry (CSI) concluded that the bright light in the sky reported by the witnesses on the 12th of September was most likely a meteor. He stated that the pulsating red-light was likely an aircraft navigation/hazard beacon, and that the metallic bodied, blood red faced, 10ft tall monster, described by witnesses, closely resembled that of an owl (17). Nickell suggested that witnesses' perceptions were distorted by their heightened state of anxiety. Nickell's conclusions are shared by several other investigators, including those of the Airforce in later years.

The night of the 12th of September, 1951 sighting, a falling meteor had been observed traveling across three states - Maryland, Pennsylvania and West Virginia. According to sceptical writer, Joe Nickell and others, three flashing red aircraft beacons were also visible from the area of the sightings at the time, which could have accounted for bizarre descriptions of the *'pulsating red-light'* and red tint on the face of the supposed *monster*. Nickell wrote m that the shape size, movement, and specific sounds reported by the witnesses were also relatively consistent with the silhouette, flight pattern, and standard call of a barn owl perched within a tree.

Some researchers concluded that the shadowy foliage which was beneath the owl at the time might have created an optical illusion of sorts. This optical trick of the light could account for the lower portions of the monster that was described as wearing a *'pleated green skirt'*.

From a conventional perspective, the slight variations on what was observed by witnesses are problematic with regards to accuracy. Specific details can be explained by varying terrestrial explanations. For example, Kathleen May reported that the monster had *'small, claw-like hands'* that *'extended in front of it,'* also loosely matched the description of a barn owl with its clawed talons that would grip a tree branch.

According to sceptical writer Ryan Haupt, he wrote in 2014 that the nausea experienced by the group could have come from *'hysteria and over-exertion,'* (19). Whilst being honest in their testimony, the shock of seeing a misidentified owl could have frightened the entire group.

Analysis:
The multiple person sighting gives his case credible intrigue and problematic issues. The witness accounts although relatively similar do have some differences. No photos or videos are available beyond an artist's impression, which hinder the case. No examination of physical trace evidence at the scene was analysed. The slight variation of how the monster looked to each witness adds to the strangeness. The question over whether the monster was a real physical entity or a result of 'psychic' projection, or neurological/psychological manifestations is yet to be appropriately determined.

The debunking attempts are highly improbable, ignoring what was being stated by multiple witnesses and instead inserting their own conventional narrative. Associating a 1-2ft owl with a 9-10ft creature is difficult to accept - for this explanation to work we need to believe that the entire group wouldn't be able to recognise the shadow of an owl or the owl itself. Also, individual and group hysteria by itself doesn't equate to visual/audio hallucinations, there is simply no official psychological research to support this claim.

The light which was observed to move across the sky did not match general descriptions of a meteor. Whereas there is no substantial body of evidence to suggest extra-terrestrials, we also cannot rule out such things due to a lack of data.

The debunking of the Flatwoods case is highly speculative. However, we should certainly not rule out the possibility of terrestrial explanations and consider the misidentification theory due to faulty memory and various human cognitive fallacies. We are reluctant to make any speculation as to the origin or nature of the observed 'monster' due to the lack of supportive evidence in this case and the extreme claims made by the group of witnesses.

Additionally, due to a poor scientific examination of the 'landing site' and surrounding area in the early 1950s, we don't know what other contaminants might have been involved at that point. Toxins, radiation, natural gas leaks or psychedelic inducing substances might have triggered neurological/psychological effects alongside mass hallucinations and hysteria.

However, we simply do not know.

Conclusions:
1). As part of the AATIP classification, we don't have enough data to verify the nature or abilities of the 'unidentified flying object' as it allegedly fell to Earth and crashed at Flatwoods.

2). The case is significantly impacted by limited data. The explanations presented cannot be accepted as probable due to the speculative conclusions reached, again, without supporting data.

3). More data is needed to conclude with a high degree of confidence.

Working Hypothesis: Unexplained – Type of Owl, Psychological/Neurological Hallucinations, Anomalous Phenomena, Other.

***

Case Report: #GLP006

As the search for answers about the Pentagon UAP programs continued, my own search into the historical UAP cases looked to other countries from the same timeframe. Again, writing case reports for UAPinfo and publishing them online, I investigated older cases from European countries. One interesting case of note came from Italy in the 50's from Italy (20).

As reported by the BBC article from 2014 (20), a case report from Italy became headline news across Italy in the October of 1954 after a reserve game between Fiorentina and Pistoiese was stopped due to a 'UAP'.

Case Report: Fiorentina Football Stadium (1954)
Case ID: #GL006
Date: 27/10/1954
Location: Stadio Artemis Franchise, Florene, Italy.

Incident:
At a football (soccer) match in Fiorentina, in front of a crowd of 10'000 fans, the referee stopped play between the two sides as the players stood and looked to the skies above them. It was reported that strangely shaped objects travelled quickly across the clear skies before stopping suddenly above them and hovered. The two 'Cylinder' shaped objects then reportedly dropped a *'silver glitter'* like substance to the ground.

Present at the football match in 1954 was a young Fiorentina fan, Gigi Boni, who would in later years state that he believed the objects to be extra-terrestrial in origin. He stated the objects *'moved very fast and then just stopped'*, and resembled cylindrical objects, like Cuban cigars as he described them (20).

Possible explanations:

Some accounts have suggested that the two objects might be 'birds' that flew and then hovered/floated on the warm rising air. Other had suggested that they saw planes that only appeared to move fast and the angle from the ground made it look as though they had stopped still. Others have suggested that the objects were balloons, whilst others say they were tricks of the light. In later years sceptical analysis attempted to link the collected objects residue material as spider webs which were common at the time however on chemical analysis no link was established.

Analysis:

The incident was witnessed by thousands of people, although it is only possible to verify a small number of witness testimony. The objects were reported as being both 'cigar' shaped and 'egg' shaped by different reports. No identifying photographs were taken of the objects. The witness's testimony did not match any explanations of floating spider webs, nor did the chemical analysis at the time support the theory. The objects didn't fit the theories of birds, balloons or planes, however with only witness testimony it becomes difficult to provide a satisfactory conclusion.

Conclusion:

1). As part of the AATIP classification: the UAP objects potentially (not verified) demonstrate 'hypersonic velocity' speeds and 'anti-gravity'.

2). The case is significantly effected by a lack of data which would verify the nature of the reported objects and their potential aerial abilities.

3). More data is needed to conclude with a high degree of confidence.

Working Hypothesis: Unexplained - Anomalous Phenomena,

Birds, Aircraft, Other.

***

Case Report: #GLP007

This case report (21), (22), is just one of many reported green light UAP instances which involve physical burns to the body. Where the beam makes contact with the skin the result is localised paralysis of the upper and lower limbs. The individual was a young female at the time with no prior mental health problems.

Case Report: Denise Bishop
Case ID: #GLP007
Date: 10/09/1981
Location: Plymouth, England

Incident:
In 1981, a 23-year-old witness by the name of Denise Bishop was returning to her home in Plymouth, England. As she got out of the taxi, she suddenly became aware of aerial lights and activity to the backend of the property. As she approached, she was confronted by an a UAP that was hovering. As reported by the witness to the media, the object was unusual in shape;

- The UAP was approximately 125ft in diameter, with an unusual aerodynamic shape (the main 'hull' apparently resembling a 'crab'). The UAP appeared dark metallic. The UAP produced pink, purple and white lights from underneath the object. The UAP hovered silently. The UAP able to direct a 'green laser beam' at the witness.

The witness attempted to unlock her front door and enter her property. At this point, a bright green 'laser-beam' came from the UAP and made contact with her left hand. This reportedly paralysed her to the spot. Despite the fact she was unable to move, she claimed to have been conscious throughout the experience. The 'green laser beam' reportedly caused a burn upon the affected area which reportedly lasted weeks. Denise disclosed the incident to both her partner and to her sister. A police report was made and investigated. The case was picked up by the local paper.

Possible explanations:
We must consider the possibility of psychological and neurological explanations. We can consider the possibility of a hoax. Additionally, we can consider the UAP was anomalous technology.

Analysis:
The unusual 'crab' shape is an interesting element to the UAP case. If accurate, it shows an un-aerodynamic shape with possible 'anti-gravity' anomalous technological abilities. The object is described as an unusual shape - which specifically is rare within Ufology case reports, however it is not rare if we classify the object under the 'other' category - alongside 'transmorphic' UAP, etc.

Denise Bishop is the only witness to this event which hinders the case in terms of its validity, primarily due to the single source. The individual experienced burns on her left hand, where she claims the green laser beam strikes her, which would be difficult to produce (in doing so would suggest mental health issue if self-inflicted). The individual speaks openly to family and files a police report suggesting the family believe her story which an important aspect of credentials to the case. There is no openly available data to support the claims of any psychological/neurological issues regarding the individual (although we have limited data to access), also there is nothing to suggest the witness was hoaxing the experience. The case is hindered by a lack of corroborated data and testimony.

Conclusion:
1). As part of the AATIP classification: the UAP displays 'anti-gravity'.

2). The case depends upon one witness, no information indicating that the individual had a history of mental illness. The object and its intentions are not clear from the reports going back to 1981. The issue of missing time is not fully clear from early reports.

3). The unusual shape is significant of the extreme variation within UAP cases.

4). More data is needed to conclude with a high degree of confidence, particularly with regard to ruling out potential psychological/neurological factors.

Working Hypothesis: Unexplained – Anomalous Phenomena, Psychological/Neurological effects.

***

Case Report: #GLP008

This case report I will mention from the UAPinfo files was my own. The 'Holly How Green Light' was the first time I had ever considered the thought of something 'Alien' (23).

Case Report: Holly How Green Light
Case ID: GLP008
Date: March, 1997.
Location: Holly How Youth hostel, Coniston water, Lake District, England.

Incident:
On a school trip in the early spring of 1997, a group of school children aged 14/15 spent a weekend in a youth hostel located near Lake Coniston. One night between 1am and 2am one boy awoke to see a green laser beam scanning the room through the window using sequenced patterns.
The individual stated the beam was under intelligent control, scanning in a sequenced pattern. The green laser then

proceeded to scan each sleeping boy individually before an incident unknown by the boy and at which point, he fell unconscious. The following morning nothing was discussed by any of the teachers or children. Following the incident, the boy developed a small scar in the shape of a backwards number 7 on his left wrist.

Possible explanations:
We need to consider sleep paralysis and the fallacy of memory. Also, we can look to 'light refractions' from external sources.

Analysis:
The claims within this report are only substantiated by one individual without corroborating evidence. The time of the encounter may suggest the individual was not fully awake or suffering a form of sleep paralysis however this was stated as not being the case by the individual at the time. The question of mistaken perception is regarded as low due to the specific nature of the claims given that the individual was claiming to be fully conscious. Reflections and refractions of external light are ruled out due to the rural location, and no source could be identified at the time.

To formally assess this case, it is imperative to acknowledge a strict guideline which adheres to contextual analysis only, any speculation must be kept to an absolute minimum. Within this case we are subject to a *'Green Laser Beam'* apparently scanning adolescent children all though we cannot know the specific intentions (or lack thereof). No person suffered any physiological or no psychological effects. Only one person (15-year-old male) remembers the encounter. The scar of a backwards 7, although appeared from the same timeframe in March/April 1997, although cannot be correlated to the incident.

Conclusion:
1). No evidence of anomalous phenomena is evident with the

data available.

2). More data is needed prior to making a formal conclusion.

Working Hypothesis: Unexplained - Possible lucid dreaming state of the boy in question.

***

Case Report: #GLP009

Possibly the most significant mass sighting in history. It has been said that if the Phoenix Lights (24) happened in 2017 rather than 1997, social media 'UFO disclosure' would have occurred overnight with thousands of handheld camera phones capturing lights and huge aerial vehicles as they hovered over the state of Arizona. This was a case report that had to be included within my UAP files, and to date is arguably the most convincing incident that indicates something anomalous occurred in the late nineties. Additionally, the inclusion of a reported *'mile wide triangle craft'* brings into question significant problems about the origin and destination of such a massive vehicle. Surely, such objects cannot simply enter our atmosphere without leaving a very significant footprint.

Case Report: The Phoenix Lights
Case ID: GLP009
Date: 13/03/1997
Location: Phoenix to Tucson, Arizona, United States

Incident:
In early evening of March 13th, 1997, people in Arizona were out stargazing hoping to catch a glimpse of the Hale-Bopp comet. A massive craft estimated to be a mile wide slowly travelled across the state of Arizona and most notably across the city of Phoenix. The craft was witnesses by thousands of people across the state and reports were made into the hundreds. According to witnesses the craft was a 'V' shape with two lights on either wing and one in the middle. The craft was

completely silent and blocked out stars as it passed overhead.

The Lynne Katei sightings (1995, 1997)

Personally, I'd recommend you watch the documentary or read Dr. Lynne Katei and her book 'The Phoenix Lights' (24). Documented is an incident in which Lynn and her husband witnessed the famous event, and three silent triangular orange oval shaped orb lights two years prior (1995) in the same area in Phoenix, approximately 100 yards from their home.

Katei describes them as three-six feet each in size, with the light of each orb contained within the orb. Katei describes how the top orb dimmed from view, and at this point she took a photo of the remaining two orbs. She believes that there was an intelligence watching her from the lights (24).

On the 22nd of January 1997, Katei reports witnessing three amber orbs hoovered on the horizon over Phoenix, this time they were horizontal. The next night on 23rd of January 1997, they hung over South Mountain, the lights blinked out then reappeared, as Katei takes a photo, another six equally shaped horizontal orbs appear in formation above the three. In total there was nine.

They were reported to be in the same formation and same location as the famous March 13th case, which would occur two months later. What impressed me is that the objects were caught on video, held formation (didn't drop in altitude) and are unexplained to a level of certainty, even to this day. The air traffic controllers at Sky Harbor Airport (in front of South Mountain) reported seeing the lights but had nothing on radar. The FAA confirmed that there were three lights at 8pm, but weren't on radar, and at 8.30pm the six appeared. Katei was told by a traffic controller they looked through binoculars at the six lights, that appeared to be attached to something as they floated, and 'slowly moved in synchrony' behind South Mountain. We don't know where these lights disappeared to, and if they didn't appear on radar, it might not have been known by the U.S. military, although I believe they know more about the Katei January 1997 signing than was ever spoken about.

Another interesting point to note is that from South Mountain to Barry Goldwater Airforce range is about 146km, Luke Airforce base is about 35km away and it is 570km from the coast and Catalina Island area by which the U.S.S. Nimitz (2004) incursions happened. Whether nuclear facilities were at Luke Airforce base or the test Goldwater range in 1997 is not known.

The famous mass sighting (13th of March, 1997)

In early evening of March 13th, 1997, people in Arizona were out stargazing hoping to catch a glimpse of the Hale-Bopp Comet in the skies over Arizona. It is thought the vast numbers of people looking up meant a higher volume of reports. The incident has been captured perfectly in one of the best documentaries ever made on the encounters that night, 'The Phoenix Lights,' based on the book by Lynne Katei of the same name. The witnesses are compelling, credible and speak about the same types of observed experiences.

1). Tom Chavez was a Fmr. Policeman and private investigator at the time, he was at 27th avenue Van Buren, Phoenix in his car, when he looked up to see an object floating at a constant speed. *"They didn't glare or emit like a landing light, floodlight type craft, there was some depth to them."*

2). Joan Mortensen was a critical nurse at the time, she stated that there was a triangle shape to her own sighting that night. *"I noticed there was a triangle shape, three huge lights, and they weren't beaming down like landing lights, they were just big balls of light."*

3). George Judson, an Interior Graphic and Fine Artist from Phoenix, reported seeing an object come towards him from the north, he described three enormous lights moving incredibly slow. *"I would estimate this object to be, several football fields, maybe a mile, maybe even two miles, it was huge."*

4).Terri Mansfield, a Hospice Volunteer, was sat with her co-workers on the patio when they reportedly saw a huge, dark. silent, object that appeared over their heads. *"We could not see the whole object, front to front, side to side, it was that big....and it just kept going and going and going over our heads, and it seemed like we could just reach up and touch it, it was that low."*

5). Mike Fortson, a former honour guard in the U.S. Navy, states the 'V' shaped object was under 3000ft. *"As it passed, we could only see the left wing of the craft, that's how low it was as it passed...and I said to my wife at the time, that's a mile long."*

6). Trudy Guyker reported the object (triangle 'V' craft) was floating over the tops of houses.

7). Tom Brunty stated that it was an orangish-amber light, *"it was almost as if the orb was crafted out of light. They are perfect in every geometric aspect that could be observed. They were perfectly, uniformly round, they were perfectly equally distanced, they blocked out stars as they moved."*

8). Kurt Russel the actor came forward and spoke with Jimmy Kimmel on his show in 2018, he said that he was flying as a civilian pilot at the time and saw the six lights above the airport with his son as they came to land over Phoenix (25). Interesting, he called the Air Traffic Controllers at Sky Harbour Airport who confirmed they had nothing on radar in the sky above the airport.

9). Fife Symington, the governor at the time, was one witness to this incident. As governor he originally ridiculed the idea of alien origin, calling a press conference and then unmasked his chief of staff dressed up as an alien. However, as mentioned earlier in the book, he called the lights he personally saw "*otherworldly*" after admitting he saw a huge 'V' shaped craft (26).

***

There were allegedly two distinct events involved in the 1997 incident: a triangular formation of lights seen to pass over the state, and a series of stationary lights seen in the Phoenix area. The United States Air Force later identified the second group of lights as flares dropped by A-10 Warthog aircraft that were on training exercises at the Barry Goldwater Range in southwest Arizona.

Possible explanations:
The official USAF explanation is 'Military Flares' which must be considered. Psychological and/or Neurological explanations must be considered. Anomalous technology is also to be evaluated as a genuine explanation.

Analysis:
The incident is widely accepted as the most documented UAP case in history, due to the thousands of witnesses and the advanced aerial vehicle(s). The vast multitude of witnesses pretty much rule out both psychological and neurological explanations on a mass scale. Additionally, we should consider psychological and neurological explanations that might include 'psychic projections', however, we do not have access to radar data to determine origin or destination which would allow us a better understanding of the UAP nature. Also, there is no known theory as to how mass psychic projections would or could occur.

The 'V' shaped craft(s), huge size and silence indicate anomalous technology (non-human technology), that include 'anti-gravity,' and possibly 'low observability' (no radar data has been made public). The 'Phoenix Lights' case documents a craft which defies our current understanding of physics, as logically, no terrestrial craft is capable of hovering silently whilst at the size of a *'mile wide'*. Lights of varying shape and colour are reported to have accompanied the UAP that night of the 13th. It is possible that this was a secret military craft, however the scale and the resources needed to build such a massive craft would be astronomical. The question is also asked, *'why fly secret advanced craft over a populated city?'*

Also, we can state with a high degree of confidence that what was reported doesn't match 'flares', as suggested by the USAF. There is limited video camera footage of differing lights above Phoenix that night or in the prior weeks and months. Also, there has been no direct clear footage of the huge 'V' shaped craft that allows for any detailed analysis.

Conclusion:

1). As part of the AATIP classification: the UAP displays 'anti-gravity' and possibly 'low observability'.

2). This is certainly a unique case and very unlikely to be flares due to the hundreds upon hundreds of corroborating statements which do not support the flare hypothesis.

3). More data is needed prior to making a formal conclusion.

Working Hypothesis: Unexplained - Anomalous Phenomena, Military Flares.

***

Case Report: #GLP010

The 'Dome of the Rock' UAP case offers that unique perspective that most others do not. The case displays 'instantaneous acceleration' on camera and has several witnesses. The UAP is caught on camera from different angles and also can be contrasted via a rare 'time-lapse' approach. The case is also unique due to the specific location, both Jerusalem and the dome of the rock are both historically significant Christianity and Islam. The case also has its criticisms stemming from an apparent hoaxed video.

Case Report: Dome of the Rock
Case ID: GLP010
Date: 13.00, January, 2011
Location: Dome of the Rock, Jerusalem

Incident:
One o'clock in the morning over Jerusalem, a bright glowing light was observed descending from the night sky. The object hovers over the dome of the rock (slightly moves from right to left) for only a few minutes before an explosion of light and then an incredibly fast vertical climb up into space within a second.

The part of the night sky in which the orb rapidly ascends is then lit up by multiple flashing red lights. The incident was captured on at least 4 known videos posted over YouTube and includes a potentially hoaxed video. Israeli Eligael Gedalyovich was allegedly one of the observers of this event and produced one of the videos (the first video in which you are able to see a man on his phone videoing the event).

Possible explanations:
We must consider that at least one or more of the UAP videos have been hoaxed. There is a strong suggestion of deception in a UAP video that displays potential CGI and edited audio. Should the other videos be real we should consider anomalous technology.

Analysis:
This case is unique as it contains multiple witnesses from different areas around the dome from the time of the incident. Most importantly the case captures advanced propulsion. The UAP is captured on 3 cameras and are all backed up with authentic audio including the appropriate reactions of people who have witnessed advanced propulsion. The three separate videos show multiple witnesses from different camera angles

and locations, at least two men (audio and visual confirmation) and a woman (audio). The time lapse of each video is consistent from the movement of the craft over the city from left to right, and consistent bright light flash. The videos appear to demonstrate a consistency between the first three.

The 4th video is proximally the closest video to the event and displays an incident which doesn't match the original 3 videos in terms of the timeline. This 4th video does not show the flash of light seen in the other videos. This video also has audio of the 'Mississippi women' who reacts more like she is watching a fire work display and not as though she has just witnessed the 'impossible'. The vast majority of media quickly attempted to dismiss the entire case as a hoax based primarily on this video despite the multiple witnesses and camera footage. A thorough investigation has not been exhausted.

The 'Dome of the Rock' UAP case is generally thought to be a hoaxed case, however this is far from conclusive. The 4th video that was used by the media in the days after the event, has unfortunately dominated the overall impression of the case. Many media sources at the time claimed the Jerusalem UAP case was a 'proven' hoax. Ben Redford wrote in 2011 that thousands of people were there at the time and no one else reported seeing it (27). However, at approximately one o'clock in the morning, people generally do not stay up in their thousands, maybe in a Las Vegas nightclub but not the holy city of Jerusalem.

Eligael Gedalyovich was the individual who recorded the 1st video footage on his camera, his friend did not want to be identified for being ridiculed. The woman in video 3 not been identified and neither has the Mississippi women in the fourth video. Interestingly the author of this article quotes the opinion of long time UFO sceptic Robert Sheaffer of 'bad UFOs' and has no other sources. The article is short and lacks contrasting perspective. Again, this view is heavily engaged in confirmation bias, not science and certainly not proven. Speculation resonating from pre-determined confirmation bias is a major issue to objective research formulating public opinion. Such approaches are dogmatic traits of unhealthy scepticism specifically when we examine the debunking of this particular case.

The conclusion the media should have reached is this: we cannot prove that this entire case has or has not been faked on the basis of the four videos. There have been witnesses, some unwilling to come forward, some questionably claimed to have been part of a media stunt, but sadly more data is needed to verify this case. Official statements producing radar reports would validate these claims and videos, but none are available. This case should remain open on that basis.

The religious connotations behind this incident are profound. The case is advantaged through two of the three camera angles vindicating each other (the individual with camera one can be seen by camera two) and the third in the time-lapse analysis. This is a case which has multiple attempts to debunk it, not aided by a potential hoaxed 4th video which is not representative of the other 3 and was presented to the mainstream media. The case is hindered by the lack of official acknowledgement or radar data and lack of witnesses stepping forward.

This case is one of the very few times that advanced propulsion has been captured in multiple time lapsed videos. More data is required to form a more comprehensive analysis.

Conclusion:

1). AATIP classification: The UAP displays, 'Instantaneous acceleration', 'anti-gravity', and 'hypersonic velocity.'

2). This UAP case is lacking in-depth supportive data to be considered reliable. More data is needed.

3). The appearance of a hoaxed video significantly harms the case and brings doubt to the other videos.

Working Hypothesis: Unexplained – Anomalous Phenomena, Hoax.

***

Case Report: #GLP011

In February 2018, four commercial pilots from separate planes witnessed a 'UAP' at an altitude of 30'000 ft. above the skies of Arizona. The FAA audio transcript was released to the Phoenix New Times news agency (28) who ran the story and was picked up other mainstream media such as the Washington Post (29).

Case Report: FAA Pilots UAP Report
Case ID: GLP011
Date: 24/02/2018
Location: Altitude of 30'000ft, Arizona, U.S.

Incident:
A *'glowing ball of light'* was reported by multiple commercial pilots whilst flying at 30'000 ft. above the state of Arizona, United States. The object was described as having no obvious flight propulsion characteristics and resembled a glowing ball of light traveling above the commercial aircraft. The pilots in this case have come forward and the FAA audio has been released to the media. One of the pilots, Blenus Green, was a former B-1 Airforce pilot. In 2018, he described the UAP as *'very bright'* and that it didn't look like an airplane.

Federal Aviation Administration (FAA) Statement:
The FAA stated that they didn't have any comment beyond what was heard in the transcript. They stated they have a close working relationship with a number of agencies and safely handle military aircraft and civilian aircraft of all types in that area daily.

Possible explanations:
We might consider misidentifications, that the pilots wit-

nessed a high-altitude balloon with highly reflective surface. Also, we might consider the pilots saw a 'light refractions' through the cockpit window. Additionally, due to the shape, light and absence of distinguished features, we should also consider anomalous technology.

Analysis:
The case was reported to have been witnessed by several commercial pilots which gives credibility to the case. The FAA have also come forward to rule out any other currently known terrestrial possibility. The object based on pilot testimony suggests the object is an unconventional propulsion craft with no visible means of thrust and has descriptive similarities to the 'Foo-Fighter' objects. We can consider anomalous technology such as 'anti-gravity', 'low observability' and potentially 'hypersonic acceleration,' given that the *'ball of light'* appeared to be un-aerodynamic, travelling at high speeds and didn't appear on radar. As stated, the UAP was not (that we are aware of) captured on radar, which suggests information is possibly being held back, the technology can avoid radar, or the ball of light wasn't there as a physical flying object. The several pilots involved are unlikely to fabricate the story due to the risk to their careers (however we accept this is speculation).

Conclusion:
1). AATIP classification: The UAP possibly displays 'low observability,' and 'anti-gravity.'

2). This case is benefitted from having multiple seemingly credible pilot testimony.

3). More data is needed prior to making a formal conclusion.

Working Hypothesis: Unexplained – Anomalous Phenomena, Misidentifications: High Altitude Weather Balloon, Celestial/ Astro bodies, Psychological/Neurological effects, Light Reflections/Refraction.

***

Case Report: #GLP012

The U.S.S. Nimitz incursions in 2004 is the most famous and most important UAP/UFO case in history and revealed to the world by The New York Times in 2017, (30). It will always be remembered as the first 'UAP case' and the incident which made the world realise that the technology involved was not Russian or Chinese or probably even human made. Essentially, nobody had that technology in the early 21st century. Without Elizondo and Mellon (others at TTSA) and the bravery of Lt. Cmdr. David Fravor, Lt. Cmdr. Alex Dietrich (who would come forward some years later in 2021), Lt. James Slaight and Lt. Cmdr. Chad Underwood as well as Kevin Day, Sean Cahill, Gary Voohris and others aboard the various Nimitz nuclear strike group vessels, we would never have woken to the UAP issue. On this basis, it was important to include the Nimitz + 'Tic-Tac' case.

Case Report: The U.S.S. Nimitz Incursion
Case ID: GLP012
Date: November, 2004
Location: Pacific Ocean, 80 nautical miles from the coast of San Diego.

Incident:
Wednesday, 10th of November, 2004. The nuclear strike group Nimitz was off the southwest coast of San Diego. Radar operator Kevin Day reported seeing slow objects moving slowly in groups of 5-10 at a time, near to San Clemente Island. The anomalous objects were at an elevation of 28,000 feet, moving at a speed of approximately 120 knots (KD).

Between 12:00 and 13:00 the USS Nimitz encountered an Unidentified Aerial Phenomenon, the object was around 40ft long, white and resembled a 'Tic-Tac'. The object was able to hover without any signs of standard aviation propulsion aka wings, rotary blades etc. The object was able to drop from 80'000 ft to 20'000 ft instantaneously.

The object was engaged by multiple F-18s and witnessed by several pilots. The first fighter aircraft was piloted by Commander David Fravor, commanding officer of Strike Fighter Squadron 41, assisted by his weapon systems officer in the back seat, and the second was piloted by young recruit Lt. Cmdr. Jim Slaight and his WSO, serving as a wingman. They were then training aboard two FA-18 Super Hornets in a routine combat exercise.

Fravor began a circular descent to approach the object, but he claimed the UFO was intentionally avoiding any short-range dogfight radar lock-on with "impossible" manoeuvres that made any engagement of the F-18 impossible. As Fravor got closer descending, he reported that the object began ascending along a curved path too, maintaining some distance from the F-18, mirroring its trajectory in opposite circles. Fravor then made a more aggressive manoeuvre, plunging his fighter to aim below the object, but at this point he said that the UAP went away with a tremendous acceleration and became out of sight in less than two seconds, leaving the pilots "pretty weirded out". Later testimony would come from radar operator Kevin Day through the Nimitz Encounters (31), a docuseries that would go on to gain millions of views over social media and drive the initiative forward.

Possible explanations:
Misidentified 'seagulls' have been proposed as an explanation for the 'Tic-Tac' UAP. Some debunkers have tried to argue that the 'FLIR1' object isn't the same object as what navy pilots reported. Others have argued that pilots Fravor, Dietrich, Slaight, Underwood were mistaken with their observations and that trained pilots don't make good observers. Also, it was suggested that the unidentified object in the 'FLIR1' video was a distant plane and that the radar tracks were a result of faulty machinery returning false data.

On a serious note, we must consider the possibility of advanced foreign drone technology by an adversary that has leap frogged the United States. The potential for 'black budget' American technology would be ruled out in a 2021 UAP Task Force report. In this case, based on the displayed advanced technology, we must consider that the 'Tic-Tac' is genuinely anomalous technology – extra-terrestrial, ultra-terrestrial, inter-dimensional, etc.

Analysis:
This case is unique as it is primarily a military encounter. The data captured in this case report involves gun-camera footage (see above video), radar data and multiple military witnesses including fighter pilots within the F-18s. The case along with the 'FLIR1' gun camera video footage was designated for public release for 2017, first reported in the New York Times on December 16th (31).
According to radar operator Kevin Day, the 'Tic-Tacs' (plural) are reported to have dropped down from 80'000ft (and beyond) to 20'000ft in 0.78 seconds which would class as trans medium travel as they pass through differing sections of Earth's dense atmosphere.

The object and UAP case fit the criteria for Unidentified Anomalous Phenomena that includes 'instantaneous acceleration', 'hypersonic velocities', 'low observability', 'transmedium travel', and 'positive lift/anti-gravity'. Despite poor attempts to debunk the case as 'birds', the alternative explanations haven't confidently provided an adequate terrestrial explanation. Additionally, much more details have come forward since 2018 (time of writing the UAPinfo report), that ensure the high value of the Nimitz case. This is the only UAP case that we should confidently conclude, with high confidence, the very real potential of anomalous technology.

Conclusion:
1). AATIP classification: The UAP(s) displayed 'instantaneous

acceleration', 'anti-gravity', 'hypersonic velocity,' 'trans-medium travel.'

2). The U.S.S. Nimitz 2004 case is the first only officially verified public case of a UAP that deploys multiple military sensory data, and military testimony. It is the most detailed and accurately sourced case to date.

3). Due to the wealth of substantiated data and verification by the DoD, this is arguably the only case to date that is close to attaining the 'Anomalous' (non-human) classification.

4). More data is needed prior to making a formal conclusion on origin.

Working Hypothesis: Unidentified - Anomalous Phenomena.

***

Conclusions

The UAP case reports give us a good range of examples that stem from the traditional 'nuts and bolts' to the 'High Strangeness' effects. One of the reasons for the inclusion of UAPinfo reports was highlight the sceptical methodology that should be applied to case reports. Essentially, we want to position ourselves between 'believer and debunker', that we can critically review possibilities without subscribing to them. We must accept that *some* UAP might be 'Anomalous' in nature, but also be sceptical of any conclusions without holistic data and an in-depth investigation. The aim of UAP case reports isn't to build a narrative of 'non-human' technology or to debunk it, the aim is to strength a scientific methodology that is effective and advocates a genuine search for truth.

References

(1). The Mutual UFO Network (MUFON)
https://www.mufon.com/

(2). The National UFO Reporting Centre (NUFORC).
http://www.nuforc.org/index.html

(3). Project Bluebook. (1947). 'Case Report: Kansas Flying Disc.'
Archive.Org
https://archive.org/details/1947-07-9668989-ClayCenter-Kansas-89-/mode/1up

(4). Bertram, C. (19th of July, 2018). 'When a U.S. Fighter Pilot got in a Dogfight with a UFO.'
History.com
https://www.history.com/.amp/news/ufo-dogfight-gorman-us-plane-fargo

(5), (5a). Project Bluebook. (23rd of December, 1948). 'Case Report: 'Flying Saucers.'
Fold3.com, Ancestry.
https://www.fold3.com/image/6388148?
terms=1948,gorman
https://www.fold3.com/image/6388145

(6). Ruppelt, E. (1956). 'The Report on Unidentified Flying Objects: The Original 1956 Edition.'
Cosmo Classics. New York.

(7). Project Bluebook. (30th of August, 1951). 'Case Report: Lubbock Lights.'
Fold3.com, Ancestry.
https://www.fold3.com/image/6982561

(8). Clark, J. (1998). 'The Lubbock Lights: The UFO Book'
Detroit: Visible Ink Press.

(9). Carlson, P. (21st of July 2002).'50 Years Ago, Unidentified Flying Objects From Way Beyond the Beltway Seized the Capital's Imagination.'
The Washington Post.
www.washingtonpost.com/archive/lifestyle/2002/07/21/50-

years-ago-unidentified-flying-objects-from-way-beyond-the-beltway-seized-the-capitals-imagination/59f74156-51f4-4204-96df-e12be061d3f8/

(10). NOUFORS. 'The Washington National Sightings'.
Northern Ontario UFO Research and Study
http://www.noufors.com/The_1952_Sighting_Wave.html

(11). Dolan, R. (2001). 'UFOs and the National Security State.'
Keyhole Publishing Company.

(12). Randle, K. (2001). 'Invasion Washington: UFOs Over the Capitol'.
HarperTorch.

(13). NOUFORS. 'The Washington National Sightings: Harry Barnes'.
Northern Ontario UFO Research and Study
http://www.noufors.com/Harry_G_Barnes.html

(14). Clark, J. (1998). 'The UFO Book: Encyclopedia of the Extra-terrestrial'.
Cengage Gale.

(15). Gilgoff, D. (14th of December, 2001). 'Saucers Full of Secrets.'
Washington City Paper.
https://washingtoncitypaper.com/article/260860/saucers-full-of-secrets/

(16). Swords, M., and Powell, R. (2012). 'UFOs and Government: A Historical Inquiry.'
Anomalist Books.

(17). Nickels, J. (2000). 'The Flatwoods UFO Monster.'
Skeptical Inquirer.
https://skepticalinquirer.org/2000/11/the-flatwoods-ufo-monster/

(18). Wenzl, R. (2018). 'In 1952, the Flatwoods Monster Terri-

fied 6 Kids, a Mom, a Dog—and the Nation.'
History.com.
https://www.history.com/.amp/news/flatwoods-monster-west-virginia

(19). Haupt, R. (30th of September, 2014). 'The Braxton County Monster.'
Skeptiod.
https://skeptoid.com/episodes/4434

(29). Padua, R. (24th of October, 2014). 'The Day UFOs Stopped Play.' BBC News. https://www.bbc.com/news/magazine-29342407.amp

(21). Stahl, F, A. (2018). 'Case Report: Denise Bishop.'
The Unidentified.
https://www.the-unidentified.net/case-report-denise-bishop-1981/

(22). Good, T. (1997). 'Beyond Top Secret.'
Pan Books. New Edition.

(23). Stahl, F, A. (2018). 'Case Report: HollyHow Laser Light 1997.'
The Unidentified
https://www.the-unidentified.net/case-report-holly-how-1997/

(24). Kitei, L. M.D. (07th of February, 2017). 'The Phoenix Lights: A Sceptics Discovery that we are not Alone. 20th anniversary edition.'
Waterfront digital press.

(25). Jimmy Kimmel Live (2018). 'Kurt Russel on Fatherhood and UFOs.'
Youtube.
https://youtu.be/RVffyAF3wz8

(26). Foxx, J. (1997).' Out of the Blue.'

YouTube.
https://youtu.be/cYPCKIL7oVw

(27). Radford, B. (11ᵗʰ of February, 2011). 'Hoax in the Holy Land: UFO in Jerusalem a Proven Fake.'
Live Science.
https://www.livescience.com/12826-jerusalem-ufo-hoax.html

(28). Stern, R. (09th of March, 2018). Hear American Airlines Pilot Discuss UFO Sighting Over Arizona in FAA Tape.'
Phoenix New Times.
https://www.phoenixnewtimes.com/news/pilots-for-ameri-can-airlines-and-phoenix-air-reported-a-ufo-over-ari-zona-10218181

(29). Bever, L. (28th of March, 2018). 'A UFO!': FAA recording reveals moment two pilots report unknown object flying overhead.'
Washington Post.
https://www.washingtonpost.com/news/dr-gridlock/wp/2018/03/28/a-ufo-faa-recording-reveals-moment-two-pilots-report-unknown-object-flying-overhead/?outputType-=amp

(30). Blumenthal, R., Cooper, H. & Kean, L. (16ᵗʰ of December, 2017). '2 Navy Airmen and an Object That 'Accelerated Like Nothing I've Ever Seen.'
The New York Times.
https://www.nytimes.com/2017/12/16/us/politics/uniden-tified-flying-object-navy.amp.html

(31). 'Tic-Tac witnesses, the Kevin Day Interview.' (12ᵗʰ of October, 2019).
The Nimitz Encounters.
https://youtu.be/_2zRabdvKnwt

CHAPTER TEN: THE ROSWELL INCIDENT AND CRASH RETRIEVALS

✳ ✳ ✳

R oswell is the crown jewel in mainstream Ufology. It has been written about in books, magazines, websites and covered in films and on television. In short, Roswell is a big case in UFO history and rightly so. Despite this, what I found particularly interesting is that most people you speak with will have heard of the Roswell crashes, but most mainstreamers will not be able to tell you anything about it. Even the infamous USAF press releases from 1947, 1994 and 1997 are unknown by the public, and really, it's not unless you get fully emerged within the literature do you get a feel for what actually happened. To give the most (non)well-known UFO case of all time due diligence, my research took its time and headed for a deep dive into data. It was the hot summer of 2018 that the challenge was taken up, I researched the 1947 wave and the climax that resulted with something impacting the New Mexico desert.

But what was it, *really*?
***

FRIDAY
06th of July, 2018
"Where it all began."

That hot humid Friday at work brought a really intense lightning storm across the rural Radcliffe coastline. The air was thick, densely sticky and to the point it made it almost difficult to breathe fully. It wasn't long before an unrelenting torrential rain lashed against the side of Radcliffe's east wing, and as the crackle of static electricity proceeded every roll of thunder, the hairs on my arms stood up. It felt more like we were in Florida's deep Everglades than the Northeast coast of a sleepy English town. Lunch break came quickly and with time to spare, my decision process switched into gear.

Research.

I had been sent a social media DM tip to look into everything I could on the granddaddy of them all, the case that dwarfed all other UFO cases. I had waited until my lunchbreak, and would need my laptop, and space to look into a topic that was stigmatised without onlooking mocking colleagues.

With only a poorly made paper-fan to cool myself, I took the time to venture over into the fourth-floor semi-deserted unit, passing over one of the glass bridged corridors in the process. The new design of floor to ceiling glass windows allowed for a long-sighted view towards the coastline, and there, the old chemical works on the Radcliffe beach coastline and beyond it, the murky grey North Sea. I stopped to observe the view, but only for a moment as the rain caught my attention as it pounded the glass. My mind asked the question.

"What is out there? What is really in our skies and in our oceans?"

The small dimly lit box room at the end of the corridor was stiflingly warm without appropriate ventilation. A few unused admin items were piled up as storage, and in the corner, a dusty old computer was hidden against the back wall.

Making space, I set up my laptop on the desk. The door was propped open with a box of old printing paper that brought some coolness to the warm room. And from outside,

the storm raged continuously, violently and was without consideration.

It wasn't long before the windows icon sounded to alert
me that the desktop was ready. In that moment I reviewed
and ordered literature, Don Schmidt, Kevin Randle, Bill Moore,
Charles Berlitz and Stanton Friedman on Amazon books.

My focus was Roswell.

When the general public thinks about association
words with regard to UFOs, they think three things: Aliens,
Area 51 and Roswell. Whether you know the history of Ufology or not, you will know those three main elements. They are
ingrained into the subconscious of the collective mind, however, not much more is known than that. At least, this was the
case in the July of 2018, even some seven months after the
AATIP revelations of December 2017.

Writing articles about AATIP, AAWSAP and the Nimitz
encounter of November 2004 was pretty much the bulk of
what I did. Everything else was just cold case reports on old
UFO cases, assigning them a quantifiable classification system. Honestly, we tried to stay clear of the mainstream Ufology quantity that was churned up and spit out of every UFO
documentary on the History channel. Something told me that
Ufology and all its treasures was buried by its own un-credible
nature, and that meant the well-known cases also were buried
with it. So, I kept away from writing about them, sticking to
UAP terminology, military encounters that could be sourced
back to a mainstream news article. At that point, The New York
Times, Politico and Washington Post were the only three that
had covered AATIP with any meaningful force. Researchers
such as Richard Dolan had shown concern that the history of
UFO cases was being forgotten about, and he was right, but for
the time being that wasn't such a bad thing.

After all, in the July of 2018 I wouldn't have considered
about talking openly about UAP with my work colleagues
at the hospital. The climate wasn't right, the civilian cases
weren't verifiable without USG acknowledgement making it

difficult to source a multitude of data.

Plus, with only the Nimitz encounter to fall back upon and with one pilot in the spotlight (Cmdr. David Fravor) we were still at the very beginning. But we had faith, things change, the storm will pass eventually.

One day I knew that the events of Roswell and other crash cases would be important as the 'process' evolved. But for now, such cases were hidden away in some humid, small boxed off room in an obscurely deserted wing, all the while a storm was raging outside.

SATURDAY
07th of July, 2018
"The cover-up."

The lightning storm from the previous few days made me think of one thing. The UFO crashes at Roswell, New Mexico, 1947. Apparently, a typical storm had somehow brought down an 'alien spacecraft', at least that was the claims of some researchers.

Yes, it seems ridiculous, and it probably was. How does a hyper advanced vehicle made by *space-aliens* travel across the universe and then simply, crash? It didn't make sense to me.

Regardless of the absurdities. How could I *not* talk about Roswell?

I'm not a *Ufologist*, but I know the basics, although I'm not clued up on every aspect of every case - the debates, counter points and revaluations of datasets. Having the advantage of not being influenced by years of Ufology, I was able to come into the issue of Roswell with fresh eyes, and an outsider's perspective. Obviously, I knew the popular culture, the films, the magazine articles, but never really looked any further and certainly didn't give it any credit. The much-shunned *Roswell Slides* and the *Alien Autopsy* video was enough to divert my interest, and then there was the stigma, the ridicule factor, the sniggering media who wrote articles without looking into what actually happened. In a way, there was an invisible line which you didn't cross, for if you did, you would find yourself being judged as a tin-foil hat wearing conspiracy loon for simply asking questions. Knowledge was limited and my only option was to turn to seasoned researchers such as Graeme Rendall and others for advice.

But what I did know is that the crashes of Roswell are important to this topic for various reasons. For one, it was said to be the official start of the 'cover-up', for another it is the topic that is most famously known. The influx of 'Flying Saucer' waves occurred from that time period and signalled the start of the modern UFO age which ran all the way to the end of the twentieth century.

The beginning of what many people believe to be the UFO cover up was only a few months after the Kenneth Arnold sighting of craft that skipped across the sky. The Arnold sighting symbolised the birth of the modern-day UFO age, and coincidentally, the birth of the nuclear age. This was also the start of the Cold War with Russia, and some even suggest all of the above are connected.

So, it is important that Roswell was addressed, and, if you are going to be a serious 'Ufologist' or UAP researcher you need to know the first 1947 crash retrieval case off by heart. Admittedly, I'm no expert, and in certainly not going to try and take on the monster as I will get it wrong. If you want a full account of what happened in 1947, look to William Moore (1), Don Schmitt (2), Kevin Randle (3), Stanton Friedman (4), Colonel Philip Corso (5) or Tom Carey (6) and others, who in my opinion brought the case back to life. You might say if it wasn't for them the Rockefeller-Clinton initiative wouldn't have chosen Roswell as the one case to look into, and for the Airforce to once again pushback against claims of crashed flying discs and alien bodies. The Airforce statements in 1994 and then 1997 of weather balloons and crash test dummies was an extreme claim as the idea of extra-terrestrials, but it worked. People believed it.

People needed to believe it.

Getting ahead of myself here. Let's go back a *couple* of years to 1947, the following is my understanding of what happened, taken from the work of in-depth research and the from the help of UFO researchers who have studied the case.

TUESDAY
01st of July, 1947
"It's above us."

I t had been two years since the Allied Forces took down the Axis power across Europe, and almost two years since two atomic bombs were dropped on Hiroshima and Nagasaki in the August of 1945. The world was ending a devastating war and rebuilding for the second time in less than a half a century that had cost the lives of millions. This was a time in which the Western nationalism and patriotism took on a different meaning, it was a time of unity, of family and of heritage, to be proud in a time of understanding for the armed forces like at no other point in history. The streets were lined with flag waving patriots who welcomed home their heroes, and solemnly mourned those who never came home. For the people could at last breathe easy, the fascist *socialist* Nazi party had been beaten, their monstrous leader committing suicide before he could be captured. And as the news broke through of his death in the days following the 30th of April, 1945, the world rejoiced that it was finally over.

However, another monster was lurking just over the horizon, the Soviet Union. Starlin had a pact with Hitler in the early days of the war, and arguably if their relationship hadn't of broken down, we might have seen a different end to the conflict in Europe. Following the fall of Nazi Germany, Starlin's Russia was emerging as the 'red threat', a communist regime that played into the hands of national security. So, when the nuclear age was born in the mid-twentieth century, the challenge of world destruction became a very real issue. Never before had humans held the ability to destroy the entire life on planet Earth and never before had frictions been so intense. The Cold War between the West and the Soviet Union ensured a strict compartmentalised policy was enforced throughout the United States Defense Departments. The scene was set for a devastating conflict that could lead to nuclear annihilation and in 1947 this was a terrifying emerging reality for the U.S. government.

The scene was set, and whilst the focus was placed across the oceans to Russia - what was about to happen couldn't be predicted by anyone. Something was happening, something unexpected, something *above* them.

Radar reports coming from White Sands testing range were made of fast flying unknowns on July 01[st,] 1947 (1). Something was in the skies above New Mexico, although it is unclear exactly how much the army knew at this point. Despite White Sands radar detectors and others picking up the objects, without visuals they couldn't be certain. Whatever they were, they were there in numbers, they were above them at high altitude and couldn't be caught, shot down or bargained with. There was a muted panic as confused questions circulated. What if the Soviet Union had developed faster, more dynamic aircraft, and what if they were carrying an atomic bomb? What if they dropped on key strategic points? Taking out a sensitive testing facility would definitely be on the list of targets.

With those speeds and manoeuvres the Russians could annihilate major cities without even a shot being fired.

They were in big trouble.

WEDNESDAY
02nd of July, 1947
'Death from above.'

T he clouds rolled back with purposeful intent as they slowly turned the desert sky black. An insidious rumble vibrated across the dry plains as the penetrating summer sun beamed down to Earth. For it was here, under the unforgiving sun, that a humid climate was building below the stratosphere. Pressure had been slowly increasing all day with densely charged quantum particles resonating and anticipating the release of what was inevitable.

The week leading up to the hot July 04th weekend across the southern state of New Mexico ensured intense thunderstorms hit hard that late Wednesday evening and into the night. In particular, the electrical storm had hit hard the rural desert fields between the small hamlet of Corona and the Captain Mountains some 65 miles from the sleepy town of Roswell. (Keep in mind the proximity, that Corona was only 158km (98 miles) from the White Sands Missile Range and 130km (81 miles) from Roswell). All of whom shared a rural corner of America which saw nuclear testing, the first of which was Trinity in the Jornada del Muerto desert in July 1945. Those exact same skies that absorbed the nuclear testing fallout, those same skies that soaked up the radioactive decay, unbeknownst to those scientists at White Sands, contained an infectious *anomaly* that could alter the entire collective human psyche.

The radioactive atmospheric effects not fully understood. Their actions still unaccountable as the desert glowed with a beautifully deadly invisible light. And it was from within those same skies that the Anomalous operated, detected, observed, absorbed and existed. The terrifying connection not yet known for another 70 years and would still not be understood fully even with increased awareness.

As the last of the daylight disappeared behind the distant mountain range, *something* unidentified flew over the New Mexico State, something that was never meant to exist. In the hours immediately before the crash, various witnesses around Roswell were reported to have seen bizarre things in the sky, those such as Mr. and Mrs, Wilmot who at 09:30pm described a *flying saucer* type craft travelling with high speed in a Northeast direction. Then two Nuns apparently witnessed something bright in the sky after 11pm - Bernadette and Sister Capistrano, are said to have reported seeing a bright fiery object appear to go to the ground to the west and slightly north of Roswell (1), (2).

An unknown object of unknown origin, sped quickly across the state of New Mexico in seemingly a rough East to West direction. Whatever *it* was that had been witnessed, was now falling down to Earth, breaking up over the desert floor at Corona and then coming to finally crash into the San Augustin plains near Socorro.

Most reported accounts place the vehicle(s), coming down late evening at around 11pm on the Wednesday. Let's consider that some UAP do indeed have low observability (one of the 5 AATIP abilities) and are able to avoid radar tracking.

Alternatively, what if some, as suggested (1), UAP could be seen on radar at White Sands. A more alarming thought, what if the vehicles electro-gravitational system was dislodged by an EMP-Atom bomb weapon. Some have suggested that potentially a classified ballistic 'V2' missile was sent high into the stratosphere to *greet* the swarm of UAP, this, the type of mission that is unacknowledged, *permanently*. Although we should be sceptical as this is speculation.

Consider that the 1940s ballistic missiles were in their infancy, the rocket technology a new concept acquired only two years earlier as Nazi Germany fell to Allied powers. Arguably, the recovered 'V2' weren't able to carry the sizeable nuclear A-Bombs similar to those first detonated over Japan. And then we must consider the range of an EMP when an Atom bomb detonates, and also, where the nuclear weapon detonates. Then we must also consider that in July 1947, there was no nuclear weapons tests at White Sands.

Not that anyone believes they wouldn't launch a nuclear attack against UAP, particularly if they believed it was the Russians hovering high above sensitive test sights, trying to gain the destructive technology for themselves. However, there is the considerable realisation that the United States military knew that they weren't Russian, maybe they already had crashed evidence of whatever the objects were. What if the U.S. military had prior experience?

And if *any* of this is true, could we blame them? These things were very real to them, watching, encroaching, probing for weakness. These were the black-eyed monsters from children's nightmares, bringing with them the dark extremity of an unwanted future. A future filled with nervous uncertainty and the fear of a technological power so radical it could incinerate the entire planet if it intended, and we didn't even know what its intentions were.

The brave men and women had just won a war against a great evil, pushed back the tyrants and dictators, and now they looked above them to something anomalous, something that encapsulated the societal subconscious fear of instant annihilation at any moment. The United States had won the atomic weapons race and developed the nuclear deterrent to supposedly bring world peace, and in the process brought with them the biggest threat in history.

And what bigger fear is there, than that of the unknown?

Death from above.

THURSDAY
03rd of July, 1947
'The Response.'.

R eports stated that something came down across the desert plains of San Augustin and debris filtered across the fields facing Captain Mountain. Possibly, the unknown object had smashed into the ground or broke up in the air above 'Crash Site A' (at Corona) before coming to 'rest' miles away at 'Crash Site B' (San Augustin or another location) however there are multiple reports of other additional crash sites around the state, almost fitting in a linear pattern, as though the object was leaving parts of it as it fell.

The research tells us that something or *somethings* had come down in the stormy night of July 02nd. The U.S. military would have known thanks to various radar surveillance (that is if they appeared on radar). Whatever *it* was, it needed boots on the ground and men in the field to secure it. If it was a Russian spy plane or an off-course top secret test rocket, the Pentagon knew that such things needed to remain secret. If this was something else entirely, well that was simply much too terrifying to even consider, such a reality too volatile for the American public's belief system.

However, the most logical explanation would be something in their control. After all, the last thing the Pentagon needed was their enemies getting wind of an operation gone wrong, or civilians finding out that a missile had blown up some poor farmers ranch house on the New Mexico plains. Even if it really was a top-secret mogul weather balloon, there would be an interest to collect and retrieve their classified property.

My mind asked the question about how much the military actually knew? Given the possibilities of previous crash retrieval cases, prior to 1947, maybe they already knew the process. Perhaps, they were ready for the Anomalous?

Or maybe they had no idea?

Crash Site A: Corona, Foster Ranch Debris Field

The more famous crash site, was crash site A. This is the debris field site on the Foster ranch, that foreman William 'Mac' Brazel found and took into Roswell. This was the object the Airforce initially stated was a 'Flying Disc', then changed to a weather balloon, then changed to a Mogul balloon and somehow involved 'crash test dummies'. This is the site that we have all heard about in books and films, documentaries and newspaper articles. This was the site that some believed was a distraction from another site that occurred, a different location with different findings.

On crash site A – the Foster/Mac Brazel site, various sized pieces of strange metal were found, some as thin as tin foil but unbreakable and then somehow returned to original size after manipulation. Other pieces were in the shape of 'I-Beams' that, according to the son of Major. Jessie Marcel had strange type of hieroglyphs imbedded into them like a form of 'alien' writing.

Mac Brazel found the pieces the day after the night-time thunderstorm as he herded sheep which refused to cross the debris field. He collected some of the wreckage and took the pieces in looking for a reward after the July 04th weekend. The closest Airforce base was the 509th bomb squadron, the only nuclear strike force team in the world at that time and who had dropped the two atomic bombs on Japan two years earlier in 1945. Within that week, they sent out intelligence officer Jessie Marcel, Lt Colonel Sheridan Cavitt and Master Sergeant Bill Rickett to the ranch to collect the debris and investigate. The military men brought it back to base and they, in their naïve wisdom, thought it to be part of a flying disc - possibly without Pentagon approval?

In those early days no-one seemed to know what to think, and most certainly, the data was incredibly contradicting. Sceptically, we should ask why Brazel changed his story after being held by the military for days after he came forward. Also, why did he wait a few days to bring in the 'alien' wreckage if it was so important? Additionally, we can ask how could the military intelligence of the 509th bomb squad not recognise a simple weather balloon that were regularly used in the area? Why are the descriptions of the wreckage different to the Airforce weather balloon explanation?

Something was wrong.

MONDAY
07th of July, 1947
'One was moving.'

Crash Site B: The Plains of San Augustin, Socorro, disc and bodies

F or over four days the intense New Mexico sun baked whatever remained on the hot desert floor. Whatever it was, laid undetected, open and completely exposed to the harsh conditions of the desert. Somehow, the U.S. military hadn't found them, or weren't looking. It wasn't until a team of civilian archaeologists that included Professor Curry Holden and soil engineer Barney Barnett had stumbled across dead 'alien' bodies and a crashed disc on the desert plains of San Augustin near Socorro, New Mexico (4) *or* was it nearer to the first crash site (Crash Site A) in Corona? The second main location (and others) have been debated and contested.

Roswell researchers have also suggested that local firemen had also arrived on the scene that included Dan Dwyer whose testimony was corroborated by his daughter, et al (7). The military had arrived on the second crash scene quickly and controlled the site, recovering whatever it was they found, and forced the civilians and their families into secrecy.

They used forceful prompts.

Either way the general consensus within the Roswell research community is that following the discovery of the debris field on the Foster Ranch, a further recovery was made that included a relatively intact vehicle and bodies, one of which, was still alive.

Despite being not the more well-known or documented, for me 'Crash Site B' should have been the main site. As stated, this is allegedly where the full-bodied craft was found by various civilians and military police, with testimony placing the full bodied 'egg shaped' or 'Disc' at Crash Site B on Tuesday the 8th of July, 1947. Almost an entire week after the Foster Ranch debris site at 'Crash Site A'.

Colonel Philip Corso would later write in his 1997 book, '*The Day After Roswell,*' (5) that the '*Grey Aliens*' were placed onto stretches and taken away, the one living alien that survived the impact crash was reportedly shot at by the military police. However, without proof or multiple testimony of such an event, we should proceed with caution when evaluating claims the U.S. military started shooting at *extra-terrestrials* in the New Mexico desert.

Sceptically, we can find issue with how the U.S. military didn't find the second site for so long? As we don't know what the radar data showed, we don't know what the military knew. The admitted 1994 Airforce report explanation - that the object was a classified Mogul balloon - meant that what came down was important to the military, and therefore they should have been out looking (as opposed to a simple everyday weather balloon).

The capture of 'alien' bodies also poses a major problem for the United States government. It would mean they covered up and lied about the greatest, most profound discovery in human history.

Not something you want on your record.

TUESDAY
08th of July, 1947
'Going public.'

I t had been a week since the reported unknowns buzzed above the New Mexico skies, which were apparently tracked via multiple radar systems. And yet despite the discovery of a debris field on the Foster Ranch, there had been no official government position on the incident, that was, until a press release was issued. On July 8th, 1947, RAAF public information officer, Walter Haut, issued the infamous press release stating that personnel from the field's 509th Operations had amazingly recovered a 'Flying Disc', which had crashed near to a ranch not far from Roswell. Questions over whether Haut was just naïve or whether this was part of a plan to distract attention away from other, more interesting crash sites were asked.

Ultimately, the story was out and for the Pentagon, who acted quickly, they went into debunking mode. General Roger Ramey then famously retracted the statement and insisted what they had found was a simple weather balloon. Jessie Marcel then posed for a picture with the weather balloon as the press took pictures. When you see the photos, you will never forget the look that Major Marcel gives as the photo is taken. Years later in the 1980s I believe it was, Marcel would admit to researchers that it was a crashed disc, and the weather balloon story was a cover up (which made sense, given that he handled such balloons and knew what a weather balloon looked like). There was a reported massive military operation surrounding the incident at the time, the debris sent off to Wright-Patterson Airfield which didn't fit a downed weather balloon.

But what was it?

TUESDAY
10th of July, 2018
"What can one take from this?"

Researching the Roswell incident was frustrating. There was just so much testimony, so many books written and so many versions of accounts with differences of opinion and versions upon what occurred that summer of 47. Most of the Roswell data in Ufology comes from 'believers', who you might argue are biased when it comes to the case, particularly when trying to argue the extra-terrestrial element. Then we equally have the problem of 'debunkers', who you might also argue suffer from researcher bias, who knowingly try to rewrite witness's testimony if it is unfavourable to their outcome.

A quick search of Wikipedia in 2018 on Roswell (8), is incredibly inaccurate and heavily biased in favour of debunkers, listing none of the hundreds of important witnesses (6), and leaves out the military proponents that negate the Mogul balloon theory proposed by the Airforce some 50 years after the weather balloon explanation.

The Airforce press conference and report from 94 and 97 was even worse, a terrible mess that simply cherry-picked data to provide a narrative that ignored all of the hundreds of witness testimonies.

The report was a whitewash.

Physicist Eric Davis (contractor for AATIP) goes into this with journalist Alejandro Rojas (@alejandrotrojas), who then floated the possibility two objects may have collided with each other but crashed in different time periods. That theory suggests there were two crashes, years apart, resulting from the same *collision* in 1947, possibly explaining the various crash sites. However, how can we validate such claims.

We probably can't.

Due to the absence of an official government report that doesn't involve crash test dummies, tinfoil, sticks and wood, we are limited in collating all the holistic data. Researchers have done a good job to bring together the facts of the case, but still inconsistencies remain with some dates, times and testimony. The worse part about the Roswell incident, is that the Airforce has seemingly changed its official story 3 times since they first admitted it was a 'Crashed Disc' and have provided a poor holistic account of the incident, cherry picking data which didn't fit the weather balloon explanation.

In 1994 the Airforce was forced to admit that the weather balloon story was a cover up for the real story, that a high-altitude Mogul balloon was actually what crashed. It was a top-secret project used to listen in and detect Russian nuclear testing.

Oh, and in 1997 the alien bodies that were reported were actually crash test dummies that didn't come into production until years later in the late fifties. The problem as I see it, is that when you look into the thorough research from Randle, Schmidt, Friedman, Cooper and others, the weather balloon and crash test dummies doesn't fit what was described by the multiple witnesses. Not one person said that it was a weather balloon from the civilian witnesses. The thinking is that General Roger Ramey put out the second story of a weather balloon to throw the media and public off the real story.

It is what they really found that scared them, so much so, the issue was buried so far away from the human psyche that it wouldn't be taken seriously for another 70 plus years.

Public information officer William Haut would later verify Jessie Marvel's story; claiming the original press release was correct. It was a crashed disc with occupants. Haut went on record to say how Colonel Blanchard took him to 'Building 84' - one of the hangars at Roswell - and showed him the craft itself. He describes a metallic egg-shaped object around 12-15ft in length and around 6ft wide. He said he saw no windows, wings, tail, landing gear or any other feature. He saw two bodies on the floor, partially covered by a tarpaulin. They are described in his statement as about 4ft tall, with disproportionately large heads. Towards the end of the affidavit, Haut concludes: *"I am convinced that what I personally observed was some kind of craft and its crew from outer space."* (2).

* * *

Conclusions

'*If*' dead non-human biological entities were recovered from Roswell (and other early crash retrievals), it would be the greatest moment in human history. Additionally, it raises problems of proof and evidence and what it means to be able to conclusively state something as fact within a high degree of certainty. We find ourselves in a strange position, in that there is the possibility that part of the U.S. government (possibly an Airforce defense contractor), has dead non-humans somewhere stashed away along with anomalous craft behind a hanger door – and yet, there is zero tangible proof of this beyond various testimonies.

Going further into it: Let's discount the argument of *'could'* the military and Pentagon keep such a secret? In my opinion, yes, they can - the Manhattan Project showed that, as does every classified program since 1947. Also, more specific to UAP – AATIP and AAWSAP were kept secret from 2007-2012 (officially). The ability of the military to keep sensitive secrets in a time before the internet, and in a time following the Second World War when people were patriotic to the cause, was undeniable. So, the Airforce could, in my opinion, have easily kept Roswell a secret. The other question of *'would'* the Airforce and Pentagon keep the secrecy of crashed UAP and bodies? Yes. I would fully expect the military in 1947 to classify such things, should they have occurred. Particularly, given that the Cold War was beginning, and this 'Flying Disc' presented as an opportunity to develop technology through reverse engineering. And what about *'should'* they have hidden away the biggest story of human history?

This is dependent on various perspectives and from the position you might hold. Personally speaking, *yes*, I believe it was appropriate at the time, however, I believe that any such secrecy shouldn't still be in operation, some 70 years later.

However, none of this matters if there is no proof that can be taken to congress and accepted by the scientific community. Condensing 70 years' worth of research into a chapter doesn't do the incident justice, nor to the researchers who have spent a lifetime uncovering the truth, or to the witnesses who have come forward to tell us what happened back in the summer of 1947.

Roswell itself is known all over the world and for good reason. It has the credibility of multiple witnesses who verify and corroborate many of the extreme claims. My issue with the case comes from many years of misinformation and secondhand testimony, memories can be easily distorted over long periods of time, and with various emotional/psychological inclusion/exclusion factors. The debate and counter debate are decades long, and far more complex than this chapter could ever do it justice. Testimony is always found to be less relatable than physical evidence in any given case which has social-psychological implications and connotations (such as the reality of UAP). Despite the Airforce denials and pushback, I'm inclined to consider that something potentially anomalous crashed in 1947.

And it wasn't a simple weather balloon. For that I'm relatively certain. Firstly, because the 509th bomb squad was the competent unit that launched the Boeing B-29 'Enola Gay' and the 'Bockstar', the two historical aircraft that dropped the bombs over Hiroshima, Japan on Monday the 6th of August, 1945 and then over Nagasaki, Japan on Thursday the 9th of August, 1945 (9). The intelligence officials from that very same unit, based out of Roswell, knew exactly what a weather balloon looked like. Secondly, because in 1994 and 1997, the Pentagon was forced to concede that the weather balloon story was a coverup (that lasted some 50 years), and that the real object was a Mogul high altitude balloon (incidentally which I also take issue with). And thirdly, and most importantly, is that the hundreds of witnesses do not allude to a weather balloon being recovered in the New Mexico desert that summer (6). They do however, in vast numbers, tell a very different story to what the Airforce told back in 1947 (the second time) – and then in 1994 – oh, and then in 1997 (10). Advocating healthy scepticism is vitally important, however, we also mustn't venture into debunking for the sake of debunking. To me it is pretty clear that the 94 and 97 Airforce reports are heavily biased towards a conventional Mogul balloon explanation, which are in clear contradiction to the voices of people who were there at the crash scenes back in 1947. Additionally, it is a difficult concept to advocate - that some persons in authority took steps to manipulate the data, swop out the real debris for a simple weather balloon. It is unthinkable.

For those who don't have a basic A-level in behavioural

psychology, a person who lies will often change their story on multiple occasions. Additionally, if one reads the poorly sourced and written 'Case Closed' reports by the Airforce for 1994/1997 (10), we see a clear intention to lead the reader to a specific conclusion, which, doesn't include any civilian or military witness testimony that contradicts the desired balloon outcome. Additionally, the calibre of military witnesses who over time would go on record to state the crashed objects weren't a balloon, but something they else entirely, was damning to the Airforce.

I'm still not comfortable stating exactly what was found, or *where* (11), or even what was recovered at the various crash sites in New Mexico, 1947 was extra-terrestrial, however we must also consider the possibility that whatever it was that came down was not human technology. The two might not be mutually exclusive. What I'm pretty confident in stating officially is that something of importance came down in the New Mexico desert, and it wasn't any type of balloon, and this case is certainly not closed.

Admitting past mistakes isn't easy. But maybe it's important all the same?

References

(1). Moore, W., and Berlitz, C. (1988). 'The Roswell Incident.'
New York: Berkley.

(2). Schmitt, D. (2017). 'The Cover-up at Roswell: Exposing the 70-year conspiracy to suppress the truth.'
New Page Books.

(3). Randle, K. (1991). 'UFO Crash at Roswell.'
HarperCollins Publisher.

(4). Berliner, D., and Friedman, S. (2001). 'Crash at Corona: the Us Military Retrieval and Cover-up of a UFO.'
Marlowe and Co. Anniversary Edition.

(5). Corso, P. Col. Ret. (1998). 'The Day After Roswell.'
Pocket Books.

(6). Carey, T., and Schmitt, D. (2007). 'Witness to Roswell: Un-masking the 60-year Cover-up.'
Career Press. New Page Books.

(7). Randle, K. (23rd of March, 2017). 'Frankie Rowe and the Roswell Crash.'
A Different Perpective.
https://kevinrandle.blogspot.com/2007/03/frankie-rowe-and-roswell-crash.html?m=1

(8). Wikipedia page retrieval. (07th of July, 2018). 'The Roswell Incident.'
Wikipedia.
https://en.m.wikipedia.org/wiki/Roswell_incident

(9). Whiteman Air Force Base. (16th of August, 2010). '509th Bomb Wing.'
https://www.whiteman.af.mil/About/Fact-Sheets/Display/Article/323963/509th-bomb-wing/

(10). McAndrew, J. (1997). 'The Roswell Report: Case Closed.'
https://media.defense.gov/2010/Oct/27/2001330219/-1/-1/0/AFD-101027-030.pdf

(11). The Plains of San Augustin Controversy, July 1947.
http://www.cufos.org/books/Plains_of_San_AgustinR.pdf

CHAPTER ELEVEN:
1950S AMERICAN POP
CULTURE AND UFOS

* * *

R esearching the 1950s era was probably the most enjoyable part of my 2018 investigation. The ambience of the Hollywood silver screen, Elvis and the birth of Rock and Roll, the motels and 'Diner' culture, the technological communication leaps with the first home televisions, the beginnings of the Cold War and the atomic age, it was all there in that decade, and underneath it all was the renewed possibilities of a world desperately trying to rebuild itself following a deadly war which simply couldn't happen again. Ever. The American government knew that the next war would be a thermonuclear war as Russian scientists made their own breakthroughs in atomic energy and weaponry, something that the Americans knew would happen eventually despite the highly compartmentalised stockpiling of classified information within the Manhattan project. Consequently, the threat of world annihilation loomed heavily over their heads, and it seemed to me, *understandable*, why there was little room for anything else in those years. You might argue the UAP were an external manifestation/representation of the inner turmoil suffered subconsciously by society, that 'interplanetary spacemen' might also pose a real threat of annihilation. After all, the intentions of these advanced vehicles and their perceived occupants wasn't known, and this was a big problem. We can understand the extreme decisions that were taken by a new generation, culture and society that was rebuilding itself.

It really was a fascinating decade.

***

WEDNESDAY
11th of July, 2018
'1950s pop culture.'

T he rich history of how the proud United States government engaged the phenomena in those early years is important to understand. Although the question of how the government engaged the topic isn't directly relevant to what UAP are in origin, it still gives us an idea of the cultural background of that era.

UFOs in the 1950s America were openly discussed, much more than any other period in the phenomena's history. We can consider that the introduction of the cinema, television, wireless radio, news media, telegrams and interlinked communities - thanks to improved motorway services, automobiles, and civilian aeroplanes, meant that people were traveling, and communicating further and longer than ever before.

An idea we can refer to as a 'quantum conscious society' was developing more profoundly than at any point in history. Such a theory might propose that the thoughts and localised cultures of thousands of people within a country, separated by thousands of miles, were becoming more linked and aligned quicker thanks to dramatically improving technology. For expose, the military upgrades of the Second World War had filtered down its technology into the civilian world, allowing for much improved communication. Even the first internet was developed as a consequence of war prior to becoming a civilian necessity.

A decade that formed the secrecy

The fifties are an interesting one at best, a convoluted one at worst, but certainly not without its strange occurrences. The historical conclusion of many established UAP researcher, is that the phenomena's reality (whatever the origin) had been kept secret by various bureaucrats and defense contractors for some time, buried away like some dirty unwanted truth that is difficult to process, a repugnant family secret that is not talked about or even acknowledged.

From 1969 until 2017, UFOs were toxic to one's professional career. The world turned its back on the biggest revelation for almost 50 years thanks to the U.S. Airforce. As a policy, they threw shade on the topic and took a debunking position at every opportunity thanks to the conclusions of the Condon report (see next chapter).

Remember Galileo's telescope? – 500 years later and humans were acting exactly the same. Preservation of conservative ideology will always trump objective reality in favour of something more pleasing, more fluent. And yet UAP had remained in the skies for all those decades since the closure of Bluebook just as the Earth revolves around the sun.

Arguably, the denial of an anomalous intelligence is an extended form of 'heliocentric' dogma. The same fallacy in human logic. The same desire to not 'believe', to refuse the due process of investigating UAP case reports holistically, to refuse to look through the telescope.

The very heart of the UFO phenomenon was always case reports. It's what the USAF's Project Bluebook, Sign and Grudge were built upon, it's what AATIP was built upon (military cases), and it's what makes the phenomena so apparent to us.

Within pop culture, UFOs were strongly associated with the early American fifties' era as that's when the issue really sunk into our collective subconscious. Films, TV-shows, books and magazines had an influence on science fiction that mirrored the 20th century space-race. This was a time in which the phenomena were showing itself, or we were widely perceiving it for the first real time in that form. Whatever was happening, our human interaction with *it* had drastically increased.

That era was significant.

The famous McMinnville case that occurred 11th of May, 1950, complete with testimony and photos, appeared on the 26th of June, 1950 - LIFE magazine edition. The McMinnville incident, which occurred over a farm in Oregon, involved an alleged metallic grey 'Flying Saucer' that reportedly performed instant acceleration (one of the AATIP five observables). Evelyn Trent and her husband Paul were witness to the saucer shaped object hovering slowly over their farmland before speeding quickly away, they both maintained their claims to the day they died. Debunkers, such as Philip Klass tried to dismiss the incident as a hoax, however his claims were limited to conjecture and speculation rather than hard evidence. To the day the event is regardless as *unidentified* by most researchers with Evelyn Trent maintaining into her old age that the object moved incredibly fast. Sceptically, we can't argue hysteria or hallucinations due to multiple witnesses and misidentified terrestrial objects – birds and balloons – do not for the testimony. The only debunking option is to claim hoax. However, having looked closely at the claims of debunkers such as Klass et al, their claims do not hold up. Psychologically, people do not maintain a potential lie like this one into their old age without significant prior mental health issues, by which, no evidence can be found to validate such theories.

The Trent McMinnville case sparked credibility for UFOs and engaged the public imagination. People in that decade believed that honest, hardworking farmers who made no money from their experience, were honest.

Why would they lie for so long?

An era of black and white photos

Many black and white famous photos were taken in

those years. For example, Guy B. Marquand, Jr., was with two friends when he snapped a famous 1951 'Flying Saucer' picture in Riverside, California (3). Marquand stated he caught the object on camera after it had returned, after making rapid acceleration away from him. Another famous picture was taken of four lights captured through the window of a laboratory in 1952, Salem, Massachusetts.

A few years later and Marilyn Monroe appeared on the 07th of April, 1952 front page issue of 'LIFE' magazine with the sub-title, *'There is a case for interplanetary saucers.'* (1).

The in-depth discussion of the UFO phenomenon is evident within the written report. The topic was taken seriously, not only by the mainstream media, but the U.S. Airforce in 1952. LIFE magazine reported that they received a response form the Airforce and proceeded to publish their statements.

1). 'Flying Discs', 'Cylinders', and 'Objects of geometric form and luminous quality,' may be now operating in Earth's atmosphere.

2). Bright green fiery 'Globes' fly within the skies.

3). The objects cannot be adequately explained as 'natural phenomena' by modern science, and are some type of artificial devices, operated by an intelligence.

***

Science fiction films involving UFOs and 'space aliens' invaded Hollywood within 1950s America. Most notably included the 1951 film, *'The Day the Earth Stood Still,'* and the 1953 film *'War of the Worlds'* which was based on the 1898 H.G. Wells novel by the same name. One of my favourite films of that genre was *'Earth vs. the flying saucers,'* (1956) which was based on a bestselling non-fiction book by Major Donald Keyhoe entitled *'Flying Saucers from Outer Space.'* (1953) (3). This was a different era, a different culture with a different perspective. The stigma of 'UFOs' wasn't established, and the topic was openly discussed as a genuine scientific endeavour whilst being a big topic in entertainment.

And all the while, UFOs were a real phenomenon.

✳ ✳ ✳

Conclusions

The 1950s really was the *'Flying Saucer'* era, a decade in which the industrial military complex intertwined with deep national security concerns. From the nuclear threat to the space race, the public's conscious awareness was drawn to new and exhilarating rocket technology that brought with it the great promise of celestial discovery and also the great horror of possible annihilation. And sandwiched in-between was the extra-terrestrials flying around in their spacecraft – or at least that was the public perception for UFOs at the time. This time-frame is an important snapshot from history, and I'm guessing that a big part of the UFO mystery is entangled within that decade.

A decade when the secrecy was developed. More importantly, a decade in which America's cognitive focus and awareness was on the phenomena.

They *believed.*

And consequently, *they* existed.

References

(1). Darrach, H.B., and Ginna, R. 'There is a case for Interplanetary Saucers.' (07th of April, 1952).
LIFE magazine.
http://www.project1947.com/shg/articles/lifemag52.html

(2). Rothman, L., and Ronk, L. (25th of February, 2016). 'See 10 Mysterious UFO Photos from History.'
Time Magazine.
https://time.com/4232540/history-ufo-sightings/

(3). Keyhoe, D. (1953). 'Flying Saucers from Outer Space.' Henry Holt and Co.

CHAPTER ELEVEN: PROJECT SIGN, GRUDGE AND BLUEBOOK (1947-1969)

* * *

Researchers say that a combination of the desired UAP technology and the concept of UAP/UFOs being a threat to national security is key to the secrecy. It is the difference between society taking the anomalous phenomenon seriously and dismissing it as mundane misidentifications. It is why we always get the *'no evidence of a threat to national security'* reply that we get from British military/intelligence agencies, because if it's real, it's a threat to them and they have to act (and vice versa). After all, if we consider the reality of such a phenomenon, we must also consider that our military and intelligence agencies would be able to detect it within our skies and have provided briefings to the executive branches of governments. That's how we are programmed to believe such a disclosure would play out - the military make a discovery; they contact the President who calls a press conference that same afternoon to tell the people. It all happens like some poorly thought-out Hollywood B-movie starring some actor you can't remember the name of.

And if this narrative doesn't happen openly and exactly like the movies, we would question its reality, the unthinkable alternative is that the system is broken. If the elected officials who represent the people aren't informed of the most important issue in history, if such sensitive data is withheld from

Congress and Parliament, then surely this is a failure within the democratic process of western civilisation. We the people, must have the information to decide how to proceed and determine our future.

To stop this from ever happening required one thing in 1953 – a bottle necked process by which classified information is syphoned off, and, whilst presenting a scientific process that is flawed by an unethical exclusion parameter design. I am not a conspiracy theorist, in fact I pushback against such outlandish claims, especially when it comes to UAP/UFOs, however, for me the conclusions of the Airforce, the Condon report and the Robertson panel (1) amounted to scientific negligence that bordered on a whitewash. This has long been the position of historian researchers such as Richard Dolan who writes at length about this issue (2).

***

FRIDAY
20th of July, 2018
'Cover-up?

T he hardest part I personally had to accept about the UAP history, was that for it to be real, it must have been covered up by someone, somewhere, in a dark shadowy corner of the DoD and Pentagon. For if UAP are real and represent something non-human, it means that the democratic process has failed on some level. The issue has been taken from the hands of congressional oversight committees and placed somewhere by which the executive government branches have no ability to act. It is a murky area - how much is a 'conspiracy' and how much is simply classification is not yet known. What we can do, is look closely at what occurred to allow the entire issue of UFOs to be moved from public awareness to the shadows.

The Robertson Panel: 14-18th of January, 1953

The July Washington D.C. incursions of 1952 really posed a problem for any Airforce group who wished to slowly dilute the problem of unknown objects. Those UFOs infiltrating North American skies - post WW2 - that didn't respond to communication or could not be shot down, were deemed to be a huge threat. And that is what happened in the summer of 1952 - unidentified threats of unknown origin engaged the most sensitive areas of America's democracy. Stalking sensitive testing facilities and nuclear bombing ranges was bad enough, but to have the anomalous swarm appear right over the capital of America was unthinkable. They had become very real in that incursion, no longer a distant military problem, but a very difficult existential and political problem to deal with.

An overt threat to national security.

The consequence meant that new life was breathed into Project Grudge, who reformed under a new name after pressure once again increased thanks to the 1952 UAP wave. The problematic Washington incursions of July meant the Airforce would need a bigger, better strategy to dismiss away the entire phenomena as nothing more than 'seagulls', 'weather balloons' and 'hoaxes'.

A secret C.I.A. backed panel was briefed in early 1953 on U.S. military activities and intelligence matters from that time, as first reported by Project Bluebook Director, Edward Ruppelt (3). The original report was officially classified as *secret*, but then it was declassified later. In the end, the Robertson Panel's final report concluded that UFOs were not a direct threat to national security. (Somehow unidentifiable disc shaped objects which were able to perform advanced technological capabilities and entered protected aerospace, even fly over the United States Capitol, are not a direct threat to national security in the nuclear Cold War – nuclear threat, era).

Of course, this was absolutely unthinkable to take seriously.

Thankfully, despite gross negligence on a historic level,

they did state that 'UFOs' could pose an indirect threat by *overwhelming* standard military communications due to increased public interest in the subject. Although, this could have been an excuse to justify keeping an eye on Ufology types.

The Robertson panel concluded that most UFO reports, could be explained as misidentifications of explainable aerial objects, and the remaining minority could be explained further with more investigation.

However, this was not the end. People were not satisfied that the explanations conclusively fit the data. From rural farmers to major city sightings, the very same phenomena were continuing to appear in our atmosphere, and by 1953, the pressure was again mounting on the Airforce for real answers. Even back in the early 1950s the multiple military pilot and civilian reports tended to contradict such mundane explanations. And this was the problem, the reports kept coming year after year, decade after decade. The anomalous phenomena were outperforming fighter planes and even interfering with nuclear weapons and appearing at nuclear test sites (see the now famous AATIP Directors resignation letter).

Something needed to be done.

The United States Airforce UFO Programs

The year 1947 was a massive UAP wave year, and the first time we see widespread acknowledgement and widely reported cases. Whilst previous historical anomalous waves had occurred, this was the first time the public's focus and attention was captured. This was also the first time in history we collectively thought *'extra-terrestrial'* at the collective subconscious level, and thought in a way that genuinely considered they might be here. The sheer volume of reports, and clear distinction of 'Flying Discs' alongside other un-aerodynamically shaped vehicles ensured that the government had to act. To address the growing pressure and issue of the UFO epidemic, the United States government created three distinct programs in concession to officially and 'openly' investigate the phenomena. Additionally, the terminology was changed from 'Flying Saucer' to 'Unidentified Flying Objects' around that time to increase the *uncertainty* around public perceptions of 'non-human' technology. A UFO could be anything from a balloon to a misidentified cloud, whereas a 'Flying Saucer/Disc' on the other hand was distinct and very much non-human technology.

Managing the social psychology was paramount to controlling the narrative. As much as you might disagree with the ethical conduct of developing and maintaining secrecy on such an important topic, you also have to appreciate the brilliance of the psychology used.

Project Sign (Saucer): 1947-1948

Project Sign was the very first, an official U.S. government project that was tasked with investigating 'unidentified flying objects' (UFOs). Following the significant 1947 wave form June to July of that year, public pressure grew on the government to provide some answers to the mystery. *'If they were aliens from Mars, the world needed to know.'*

The official project was undertaken by the United States Airforce and was active for most of the year 1948. Project Sign's final report, published in early 1949, stated that while some UFOs appeared to represent physical aircraft, there was simply not enough tangible data to determine their origin.

Of the three USAF programs that studied UFOs, it was Sign that was the most sympathetic to the non-human explanation.

Project Grudge: 1948-1951

Project Grudge was another short-lived project by the U.S. Airforce to investigate unidentified flying objects (UFOs). Grudge succeeded Project Sign in February, 1949 and was then followed by Project Bluebook in 1952. The project formally ended in December 1949 but continued in a minimal capacity until late 1951.

Project Bluebook: 1952-1969

Project Bluebook was the third in a series of systematic government studies regarding unidentified flying objects (U-FOs) that was conducted and regulated by the United States Airforce. It started in 1952 after a significant UFO wave swept across America, climaxing with the Washington incursions that prompted answers from the military. Bluebook was the third study of its kind (the first two were projects Sign/Saucer, 1947, and Grudge, 1949). A termination order was given for the project in December 1969 after the Condon report investigation. All activity for the project ceased in January 1970. Bluebook was criticised for its lack of scientific objectivity with many feeling that the entire study was set up to fail and a publicity stunt for congress.

***

Managing the psychology of awareness

Prior to the most recent 'UFO' programs - AATIP and AAWSAP being revealed, the USAF and other agencies had historically claimed the United States government was no longer investigating the issue of anomalous aerial vehicles. But this, as it had turned out, wasn't exactly true. When the three United States Airforce programs (Sign, Grudge and Bluebook) closed in 1969 after running for 22 years, the issue was instantly relegated to fringe conspiracy. For 50 years no one could get funded, or have academic institutions look into their research and data on UAP.

Then through the Obama administration, Senator Harry Reid headed up a new effort and charged DoD with investigating UAP as the activity increased around nuclear strike groups of the west and east coast. And it happened in secret, it happened when officially the mainstream media still believed that the U.S. government was out of the UFO game. If it wasn't for AATIP Director, Lue Elizondo going to congress and resigning, none of this would have happened and the world would still blissfully believe that UAP weren't real.

Managing the threat narrative

The most famous program was Project Bluebook, which came to an end after it was officially declared that UFOs *posed no threat* to national security. And this is an important point that many old guard Ufology types don't like to admit, and certainly don't accept. That the 'threat narrative' is the key to whether or not the government is legally responsible to engage investigation of UAP. For if an unknown technology exists, and are in our skies, then that would be considered a potential threat (regardless of whether they are or not).

It is a very effective strategy for playing down importance and awareness of the general public. Unfortunately, I was sad to hear that some Ufologists have been manipulated into thinking the threat narrative itself is part of some false flag conspiracy. Seemingly, some people in the early 2000s and beyond, went to a lot of effort to implant this particular conspiracy storyline within Ufology. Essentially, it meant that should one day a small breakaway group from within DoD, with access to data and materials, try to engage congress and the public sphere - then they wouldn't be supported by Ufology due to the pushback against the all-important threat narrative. Without the support of hundreds of thousands of Ufologists, the pressure wouldn't be put on the system. Game over.

Conspiracy was used very effectively as we found out when we ourselves tried to gather support for engaging congress using the threat narrative. In fact, the small DoD group of mercenary activists trying to leak UAP videos and push UAP transparency became the enemy of Ufology. A few well-crafted aversion techniques that played to UFO-types fears and it became self-sustaining.

This aversion strategy is decades old. He who controls the spin on the threat narrative controls the disclosure discourse. Take the U.K. Condign report (2000), which again dismissed any future Ministry of Defence (MOD) investigation due to a lack of a threat to national security. The MOD borrowed this concept from the 1968 Condon report conclusions. What can we say?

They were bloody clever.

The Condon Committee report

The infamous Condon Committee was actually the informal name of the University of Colorado UFO Project. These were a group funded by the United States Airforce from 1966 to 1968 at the University of Colorado to study unidentified flying objects under the direction of the now famous physicist Edward Condon. The result of its work, formally titled, *'Scientific Study of Unidentified Flying Objects'* (6), and known as the 'Condon Report', appeared in 1968 as stated earlier.

These findings are that no 'UFO' ever reported and investigated by the Airforce has ever indicated a threat to national security. This is accurate from the perspective that none of the unidentified aerial vehicles have been overtly violent towards humans (at least not a large scale). However, when we consider what DoD believes to be a threat, we must consider intent vs. behaviour vs. capability. And the *threat* narrative is key. The potential *threat* is what determines whether the military take UAP serious as a genuinely anomalous phenomenon.

Buried within our collective subconscious, we know that *if* some external intelligence *arrived* here on Earth, it would be treated seriously by the world's military forces as a first point of contact. The potential threat is assessed by them and from there we move forward. If the worlds military, the DoD, the Airforce and others, state that there is no threat, then it also says to us civilians that there is equally nothing to the phenomena. Which essentially is what the Airforce did in 1969.

But how can we know the intentions of the anomalous now or in the future?

So, in the case of UFOs or UAP, as they are now called, we simply don't know the future intent (intention has the potential for change).

On top of this, DoD via the Airforce have historically minimised the 'capabilities' of UAP through poorly applied debunking methodology. This has meant that when a UAP potentially displayed the 'AATIP five observables' for example, the case report analysis dismissed them, painting a conclusion of terrestrial explanations, thus removing the 'capabilities' element from the equation of 'threat to national security'.

The Condon report also provided a conclusion that 'no evidence' had been found by the Airforce that suggested 'Unidentified' reports represented a technology that was unknown by modern day scientific knowledge. This is the most problematic conclusive statement which is provided and is inherently false. Firstly, we can ask what exactly constitutes *'evidence'*? Does the military and civilian report testimony within Project Bluebook's files not count as 'evidence' of advanced anomalous technology?

And if not, *why not?*

We can highlight how the poor methodology approach used within the Condon report completely syphons off the potential for anomalous technology (which we will discuss later in this chapter), via the clever and yet intellectually dishonest constructed research approach.

Essentially, any objective, holistic approach would have identified the various technological categories that we have identified ourselves through the five AATIP observables – 'low observability', 'trans-medium travel', 'hypersonic velocity', 'anti-gravity' and 'instantaneous acceleration'. And yet there are no subsections or statistics within Bluebook, or the USAF sponsored Condon report which incorporated and accounted for such advanced technologies.

They didn't find anything because they didn't look, and

they didnt look because arguably, they didnt want to find such things.

Finally, the Condon report states that there was 'no evidence' that the 'Unidentified' case reports were extra-terrestrial vehicles (6). My issue with this statement would be based around *'what constitutes evidence of extra-terrestrials'*. What radar data is provided alongside each individual case within Bluebook to corroborate whether or not these UFOs were leaving orbit (and even then, how can we take that as a conclusive indication of extra-terrestrials). If we are to assume that the reported 'Flying Discs' are extra-terrestrials, where is supportive data to determine origin and destination? When we look back through case reports within Bluebook, there is no additional data to suggest that these objects are extra-terrestrial, and also, there is no data to suggest that 'Flying Discs' are *not* extra-terrestrials either.

And yet the conclusions of Condon state firmly there is 'no evidence' of extra-terrestrials without adding the very critical point that they didn't have the relevant data to rule it out either.

From my perspective, the entire report suffers with intellectual dishonesty and narrative building – there is a conclusion in place prior to investigation and the entire report is orientated around getting to that conclusion.

The consequences

The following January, The New York Times ran an article (5) that dismissed the extra-terrestrial hypothesis based on the findings of the Condon report. In the article, scientific critics were labelled as 'enthusiasts of UFOs', and the stigma began. The age of the UFOs was over.

Let it be noted that these three conclusions within Project Bluebook along with the Condon Committee formulated the decision to officially end research funding of projects into unidentified flying objects. This is historical fact and will serve as a benchmark for the lack of official UFO research. After that fact the topic became lost to fringe and second rail science. Documentation regarding the former Bluebook investigation was transferred over to the Modern Military Branch, the National Archives and also the Records Service. The files are available online through various companies and a quick scout through the files reveals there is something interesting in the testimony and data.

Since the termination of Project Blue Book, nothing significant has occurred that would support a resumption of official investigations by the Air Force. That is, until DoD programs AATIP and AAWSAP were disclosed in 2017 and 2018 respectively.

Criticisms of the methodology and conclusions

The conclusions of the Condon report do not match what is reported in the Bluebook case files, specifically case report #14. In fact, they directly contradict the final conclusions, the same conclusions that shut down Bluebook and ended the world's credible interest in UFOs. It was sneaky science, the type you would expect our favourite pseudo-debunker to pull off and get away with because the psychology of stigma strengthens their argument.

Time after time, our research shows military and civilian cases of 'Flying Discs', and other strange lights that defy obvious explanation, whose reported abilities defy any known human technology of that time period (or even now), and yet these cases have been dismissed through a needless convoluted scientific process that from the outside only appeared to 'muddy the waters'. For anybody applying the sceptical approach, one must also apply such close attention to the Condon conclusions with regard to data analysis and how they completely sidestepped report #14.

The report shows that special report #14 examined over 3200 cases and labelled them either 'known' or 'unknown' or 'insufficient information.' The 'knowns' and 'unknowns' marked down from excellent to poor - cases categorised as 'excellent' would involve experienced witnesses such trained military and airline pilots, multiple civilian or military witnesses with some form of corroborating evidence such as radar data or photographs. Even with report #14 the marking criteria was in favour of a terrestrial explanation.

Also, as we look over the report (5), the 3200 cases were broken down into six different characteristics by the Battelle scientists into colour, number, duration of observation, brightness, shape, and speed which were then catalogued between 'knowns' and 'unknowns' to see if there was a statistically significant outcome. A major problem was that in order for a case to be categorised as 'known', only two data analysts had to independently agree on an outcome for that case. But, for a case to be categorised as an 'unknown', all four data analysts had to agree on the outcome. This is quite astonishing. This isn't a scientific process which seeks out objective truth, this is stacking the cards in a certain favour. Additionally, labelling something conclusively as 'unknown' from the start is quite unambiguous, it generalises anything anomalous under a category which may be classed as uninteresting - when it might not be. Genuine reports of 'Flying Discs' then have the potential to be falsely associated together with unidentified objects such as balloons and birds etc, that probably could be identified with more data. The result of this is that 'unknowns' are looked over and downplayed. Suddenly the media and public are talking 'unknowns' instead of 'Flying Discs' and nobody is talking about the advanced technology displayed.

This trick is still used today by Pentagon spokespersons who use the classification 'Unidentified', rather than 'Flying Disc,' or 'Tic-Tac', which bring directed awareness to the anomalous phenomena.

A credible Condon investigation methodology would have identified each 'unknown' aerial vehicle shape by its own category (Disc, Tic-Tac, Cube, Pyramid, Triangle, etc), thus as a hallmark of that scientific conclusion and bringing attention to those report collections. Essentially, they don't do this. They switched focus away from the hundreds and hundreds of 'Flying Disc' reports – which clearly indicate anomalous phenomena and the advanced anomalous technology.

Honestly, I personally don't believe that this wasn't some overt conspiracy, at least not by the scientists involved, this was a simple case of biased research ethics. A poor methodology and report was applied that faced no peer review research, no scrutiny from the scientific community and was completed in a way which suited those who were funding the investigation, the United States Airforce. Despite the debatable use of syphoning information within an objective research study, the main results of the statistical analysis from #14 were quite hard to take.

The found that 69% of all cases were determined to be 'known' or identified. Then only 9% were due to 'insufficient data', and the final 22% fell within the 'unknown' category.

With regard to the 'known' category, a massive 86% of the 'knowns' would turn out to be balloons, aircraft or celestial explanations. Only a small 1.5% were determined to be psychological explanations. Hoaxes came under 'miscellaneous' and made up 8%. It was assessed that the significantly higher quality of case, the more likely it was to be determined as 'unknown'. Additionally, 35% of the higher quality cases were categorised as 'unknowns', in direct contrast to only 18% of the lower quality cases.

Critics of the UFO reality tried to argue that report #14 proved that the phenomena wasn't real, stating that the 'unknowns' would be identified with more data. This was arguably a poor scientific claim, given that, as the official conclusions show, there is a distinction between 'knowns' and 'unknowns' by a high statistical significance.

But yes, I do agree that we must accept that none of this suggests some non-human technology by design of the flawed methodology. 'Unknowns' by definition are not symbolic of '*Aliens*'. Again however, we could highlight the direction of the entire report was postioned in a way to not find non-human technology.

The Low Memo, 1966

In the July of 1967, a gentleman by the name of James E. McDonald, learned from a Committee member about a memo that had been written the previous year on August 9, 1966. As detailed by Harkins and Saunders (7), the '*Low Memorandum*' detailed how Low had apparently reassured two University of Colorado administrators that they could expect the study to demonstrate that UFO observations had no basis in reality. Historian Richard Nolan's coverage of this is very compelling and well worth an in-depth review of what occurred. He notes a few important points about the objectivity of the report. Mainly, that In late January 1967, Condon was reportedly quoted by the Elmira-Star Gazette in which he said in a lecture that he thought the government should not study UFOs because the subject was '*nonsense*', adding that he wasn't supposed to reach such a conclusion for another year (2).

For anyone who has worked in professional research before, they will recognise this as is intellectually dishonest. You do not start with a conclusion and work backwards, that is not how science works.

However, objective science seemed to be low on the list.

The gaping hole left from Bluebook's conclusions.

Bluebook's Special Report No. #14 contradicted the official conclusions of the Condon Committee. It suggested further investigation was required into the significant 'unknown' element. This, however, was seemingly not in the plans of committee leader Edward Condon and the board members who seemed to have a narrative already in place ahead of time. This doesn't mean those involved were part of a secret conspiracy, but it does mean that significant researcher bias could have played a part in the process.

In any case, the closure of Bluebook was what killed UFOs for the next generation and the one after that. Academia and the scientific community now do not take the subject seriously and instead it has been left to well-meaning amateurs. But amateurs all the same.

The field of 'Ufology' was a wild west of confabulated half-truths from profiteers selling snake oil to those wanting to buy it. Tales of space aliens and 'insiders' is common with no real way to establish validity. The official withdrawal from investigation has left a gaping hole to which conspiracy was born and nurtured. Not that there aren't good, thoughtful researchers in the field such as David Marler, Richard Dolan or Stanton Friedman, etc.

Without the UFO researcher, 50 years of good data would not exist. We look to the likes of MUFON and others as an example. Data needs to be collected and analysed professionally, appropriately and without bias.

* * *

Conclusions

Project Bluebook was a success for the Airforce - if their intentions were to successfully prove that a scientific investigation had run through the process and then concluded there was nothing to the UFO case reports. My personal feelings are that some in the Airforce and elsewhere wanted the problem of UFOs to go away. Whether they believed them to be extraterrestrials or whether they saw them as a whole 'bunch of baloney' and 'nonsense' is undetermined. Poor methodological research was applied in a way which meant the recommendations were only ever going to reach one conclusion, and that wasn't in favour of anomalous technology. Either way, the closure of Bluebook ended the topic of UFOs for the general public for over 50 years. It wouldn't be until the emergence of AATIP and the UAP revolution in late 2017, would the world once again reconsider the prospect of non-human intelligences, here on Earth. No matter how it is played out, what occurred in the Condon report will not be forgotten in future generations.

The closure of Bluebook is important as it essentially shuts down the interest and credibility of UFOs, relegating the issue from the mind of society, banishing it to the fringe. Humans collectively changed their cognition towards the phenomena from that moment – potentially, a little understood part of this mystery.

References

(1). Greenewald, J. 'Report of Meetings of Scientific Panel on Unidentified Flying Objects Convened by Office of Scientific Intelligence, CIA.'
The Black Vault.
https://documents.theblackvault.com/documents/ufos/robertsonpanelreport.pdf

(2). Dolan, R. (2001). 'UFOs and the National Security State.'
Keyhole Publishing Company.

(3). Ruppelt, E. (1956). 'The Report on Unidentified Flying Objects.'
Cosimo Classics. New York.

(4). United States Airforce. (1954). 'Project Blue Book Special Report #14.'
Archive.Org.
https://archive.org/details/ProjectBlueBookSpecialReport14

(5). Sullivan, W. (1969). 'U. F. O. Finding: No Visits From Afar.'
The New York Times.
https://www.nytimes.com/1969/01/08/archives/u-f-o-find-

ing-no-visits-from-afar-ufo-finding-no-visits-from-afar.html

(6). Condon, E. (1969). 'Scientific Study of Unidentified Flying Objects.'
E.P. Dutton.

(7). Harkins, D., and Saunders, R. (1968). 'UFOs? Yes!
Where the Condon committee went wrong.'
Signet Books.

CHAPTER THIRTEEN:
ANOMALOUS TECHNOLOGY
AND THE FIVE AATIP
OBSERVABLES

* * *

W hat separates us humans from animals are higher emotional and cognitive processes. The neurological synaptic structures are densely compacted within our biological brains. Some argue that we have a higher state of consciousness, that we can *choose* to ignore our primal self and our 'lizard brain'. We believe ourselves to be more emotionally developed, cognitively superior and more acutely deliberate within our planned actions when engaged tasks. We can see the future consequences of a multitude of actions and act accordingly. Seemingly, our DNA has evolved well beyond other primates.

When Charles Darwin wrote the *'The Origin of Species,'* in 1859, he contemplated the very first ideas that the survival of the fittest was an evolutionary biological process that allows the most effective/adaptive DNA gene pool to flourish at the expense of the weak. Whilst I'm not going down the historical rabbit hole of extra-terrestrial interference upon human DNA, we should still consider that some genetic mutation (random or not) in our history altered mankind is significant.

These series of mutations which occurred over millions of years allowed the development of modern humans, and most importantly, the increased cranial capacity and cognitive ability for 'tool making'. The first tools within the 'Stone-age' were mankind first primitive technology.

Our ability to manipulate our environment, to destroy and build, and to create complex tools have meant we far out-match our hairy primate cousins who for whatever reason, never developed past Chimpanzees.

Our own understanding and application of technology sets us apart. Interestingly, in the last century alone, we have arguably made more *significant* advancements than in the previous 1000 years combined. The age of technology across the 20th century dramatically changed how we life our lives in many differing ways. It is almost hard to believe that just over a hundred years ago there was no aeroplanes, no computers, mobile phones, televisions, internet and the main mode of transportation was the horse and cart. In fact, my Nanna told me once that she got her driving license with a horse and milk cart. In many ways, that was a different era completely.

Currently we are at the beginning of the '3D printer' age (imagine this technology in another millennium), in which our computerised technology can physically print functional, highly dynamic parts and objects. Our mastered technology is the pinnacle of this world, and all others (so far as we know). The truth is that there was another technology operating in our skies, undetected, or maybe even *undetectable* to us for the longest time. A technology beyond us, even to the point we struggle to recognise it.

Some argue that as our brains evolve, and once con-sciousness reaches a certain level, we start to become aware or even *conscious* of other extra-aspects of reality. We can argue that our human technology is a symbol of that raised con-sciousness – consider that we now have the devices and instru-ments to track and detect the anomalous phenomena like at no other point in human history. We are starting to become aware of them, who they might be and what they can do beyond the religious hoodoo of previous centuries. We also are able to define them with more accuracy thanks to our technology.

Most importantly of all, we are now able to closely observe UAP vehicles as they outperform anything we could hope to throw at them, and that shows us that the impossible is actually possible. Maybe we too might have this anomalous technology one day, should our own global consciousness be raised high enough.

***

SATURDAY
21ˢᵗ of July, 2018
"Tucker."

Remembering back to the hot summer of 2018, the conversations with the team helped with UAPinfo research ideas. Although, it wasn't a picnic, and certainly wasn't a simple case of researching concepts without concerns. Obstacles seemed to present themselves frequently within the team - but the team themselves were good intelligent people, dedicated, engaging and motivated. These were the people who created UAPinfo, the UAP revolution and the social media platform of 'TwitterUFO'.

Sven was always discussing advanced quantum consciousness ideas – honestly, I didn't understand them as they were way too advanced for me. Danny was always on the front foot, looking for the 'nuts and bolts' data on the 'Tic-Tac,' whereas Christian was focused on graphic design concepts for the UAPinfo artwork stuff. Keith was speaking with important people and always formulating ideas.

Those were some of the good days, the weird days, the days of disclosure that brought out our imagination and thirst for data. Although, there were issues and our unofficial moto of '*nobody ever really quits*', was in place for a reason - UAPinfo members kept quitting and returning. Fractures, arguments and fights were always popping up within the team. Sometimes, things just don't work out and people part ways.

***

Almost seven months had passed since Luis Elizondo was revealed as the director of AATIP, and, it hadn't been easy, in fact it was a constant slog against trolls and the disgruntled on social media. The truth is that TTSA and Mr. Elizondo received pushback from the old guard Ufologists immediately, they believed him to be a 'CIA PSY-OPP' agent with a *'limited hangout'* initiative, all of which we knew wasn't true – and by 'we' I mean the very first people of what would become 'UFOTwitter'. Even today, most people are unaware that UFOTwitter/UAP research community was born from TTSA, it's what started it all, even our own group of UAPinfo. For the first half a year, Mr. Elizondo was very limited as to the engagement of mainstream Ufology, and despite a few appearances on Coast2Coast, it wasn't until the July of 2018 that his first major engagement of Ufology occurred. Whilst the AATIP-FOIA debate raged across social media, I stepped back slightly with no personal means of gathering such data. I wasn't that type of 'UFO' person, and to this day I'm not a 'UFO researcher' and I certainly wasn't much good with stats and figures. Additionally, I didn't have the patience or the interest for contacting spokespersons or chasing down leads. Better researchers were better at that field of research than I could ever be. So instead, I decided to find where my own place might be in the world of UAP, how could I both contribute and learn at the same time. Maybe there was a research place for me in Ufology, however, something inside didn't want a place in *Ufology*. I wanted something different entirely that still focused on UFOs – a platform which asked a different type of question but without subscribing to it.

In the July of 2018, the very notion of 'UAP Activism' hadn't even dawned on me. Much like everyone else, I was still just following events as they happened, and it would be some time until my true role (of annoying UFO cultists) would come to me.

***

When I awoke that Saturday morning, it was to the notification that Fox News anchor, Tucker Carlson, had done another segment on the issue, this time his guest was British UFO representative Nick Pope (1). Despite his political viewpoints, which seemed to upset a few people on social media, it has to be said that Tucker Carlson is the first mainstream media personality to take the phenomena seriously. At least that is true in this UAP-Revolution/Golden Age of UFOs (that begin December 16th, 2017). But it brought up a good point which still stands today - leave your political perspective out of UAP research. Carlson would push the issue forward within the right-wing media and even asked President Trump the UFO question in later years.

Credit to him for that. He was one of the first.

FRIDAY
27th of July, 2018
"That UFO conference."

The MUFON symposium was held some eight months following the December 16th revelations of AATIP. At the time Luis Elizondo was still highly questioned and pursued, after all, he was the centre piece of a bizarre initiative to inform the world that the UFO reality was science fact, not fiction. At the time of the keynote lecture, I was on social media and spoke to a guy who ran his own 'Twitch' show about UFOs. He had somehow got a slot to stand up and ask Lue Elizondo a question about 'UFOs' at the symposium. Me being me, I interjected, and suggested to him that rather than ask the former AATIP director a question about something or other, that instead, he should simply thank Lue for coming forward. Which the guy actually did to his credit.

SATURDAY

28th of July, 2018
"Morning after."

At work the following morning and the night before was still on my mind. Sitting in the kitchen on
my lunch break the following day, I managed to watch the entire MUFON presentation. Lue Elizondo ran through AATIP and
its purpose within DOD, essentially telling the story of why
such a program was important. Unlike other government personnel who had come forward on UFOs over the years, I found
that Elizondo, in comparison, was doing so for the long-term
benefit of the Department of Defense, and he did so legally. Mr.
Elizondo stated on many occasions that he would not violate
his national security oath at any cost.

AATIP was unclassified (at the time) and so were the
three videos at the time of release and he certainly wasn't leaking anything classified. In fact, the way he and others ensured
national security wasn't impacted was pretty impressive.

Edward Snowden can be used as an example, to contrast
against Luis Elizondo - Snowden took classified information
from NSANET and leaked it, illegally. And here is the careful distinction. The actions of Edward Snowden significantly
harmed the DoD, despite the highly immoral and unethical
considerations of 'wire-tapping' civilians. The difference between Elizondo and Snowden is that Elizondo took steps to ensure he did things legally to benefit DoD long term, Snowden
on the other hand is exiled to Mother Russia.

***

Also, in the July of 2018, my personal UAP hero (investigate journalist George Knapp) was able to release an important document (2). The Harry Reid/William Lynn 111 letter
showed that AATIP was 'Aerospace' and that in 2009 Senator
Reid had requested AATIP apply for a 'Special Access Program'
status. It was denied (one theory is that if it had achieved SAP
status, we might have never heard of AATIP). This document

conclusively showed that Reid wanted AATIP to become an SAP, which meant they would have had access to whatever is behind the 'hanger doors', which is essentially all the deeply buried UAP secrets. So, despite the run-around for researchers, we in July 2018 had official statements on record from Pentagon spokespeople saying officially that AATIP investigated vehicles with extreme manoeuvrability and *unique phenomenology - as* seen within credible Navy pilot reports.

It is important to touch upon the point that by the July of 2018, the DoD were still acknowledging that AATIP had been run by Luis Elizondo. Although technically, they never claimed AATIP to be a UAP program (at that point), that came from Elizondo, Senator Reid and the anonymous intelligence sources gathered by The New York Times and Politico.

SUNDAY
29th of July, 2018
"Anomalous technology."

Here is the thing. If AATIP was a real UAP program and Elizondo was the Director, it meant that the issue was very real. Everything hung on Mr. Elizondo and his reputation. It also meant that UAP technology was real, the genuinely anomalous technology that simply wasn't human by its own definition. The technology was the whole entire game, the cornerstone of the secrecy, the diamond in the rough. Whoever owns the UAP technology that powers the anomalous phenomena will rule the world indefinitely.

This is the technology of the Gods.

You might imagine that some factions in DoD did not want employees, former or current, speaking about this extreme technology and what it can do. When Mr. Elizondo came into the picture, he made waves as a former Department of Defense employee. A former counterintelligence officer and a program director that included AATIP. This was the guy who ran the Pentagon's secret program that investigated Unidentified Aerial Phenomenon (UAP) also known as UFOs, or anomalous vehicles that were penetrating nuclear strike group airspace with impunity.

The previous day Lue had gone on stage at the 2018 Mutual UFO Network symposium and talked about AATIP (mentioning AAWSAP as the program from which AATIP evolved), and he mentioned the five observables (3).

> One: Hypersonic velocity - without signatures
> Two: Trans medium travel
> Three: Low observability
> Four: Sudden and instantaneous acceleration
> Five: Anti-gravity

When we historically think about UFOs and what they can do, we think about one or more of the observables. They represent a technology which we simply don't have and what was once reported as science fiction, or at least it is to us in the 21st century, is now science fact. Consider the implications of a high-level DoD official exclaiming the reality of such concepts within a secret government program.

***

I think I must have watched that MUFON symposium video at least three times back-to-back, over and over to try and understand how AATIP interpreted UAP technology. Simply put, how can the abilities of the 'Tic-Tac' and 'GIMBAL' objects be possible via linear thrust propulsion? The reported speeds, right angle turns, and hypersonic dead-stops would liquefy the occupant of an aviation vehicle under normal circumstances. So, with this in mind, it left AATIP to conclude that this technology cannot be using conventional physics. But if the technology isn't ours…. then whose is it?

Did Russia have this technology in 2004, or what about in 1952 or 1947?

***

The distinction of the five observables being part of AATIP was profound. It showed us that such a UAP technology existed and was being investigated by DoD. In our own case report history, we see that in some cases the UAP was able to display one or two of the observables, in other cases the UAP displayed all five. Any of these technologies on their own would be a leap forward and revolutionary, but having all five is something radically different, and, beyond next generation. Maybe even beyond the next few generations. What about other, as of yet known abilities?

What about: *'Trans-morphia.'*

Trans-morphic abilities would be the intelligent ability to create and change your physical makeup and appearance at the quantum level whilst in motion (or motionless). Let's be clear. This does not exist within a human capacity. We simply don't have an understanding, or application of a technology that morphs matter at the atomic layer into something new. This concept, as an ability, doesn't exist to us right now. At least not beyond my own pondering and unconventional imagination. As you might think, this would be too extreme for the first phases of any planned disclosures for the general public. That's even if 'Trans-morphia' is a viable ability of genuine UAP.

This technology surely is far, far, far beyond us right now. Nanotechnology doesn't exist at the atomic level; we can't change the makeup of an atomic cluster.

However, such 'trans-morphic' UAP *cases* do exist officially and are recognised historically. Unfortunately, what we have is very poor data, if at all you could call it data. We have a random assortment of cases that aren't true cases, information which can't be classed as verified information. We have tabloid-level stories that have no evidentiary sources or supporting information. Any normal person would dismiss the idea out of hand, but I'm not normal, and I'm certainly not one to dismiss and interesting concept, no matter how insane it might seem.

Cases of Trans-Morphing UAP technology

This is where we get really interested. Whilst the vast majority of such cases are stepped over my mainstream Ufology, for me the ideological implications of something that can transform itself at the quantum level is incredible. If you are a pseudo-sceptic, you might look at 'Flying Discs' and 'Tic-Tac' reports and dismiss them due to the cognitive barriers and surjective bias that such things simply can't exist, therefore they don't exist – then proceed to explain them away with Seagulls and balloons. We aren't even talking about anything truly exceptional beyond the 'nuts and bolts' vehicles with physical substance here either. We all know debunkers love to talk extra-terrestrials.

Philosophically, we should now imagine that there is a phenomena beyond that ideology, maybe a phenomenon that can manipulate localised space/time to its own desire. Hypothetically, this would be an extreme form of nanotechnology at the atomic layering, rearranging and restructuring the fabric of its own physical makeup. Imagine, it is creating a multitude of Earthly elements from the quantum level, clustering and forming atoms to bind together to form what we crudely know to be objects. Complete mastery over chemicals, metals, fabrics, materials, cells, 'genetic biological tissues' or even 'conscious beings', and instantly interjecting them within reality much the way our '3D printers' print out new objects for us to use.

This hypothetical UAP technology would be God-like and, *'for them, reality is negotiable'.*

Can we also consider that the anomalous phenomena could be 'secreting' themselves into our collective conscious universe using the building blocks of the periodic table as a painting palette for some unknown intention?

Possibly they or *it*, might do this at the exact point of

origin into this universe, or at some point whilst they/it is here.

Simply, unimaginable.

As you might consider, these case reports are not really promoted by mainstream Ufologists, it's hard enough to get the world to accept solid formed shapes never-mind this beyond radical idea, if that's what it actually is. The other problem is that we know the mainstream will always look at such cases and determine that they must all be balloons and other weird assortments floating and changing shape under atmospheric conditions – which makes sense and I'm sure accounts for the vast majority of reports are exactly that.

Again, we are faced with the same old theme of the data not being good enough even remotely start concluding.

The National UFO Reporting Centre (4) has a wealth of case reports going back to the 1960s, and in particular 2357 reports of '*changing shape*' UAPs. I read a rather impressive triangular shaped UAP by researcher David Marler (5), who cites various cases of 'shape-shifting' triangles, however, unfortunately doesn't give any further details which make it difficult to pursue and evaluate.

Instead, we looked into what we had available. If one looks across the internet there is a wealth of UAP cases on which unknown objects are said to have changed in shape, size and colour. These cases are very frequent, but poorly analysed and poorly collected.

One 2007 case reported over India, stated a round aerial object changed shape to a triangle and then into a straight line, it also '*emitted a bright light that formed a circle - almost a halo - and also radiated a range of colours*' (6).

And then in 2020 over Bogotá, Colombia reports stated a 'hexagonal shape' changed into a 'black cube' shape (7). In 2018, there was the strange case of an aerial object over New Jersey, America, that appeared in which a long black object that changed shape quickly (8).

The Daily Star reported in 2020 that a 15-17-minute-

long video made its way to YouTube (9). The apparent unknown aerial object in question, *'shows the bright round orange
object changing its shape to a triangle or a boomerang.'*

Another case from 2020, this time in Rio de Janeiro, Bra-
zil (10), involved video camera footage that captured an object
morphing from a five-pointed star to a pyramid in a matter of
seconds. The audio sounds authentic, however the case lacks
in-depth and on-record testimony that gives context to the
aerial objects.

Naturally, without the context of such cases we are left
with considering hoaxes and misidentifications. The internet
is flooded with these types of cases.

The problem is we cannot appropriately identify such
a technological phenomenon from birds, balloons or drones,
currently. We simply dismiss 'trans-morphing' UAP and such
things as balloons or errand plastic bags that change shape
with the wind at high/low altitude. Unfortunately, there isn't
enough available data in these cases to even compile a cold case
review and UAP case report. Rumours are that TTSA are developing a system which might use artificial intelligence (A.I.)
to identify such unknowns, but nothing had come forward in
2018.

The other issue, as with most of these encounters and
cases, is that they are firmly planted within the civilian world
and even within mainstream Ufology and are not well understood. They are complex in their own right and rightly open to
critical evaluation. If we look at such cases, we could point to
a lack of witness testimony, a lack of military testimony and
a lack of sensory data, clear pictures, gun camera footage and
radar data which would help us grasp what exactly is being
observed.

Should this proposed technology exist, it may have
gone completely under the radar due to its untenable nature.
The closest thing we currently have in the civilian world to
understanding this extreme 'nanotechnology' type of ability
is when Tony Stark 'morphs' into Iron Man in the beginning

of the brilliant Avengers film: 'Infinity War'. Beyond that, we don't have any real technology within aerospace that would explain this ability, if it even is a *technology* at all, and not some living plasma-based life form.

This might be a conversation for future generations. Essentially, we would need military case reports and data to fully understand what exactly these things are truly capable of doing. Plus, we would need to see the atomic layering to give a baseline of how such structures are created, maintained and changed. The gravitational 'Strong Force' keeps atoms glued together (it's why our bodies and objects don't separate). As atoms themselves are affected by gravity and produce their own gravitational field, such a trans-morphing ability would need to be able to affect the gravitational field of Earth and the individual fields of the atom themselves. Then the subatomic particles that would make up a 'Flying Disc' would need to be arranged, clustered together at the quantum level to form that object in this reality.

***

Now much has been wrote about the long-term change of the historical UAP appearance - I strongly suggest you read all of John Keel and Jacques Vallee's work and the inter-dimensional + ultra-terrestrial theories.

If we look at how the appearance of the phenomenon has changed from decade to decade, century to century we might get a better picture and even apply 'trans-morphia' as an explanation, however radical this seems.

At the end of the 19th century the 'Mysterious Airships' reportedly performed amazing abilities well before the first aeroplane. The wave of airship objects changed with time (despite outliers being evident in other minor waves).

The classic waves of 'Flying Discs' that appeared in the 1940s and 1950s changed in frequency, replaced by the giant 'Black Triangles' that started in the 1960s and was more known throughout the 1990s – see the research and literature around the 'Belgium wave'.

To link all of these phenomena might seem premature, and it would be scientifically foolish to associate cold cases without hard evidence. Having said that, the point still stands, what has been *reported* by multiple witnesses over the past two centuries has changed. This change of physcial shape through civilian reported observation has led most researchers to ignore the disclosed objects that don't fit their narrative. If there had been military witnesses instead of civilians, this might have been different as pilots and others in service are trained observers. Essentially, they hold more credibility in the eyes of the public.

Going forward, we can ask how accurate it is to associate UAP with 'trans-morphic technology', a possible *craft* that has the ability to literally change its shape?

Instantly?

This is the stuff of science fiction and is actually the case with regards to Hollywood. Remember the film, '*Flight of the Navigator*', as a kid I loved that film and in my naïve innocence had no idea the craft was based on Ufology reports of 'Flying Saucers.'

Back in 1987 a film was released that incorporated a silver 'Flying Saucer' object that was able to change its shape based upon its propulsion needs. This was a fictional concept, one that implied an alien vehicle morphs its own shape to intentionally engage a specific task. To go faster it must become more streamlined.

With regard to the craft's propulsion, the film's story ensures the 'Flying Saucer' morphs for our benefit as the viewer - rather than for a sense of rationale or logistical appropriate aerodynamic function. Aka, in reality the craft wouldn't need to morph into an aerodynamic streamlined shape as the craft isn't using chemical/linear thrust propulsion to cut through Earth's thick atmosphere like a plane or rocket would (which is proven in the film by the craft's vertical climb into outer space in seconds).

This interested me as theoretical concept. Although the film was fictional, the inaccuracies actually mirrored what we are seeing within the current day phenomenon. Despite hypothetically being well in advance of human technology, this anomalous phenomenon is flawed, and flawed in ways it *shouldn't* be flawed.

For example, we have the 'Mysterious Airships' of the late 19th century which make no sense aerodynamically and shouldn't have been able to fly in the way they do. Then we see hyper advanced anomalous vehicles outperforming navy fighter jets, and yet they allegedly *crash* in the New Mexico desert (see chapter on Roswell). Some have suggested that human technology brought them down with electro-magnetic-pulse (EMP) weapons.

I struggle to accept this. Even if EMP weapons can affect their navigation systems etc, they definitely shouldn't. These are vehicles that have an understanding at the quantum level, are potentially thousands of years more advanced in technology and yet they get brought down by an EMP device in the early 20th century?

Does that sound right to you?

No, me neither.

Then we see reports of 'Flying Discs' rotating in mid-air to a standstill before taking off at grey speed - but they are 'wobbly' in lower atmosphere and 'clunky' in rotation ('GIMBAL', 2015).

We see reports of pointless little grey men inside and outside a 'Flying Disc' craft but for no obvious reasons - arguably they don't need to be in there - why not simply send the hyper advanced probes to collect data?

Why do they pretend like proximity is relevant to them and whatever their mission is?

We have 'Tic-Tac' objects which interact with pilots, employing human mirroring techniques. The 'Tic-Tac' doesn't need to be affected by humans in any way. Cloak and avoid should

For a technology well beyond human understanding and application, some of these technological behaviours and unforgiving errors don't make sense to me. And this particularly the case if *they* are able to manipulate space-time at the quantum level.

Hypothetically, anything with the ability to change itself at the atomic/quantum level should be, in theory, indestructible, impervious, unaffected by the elements of Earth as it goes about its unknown agenda. Anything that understands and manipulates molecular atoms at the quantum level shouldn't crash in the desert or wobble on low atmosphere, clunk in rotation, or be influenced in behaviour by the appearance of an F-18 fighter jet.

If the anomalous phenomena have 'trans-morphic' abilities, then nothing should be able to effect it. And certainly nothing us primitive primates could think up in the 20th century. So, either it doesn't have such an advanced technological ability, or it does, and if it does then we are missing a massive part of this puzzle and UAP is even more complex than we first thought.

Again, the problem as always, is proving such things in a world which doesn't accept UAP.

MONDAY
30th of July, 2018
"So... what are they?"

At work the next day, I sat in the warm box room on the far side of the hospital. My mind was contemplating the possibility that this technology was in fact 'alien' to us, but then maybe not even extra-terrestrials.

Or they might be? I honestly didn't know anymore. Without data and official reports and a government position, we couldn't ever know.

One thing Luis Elizondo had always stated, and had

reaffirmed the statement at the MUFON conference, was that he wouldn't conclusively say that UAP are extra-terrestrials. In fact, he wouldn't say they were anything beyond a phenomenon that required more data and open transparency. He didn't want to influence the jury and I've never asked him because I know the answer I'll get.

He stated this was his position because he didn't want to influence other people, quite refreshing and noble in contrast to other old guard Ufologists who are happy to tell you what UFOs are with no regard for the consequences. Personally, my belief was that he probably knew that the UAP issue was possibly something else, something non-human. Something more complex, however, this was just my unfounded speculation.

Having spoken a few times with Doctor Garry Nolan (a close associate of notable UFO researcher Jacques Vallee) I quickly started to formulate the idea that the phenomenon was possibly inter-dimensional or trans-dimensional - from somewhere else, maybe another dimension or multi-verse, but again this is just hypothetical. To transverse realities, universes, dimensions and worlds you need a technology that can do so.

And we do not have such things.

* * *

Conclusions

The revolutionary five observables of AATIP are the desired technology of any black budget special access program. Whether or not some Airforce defense contractor already has *some* of these abilities displayed by the 'Tic-Tac' UAP is still very much contested. We simply don't know despite the claims of some in the field of Ufology that aren't backed up by verified sources. The truth is no matter what advanced technology the government may or may not have, there simply hasn't been any concrete evidence to conclusively state that the 'Tic-Tac' in 2004 was human technology. In fact, the claims have been highly disputed by those such as Christopher Mellon who worked under the Bush administration and was a part of a congressional oversight committee, the Senate Select Committee for Intelligence (SSCI). Additionally, we cannot associate any 'trans-morphic' abilities to UAP because we don't have solid data. The problem, as always, is we don't have a scientific process to identify the unidentified technology.

References

(1). Carlson, T. (2018). 'Expert: UFOs frequently come close to hitting airliners.'
Fox News. Youtube.
https://youtu.be/1ruFixSu0wA

(2). Knapp, G. (2018). 'William Lynn AATIP Document.'
8NewsNow.
https://www.8newsnow.com/news/exclusive-i-team-obtains-some-key-documents-related-to-pentagon-ufo-study/1324250087/

(3). MUFON Symposium. (2018). 'Lue Elizondo presents the history of AATIP.'
To The Stars Academy of Arts and Science. YouTube.
https://youtu.be/D3r6SmrCUM0

(4). The National UFO Reporting Centre (NUFORC).
http://www.nuforc.org/webreports/ndxsChanging.html

(5). Marler, D. (2013). 'Triangular UFOs: An Estimate of the Situation.'
Independently Published.

(6). 'UFO puzzle has city in a tizzy.' (2007).
Times of India.
https://m.timesofindia.com/city/kolkata-/UFO-puzzle-has-

city-in-a-tizzy/articleshow/2500882.cms?referral=PM

(7). 'VIDEO: Colombia witnesses 'shape-changing UFO' in broad daylight.' (2020).
India TV News.
https://www.indiatvnews.com/amp/trending/news-video-colombia-witnesses-shape-changing-ufo-in-broad-day-light-615584

(8). Parsons, J. (2018). 'Bizarre shape-shifting UFO caught on video seems to defy explanation.'
Metro.co.uk.
https://metro.co.uk/2018/08/21/bizarre-shape-shifting-ufo-caught-on-video-seems-to-defy-explanation-7866504/amp/

(9). Tiffany, L.O. (2020). 'Orange 'UFO' spotted 'changing shapes' as it hovers in night sky.'
Daily Star.
https://www.dailystar.co.uk/news/weird-news/orange-ufo-spotted-changing-shapes-22671288.amp

(10). Martin, S. (2020). 'Alien news: Shape-shifting UFO seen over Rio de Janeiro – claim.'
Express.co.uk.
https://www.express.co.uk/news/weird/1316545/alien-news-shape-shifting-ufo-video-space-aliens-conspiracy-the-ory/amp

CHAPTER SEVENTEEN:
CLASSIFIED INFORMATION

* * *

Y ou don't really understand just how important classified information is to people who hold a security clear-
ance until you listen to someone like Christopher Mellon or
Luis Elizondo. In a way, his decision to come forward about
AATIP and UAP has allowed people such as myself, who have
semi-researched UFOs, to really appreciate the real-world implications of such data. The way they carefully approach data,
what they can say and what they can't really hits hope with
others in Ufology at the time who were saying the most extremely crazy things about 'secret government alien bases' and
'deep state conspiracies'.

Personally, up until that point, I had never given a second thought to information which is classified, declassified or
unclassified. In a way it is this process which allows governments, rightly or wrongly, to keep their secrets, to stop leaks
to the enemy on sources and methods. As you might imagine,
classified information is a big deal, leaking it can mean you go
to prison for a long time. Take Edward Snowden for example,
in 2013 he leaked classified information from a classified system (NSANET) and in the process got himself exiled to Russia.
Some call Snowden a hero, others call him a traitor, me personally, I have no opinion beyond the fact that he has destroyed his
own life, and that is something I have no intention of doing.
Not even with significant UAP information would I handle or
release what I believe to be classified information.

It wasn't worth the risk.

***

THURSDAY
05th of August, 2018
'AAWSAP'

A ugust was a difficult month for me and my family, and in a strange way it was good to have a distraction in researching UFOs. When you get into the topic of UAP, it isn't just lights in the sky, *'it's lies on the ground'*, well that's what Ufologist and political activist Steve Bassett (of Paradigm research group) says anyways. Apparently, it's a truth embargo rather than cover up. To me it doesn't matter what terminology you use because in the end it's all the same, the governments of the world have neglected to take seriously the biggest issue in history.

At least, openly, they have.

The closure of the Airforce's Project Bluebook in 1969 stated that there was nothing to the issue and that the UFOs weren't a threat and therefore nothing to worry about. The U.K.s Defence Intelligence Agency issued a report in 2000 which did the exact same thing, it said basically, that there was nothing to worry about, we won't take the issue further because there is no threat (1). You might imagine that *if* the U.K. and U.S. governments had been studying UFOs after these respected statements, this would have happened under extreme secrecy and high levels of classification.

When Pentagon programs AATIP and AAWSAP were finally leaked in 2017/2018, it was exactly as we had thought. Their investigation of UAP/UFO was hidden away for years at the unclassified and classified level, and no-one had any idea.

In mid-August of 2018, Keith Basterfield's blog, "Unidentified Aerial Phenomena – scientific research" published an article that referenced the 'Advanced Aerospace Threat and

Identification Program,' (2). The obscure reference came from the April 9, 2018, Congressional Record. The letter from the Chief Congressional Relations Division read that all products produced and listed under the Advanced Aerospace Threat Identification Program (AATIP) to be made available to the Committee on Armed Services (2).

This was one of the first times that we saw sensitive information on AATIP being openly channelled into the public sphere and more importantly, it showed interest from the American congress on a program that studied UAP (UFOs). As you might imagine, the information surrounding AATIP was kept tightly in-house by those in the Department of Defense prior to December 2017 and certainly in the months following. AATIP existed at the unclassified and classified level. There was a high sensitivity and secrecy to the entire issue over the study of UAP. My guess was that if AATIP was unclassified when it leaked to The New York Times in 2017, it certainly would have been fully classified after it broke.

Some stories persisted that even General James Mattis (Secretary of Defense, DoD), was only made aware of the program, and the revelation of The New York Times the night before it broke on December 15th, 2017. But we've got no concrete proof of that, and if there is a link somewhere in the bowels of UFOTwitter, I can't exactly remember where, apologies. What I do have a link for is the resignation letter of the AATIP Director, Luis Elizondo, which was taken to the Times alongside other documents verifying the program.

How we released the AATIP Director's letter of resignation

The now famous story of UAP truth advocate, Mr. Elizondo's resignation is one for the history books. He, along with Christopher Mellon and others, were unable to get senior DoD management to take seriously the UAP issue and potential threat to nuclear strike groups. It was a strategy which was quite brilliant.

Prior to 2017, DoD leadership wasn't willing to allow the Secretary of Defense, James Mattis to be briefed on the issue of UAP. They cited stigma and negative professional prospects, considering the notion that this topic is highly toxic for one's career. Which is very true, hence my own alias of Andreas Freeman Stahl.

Consequently, Lue Elizondo resigned from his position at DoD and Director of AATIP and went public to raise the issue to congress and the public. He became a hero to the American people, taking arrows in the process.

Our role in UAPinfo would then occur through sheer coincidence. At the time, ourselves and maybe only UFOJoe and UFOJesus were the only groups that had a substantial following outlet on social media who supported Elizondo and TTSA.

It was then In the August of 2018, that the Elizondo resignation letter (3) was leaked to Twitter by myself and the now defunct group UAPinfo (that included researcher Danny Silva) and a gentleman called Jay (@Jay09784691) (4). Without Jay, we wouldn't have known about the website or resignation letter.

This was not a verified release and came about by an accidental open website belonging to Christopher Mellon (TTSA colleague and close associate to Luis Elizondo). I was a part of the UAPinfo group, and followed the link provided by Jay into Mellon's website. Here I rather unwittingly took copies of the data which was on the website (I won't repeat the sensitive data that was found, or the names of the people involved even though some are now public).

We published Mr. Elizondo's letter to our UAPinfo website and it got out into the Twitter sphere and that was that.

When we realised the leak was a mistake, the decision was taken by myself and others in the group UAPinfo to delete the published article containing the resignation letter (and other sensitive details) - we did not wish to handle potentially classified or sensitive information. The details of a certain female navy pilot were also kept hidden by ourselves for over three years. We could easily have used her face and details as part of research and activism efforts but decided not to. People have the right to privacy, even when it comes to UAP.

Even though the Mellon website closed within the same afternoon, by this point it was too late, our extended group had published details to the internet for several hours before deleting the article. The letter had already been copied and pasted from the published UAPinfo article before I deleted it. I would later apologise to Lue for the accidental release in an email correspondence interview for UAPMedia (5).

＊ ＊ ＊

Conclusions

Thanks to the entertainment media over here last 50 years and Ufology itself, people in the public sphere believe that if UFOs are real, then the government must be involved in a conspiracy. But how accurate is this? How much do people confuse classified information with being a conspiracy?

Well, we can say with some degree of confidence, that the reality of this anomalous technology has been kept secret, even covered up, by someone or some group of people in dark programs doing their patriotic work for the sake of national security. At least that's how I imagine they would see it, should this be the case. But again, this doesn't necessarily mean that UAP secrecy formulates a *'conspiracy'*, after all, a conspiracy is an illegal act committed by a group of individuals with intention. What we have seen with Project Bluebook, Grudge, Sign, AAWSAP and AATIP, is that they were all legal programs ran with oversight of either the Airforce, the Defense Intelligence Agency and/or congress.

Take AATIP for example, the funding was legitimate (although not advertised in wider circles), the viability and results of the programs overseen by a representative who reported to congress committees, so they could make a call on whether such a program is relevant to national security and the American people. The information around AATIP was classified, which meant anything within that program was legally kept secret and therefore, not a conspiracy.

The problem comes with any claim that suggests certain programs which significantly effect national security, such as dead *'alien'* bodies and crashed 'Flying Discs' in defense contractor underground bunker or lab, should have congressional oversight. This is particularly true if such programs are receiving millions or billions in taxpayer dollars. Such sensitive issues for the human race should surely be in the American government's hands, not a private aerospace defense company who have no obligation to the American people. So, if, this was the case, and I'm not saying that it is, there may be a few legal questions asked if congress become involved at that level.

As for myself, or any team I have ever done research for, we will not handle classified information, and as we have shown, we also treat sensitive information with the utmost respect.

References

(1). Defence Intelligence Staff. (2000). 'Unidentified Aerial Phenomena in the U.K. Air Defence Region: Volume 3.'
Project Condign.
https://webarchive.nationalarchives.gov-
.uk/20121109132817/http:/www.mod.uk/NR/rdonlyres/
EBC81730-9FFF-4384-B9E0-C3679B5F0C8D/0/uap_vol3_pg-
s1to9.pdf

(2). Basterfield, K. (15th of August, 2018). 'Reference to the Advanced Aerospace Threat and Identification Program found in a 2018 issue of the US 'Congressional Record.'
Unidentified Aerial Phenomenon- Scientific Research.
https://ufos-scientificresearch.blogspot.com/2018/08/refer-

ence-to-advanced-aerospace-threat.html?m=1

(3). Stahl, F, A. (2018). 'Letter of Resignation.'
The Unidentified.
https://www.the-unidentified.net/aatip-files-luis-elizondo-resignation-letter-from-ousdi/

(4). @ Jay09784691. (06th of August, 2018).
Twitter.
https://twitter.com/Jay09784691/status/1026408326412873728?s=20

(5). Goldsack, A. (27th of January, 2021). 'Past, Present and Future with Luis Elizondo.'
UAPMediaUK.
https://www.uapmedia.uk/articles/luis-elizondo?format=amp&__twitter_impression=true

CHAPTER FOURTEEN: RISE
OF THE SKINWALKER

✻ ✻ ✻

Skinwalker Ranch wasn't even on my radar before the spring of that year, and probably wouldn't have entered into my consciousness if journalist George Knapp hadn't been involved and co-wrote 'Hunt for the Skinwalker' with Colm Kelleher. Additionally, the upcoming Jeremy Corbell documentary in September was causing excitement. Making bold, extreme predictions is more the style of 'UFO-Jesus' than myself, basically because I've never been very good at doing so. Having said that, my inner self tells me that places around the world, such as 'Skinwalker Ranch' might possibly hold the keys to future generations unlocking the secrets of Unidentified Anomalous Phenomenon. My statements here aren't made through peer reviewed research or appropriately applied methodology, they are made through unverified data, unsourced understanding and vague hearsay testimony that cannot be evaluated or assessed by the scientific processes of a professional field. And yet despite this, I believe I'm right, which is contradictory to my own beliefs about how information should be disseminated. The truth is there is something hidden at the quantum level within such geographical areas, something concentrated that produces or attracts multiple anomalous phenomena.

But what really was the secret of Skinwalker Ranch?

***

WEDNESDAY
08th of August, 2018
"Another direction…same location."

As that first *UAP-summer* came to an end, I had decided to put AATIP and Mr. Elizondo to one side and set off on a journey to really discover the true nature of the anomalous phenomena. Looking behind the mask of the extra-terrestrial and seeing who is really there, alternative explanations and all that 'woo'. This was easier said than done, and I can promise you that if you simply look for the origin of UAP as a consequence of interplanetary space vehicles, you won't find the full truth about the anomalous phenomena.

As much as I found both Elizondo and AATIP important, they represented the 'nuts and bolts' part of UAP, the 'disclosure' part the general public could easily digest and get started with. After all, with this UAP topic, the safe bet would be to simply declare aliens with all their stigmatised connotations and be done with it.

Thinking back, I could have easily stated that UAP were extra-terrestrials, underlined it and happily gone about my day. But I didn't do that. When I tried to picture another world with advanced life in some hyper developed city with George Jetson styled vehicles, my mind wouldn't let me. Something is really weird about this universal reality of ours, something doesn't quite add up like it should. Intelligent life on other planets?

Why couldn't I picture it?

For myself, someone with a good imagination and the ability to see things clearly, I was drawing a blank. Something was telling me that wasn't the answer to the UAP mystery and the more I looked into case reports the more associated para-normal phenomena started to reveal itself.

Something wasn't quite right.

***

A strange thing happened over the summer of 2018, somehow, thanks to our links at UAPinfo, I managed to speak, via social media, to a scientist who had a good working knowledge of UAP and associated phenomena. Honestly, I don't remember exactly how that came about, but my conversations with various individuals really helped my understanding of what the phenomena might be. It was on his advisement that I read information about ultra-terrestrials and further explore the 'high strangeness' of case reports.

- ultra-terrestrials are apparently intelligent beings who inhabit Earth and are hidden to us, apart from when they fly their advanced anomalous vehicles.
- 'High Strangeness' is the weird paranormal associated phenomena that often accompanies UAP cases.

The recommendation of literature was for two influential researchers, John Keel and Jacques Vallee, both of whom strongly suggested that the UFO phenomenon can't be simply explained in terms of the crude extra-terrestrial hypothesis. A direct contrast to the most commonly held Ufology belief in 2018 - that UFOs equated to extra-terrestrials coming in spaceships from another planet. Simple and yet without the data to conclude.

By summer of 2018, I had agreed with Jacques Vallee and John Keel that the UAP issue is highly more complex than extra-terrestrials, although I still couldn't rule out interplanetary visitors either.

The book 'Passport to Magonia', (1) by Jacques Vallee in 1969 was influential to my own thinking. It was the first time that collected case reports from history show sequential patterns in data but also accounted for from within differing historically reported paranormal encounters and phenomena.

The 'Mysterious Airships' of 1896/97 for example, consisted of a UAP wave that included advanced aerial vehicles that presented different occupants and airships each time, appearing mainly across the eastern part of America. The cases shown by Vallee display various individual's perceptions of their own experienced encounters with different phenomena. Strangely, the circumstances within those experienced encounters are different (different appearance of entity, vehicles, etc), but the baseline fundamentals are the same, aka, similar psychology of behaviour and attitudes displayed by the different anomalous phenomena. These are the same attributes across many years and even decades. A strange phenomena engagement of humans that follows different routes, but allows for the same end result, *belief and acceptance* (very much humanistic behavioural traits).

Common themes are prevalent in Vallee's work as he collected the historical UAP sighting and encounter data, such as perceptions of *abductions*, the isolation of the individual, the broken-down vehicle scenario, the sequenced appearance pattern and the observations of what we now know as the advanced 'five observables' AATIP technology.

However, despite this, this still doesn't equate to a causal and physical link that can be proved. After all, we are dealing with cold cases that lack an in-depth sensory array of historical data to distinguish and develop theories of origin. No doubt Vallee was onto something, *hypothetically*. But we just can't prove it or add to it without overlapping datasets. Again, to say there is a link between the strange encounters throughout history, etc is non-sensical by any acceptable scientific framework in 2018. For one, these are unproven entities/vehicles, and we would have to first prove each entity existed within its own right, then somehow find evidence to link them as one phenomenon.

The only real established link is that it is a human being who is experiencing and reporting the encounters in each case. Sceptics would therefore tell us that all of the historical UFO case reports going back throughout history are unrelated and that there is no significant connection in Vallee's work and therefore the *high strangeness* throughout reported cases is simply coincidental and a product of human cognitive fallacy. This may be true and shouldn't be overlooked with regards to neurological, socio-psychological factors. Certainly, this idea shouldn't be dismissed. What the sceptics have got right, is that we would need more appropriate in-depth data.

From this we could push alternative theories to the extra-terrestrial hypothesis - something other than cold cases from history that couldn't be fully assessed and analysed.

Having said that. I happily came across something else in my UAP journey, something which began to make me think closely about the cases of high strangeness and the paranormal. And that was small property in the middle of nowhere in Utah.

THURSDAY
09th of August, 2018
"The world can be thin."

T he very next day I picked up where I had left off. Possibly, I had found an answer to high strangeness cases within UAP. A bold claim, but a claim to be evaluated, nonetheless.

Something I had overlooked in The New York Times article (2) from December 2017, something I hadn't even fully grasped at the time, and then the realisation hit me - AATIP studied UAP and was born out of AAWSAP, and AAWSAP was at the heart of a geographic location.

Skinwalker Ranch.

The most bizarre question that I was seriously forced to ask, was how UAP could be linked to a small piece of land in rural Utah, America. What possible interest does a random farmland and a cattle ranch in Utah have for these reported phenomena? Well, as I re-researched anything about everything associated with AATIP and AAWSAP, it became clearer that the Department of Defence had given serious consideration to that very same small ranch in Utah.

But *why?*

Really the issue of Skinwalker started when I was first reading the December 2017 New York Times article (2). I found that AAWSAP/AATIP creator, Senator Harry Reid, and his UFO interest came through Robert Bigelow (a billionaire from Nevada) who just happened to have purchased a small ranch in Utah in 1996. Mr. Bigelow bought the property because he was made aware of the strange paranormal phenomena that frequently occurred in that area. Mr. Bigelow then used the ranch as living laboratory with his team of scientists.

***

To aid my research, I looked into lectures by investigative journalist George Knapp and then took the time to read through, *'Hunt for the Skinwalker'* (3), which I strongly suggest you add to your reading list also. There were many other good blogs from 2018 which gave an accurate understanding of the Skinwalker situation, Joe Murgia and Keith Basterfield being two of them (4), (5). This was important coverage, considering, this was a time prior to mainstream acknowledgement or even mid-level journalist interest. This was a time when UAP blogs pushed AATIP agenda into the world.

Prior to the creation of AAWSAP, the former director and DoD scientist, whose career would come to be ruined by some elitist types (6), had an experience of his own on Skinwalker Ranch. Apparently, as discussed in an earlier chapter, the DoD scientist saw a multi-coloured Mobius Loop/Tubular Bells object that was able to change shape in front of him. Visible only to him, and a significant vision.

It was enough to convince him to speak with Senator Harry Reid about the creation of a permanent program after going back to D.C. Without that exact moment in history, our timeline might not have given us AAWSAP or AATIP.

***

Rise of the Skinwalker

Ok. So, to quickly skim over the story, a farmer by the name of Tom Sherman moved his family onto a northern Utah cattle ranch in the early 1990's. They were plagued with paranormal experiences ranging from giant bullet proof wolves to shadow creatures, Bigfoot, strange beings, cattle mutilations, coloured orbs and then the traditional metallic flying discs that have been reported for the past 70 years across the world. Strange lights above the pasture would be seen and illuminated at night. Lights would come from the ridge; metal machinery would sound from underground and even exotic tropical birds would be seen in the trees. Most alarming was the cattle mutilations which were destroying not only Tom Sherman's prised livestock, but also his livelihood. And then there was alleged poltergeist activity and the shadow men at the foot of the bed, not to mention the knocking sounds late at night.

And of course, UFOs: 'Triangles', 'Discs' and various 'Orbs' that would zip overhead and, in some cases, come through what seemed to be a portal, with another visible sky on the other side. I don't do the story of Skinwalker Ranch justice, again, I would strongly recommend you read the 2006 book by George Knapp and Colm Kelleher (3) for full details.

Anyways, the occurrences became so intense that the family suffered serious psychological stress. This after all was weird paranormal mythology rolled into one highly difficult to accept reality, a reality that didn't make sense. The Sherman's weren't paranormal investigators or UFO people, they were farmers.

And it doesn't make sense, at all. Consider how dark shadow creatures, bullet proof Dire Wolves, Bigfoot, weird yellow eyed creatures, portals opening and closing, triangular shaped UFOs, 'Flying Saucers', crop circles, cattle mutilations, poltergeist activity and strange blue orbs, all are more frequently seen in one area of the world than most others. If this was all true, then what can we conclude about this geographical area?

What conditions allow for all this activity?

As you might imagine, the Sherman family that had the ranch in the 90s, were freaked out. Thankfully for them, local businessman Robert Bigelow bought the ranch from Tom Sherman with the intention of turning the property into a living laboratory to report and record the extreme occurrences being stated by the witnesses. Bigelow created the National Institute for Discovery Science (NIDS) who set up their technical equipment and started recording the events from the area.

In The New York Times article, they report that Senator Harry Reid's interest in the phenomena came from Robert Bigelow and his research at Skinwalker Ranch (2).

As reported in the bombshell AATIP article of 2017, it was apparently Skinwalker Ranch that instigated the official investigation. The Defense Intelligence Agency (DIA) took an interest in the property and the strange phenomena that was occurring in that location. Senator Reid held a meeting with Mr. Bigelow and secured secret funding for a program. Now, whether that was the Advanced Aerospace Weapons System Application Program or whether that was the Advanced Aerospace Threat Identification Program is still not clear due to the mixed timelines and various stories given. However, we do know that there was an official government program that investigated paranormal activity, after Bigelow's NIDS. At the time I remember speaking with filmmaker Jeremy Corbell and asking him if we (UAPinfo) could cover his upcoming film, 'Hunt for the Skinwalker' (same title of George Knapp's book). Jeremy agreed, and we started promoting the film's release from our UAPinfo website prior to its release in September of 2018 – which brought more conspiracies aimed at us from disgruntled old guard Ufologists, but at least we were used to it.

***

Following on from the unexplainable Skinwalker Ranch, the emerging #UFOTwitter platform (a subculture created to sidestep Ufology) was starting to investigate the very real consideration that the UAP phenomena was possibly involved, influenced or even behind most genuine paranormal activity. Admittedly, this was a driving focus of my own research at the time, and I ventured into some obscure literature to understand how a phenomena such as 'poltergeists' – the German word for noisy spirit, could be possible. This was fringe stuff. How does one even come to terms with the idea that inanimate objects move without applied external force? Never-mind the concept that some invisible entity might be involved. What is the causal relationship to unidentified aerial vehicles that deploy the possible warping of space-time?

I have a hard time accepting this unverified relationship without more data, much like I struggle to accept evil entities are playing tricks on farmers in Utah for 'shits and giggles'.

Demons aren't real, at least beyond a subjective cognitive process within the human mind. Dead spirits and poltergeists should be treated with healthy scepticism also, just in the same way we should approach UAP case reports. Some reports suggest that the anomalous phenomena follow you home from Skinwalker Ranch, and I've even been told that a scientist was badly infected by something there. Other reports from Mr. Knapp and others, suggested that the more aggressive you are towards the phenomena the more it reacts to you. In consideration, of this hypothetically suggests an 'infection model', that once you are exposed to the anomalous, it alters your genetics.

Again, *where* is the data?

***

In the late summer of 2018, I wasn't convinced of any unifying correlation theory with UAP and the paranormal, however, I'm very open to the real possibilities that these reported phenomena occurred in some fashion. But concluding within a certain degree of confidence requires data, lots and lots of data, and data which is irrefutable, data that can be replicated and studied. Currently, we don't have that, we don't have peer reviewed papers that examine electromagnetic fluctuations on the property or clear footage of paranormal activity or a big juicy 'Flying Saucer UAP or anything else. We have stories of classified data form AAWSAP and BAASS. And this is where I find myself with the paranormal, high strangeness, UAP and anything else. I can't prove a link, but I also can't discount it and wouldn't bet against it. In twenty, maybe thirty years I wouldn't be shocked to see that evidence has come to light, and that all of this is common knowledge. Maybe people will look back at us and laugh at how we couldn't see it, how obvious it should have been.

For now, however, we must try to incorporate the limited data from Skinwalker into the equation. We simply can't dismiss data because it throws our theories about extraterrestrials into question. Arguably, what Skinwalker shows us, is that the anomalous phenomena are incredibly complex beyond all scope and practice, beyond our current understanding of physics and even how we understand the very fabric of reality itself. It becomes important to look at various cases in which something highly strange and unexplained had occurred. And yes, the cases do exist, but more so they exist in the realms of the fringe paranormal, which has mostly been kept separate from historical UFO incidents by mainstream Ufology researchers. The irony is that Ufologists see Ghost Hunters, Demonologists, Parapsychologists as something separate and not credible. Anything considered in these realms is considered 'woo', and not to be mixed or matched with the nuts-and-bolts style of research.

FRIDAY
10th of August, 2018

'Highly strange?'

S kinwalker Ranch is a difficult themed problem to master. Firstly, we are stuck with the problematic situation of not having access to hard data to analyse and evaluate. Whilst I personally believe that most of the data obtained through AAWSAP's contractor 'BAASS' is still highly *classified*, we still can't be sure what exactly is held within the locked cabinets of the Pentagon. Maybe, nothing of real significance?

In any case, we have testimony of Bigelow's original research team – the National Institute of Discovery Science (NIDS), the testimony of the Sherman family prior to Bigelow's team coming, and finally we have the AAWSAP investigation and contractor BAASS. All of which leaves us with nothing tangible – much like the snapshots of the anomalous phenomena itself, it can't be verified through repeatable testing and most of the cases are now 'cold cases'.

Funny how we are in a 'grey area', looking to what might be real, but never having the data to make it real.

What is reported at Skinwalker Ranch, however, is troubling from many various discipline perspectives. If we are to believe that something anomalous was/is operating in such a condensed geographical area of Utah, on some obscure farming ranch in North America, then we are faced with various difficult questions about UAP origin, the paranormal, the implications upon human consciousness and even how we understand objective reality.

And most importantly of all, we are faced with asking what are the conditions that enable a high increase of activity in one place?

In this condensed location, UAP are often reported alongside a multitude of paranormal phenomena that defy logic. Whilst we absolutely mustn't completely subscribe to the paranormal events of Skinwalker Ranch without further holistic data that can be verified, we must also not dismiss the concept either. We should follow a path that is highly sceptical of such claims in a way which advocates the scientific process.

MONDAY
13th of August, 2018
"Icing on the cake."

Without George Knapp, documentation and the testimony of Senator Harry Reid with regards to AATIP/AAWSAP and Lue Elizondo would not have come forward. The probability is that the sceptics and angry ufologists would have won the day, the initiative would have died, and Mr. Elizondo would have been taken down by the potential misinformation of Pentagon spokespeople.

Thankfully, George and his team are resilient. Throughout 2018, investigative journalist George Knapp played a vital role in shaping the landscape of UFOTwitter. Time after time after time in 2018, George Knapp and his team interviewed key people in the initiative that included Luis Elizondo, Eric Davis, Senator Harry Reid, Doctor Hal Puthoff. He, along with the Ninja Viking Jeremy Corbell, pushed home the exposure of Commander David Fravor (Navy Pilot of the F/18 that engaged the 'Tic-Tac' UAP). His appearances of Coast 2 Coast AM have been instrumental to the credible UAP conversation, taking the concepts of the bizarre and making them reasonable. He was and always will be one of my true idols. George used strategy, sitting in information, releasing it at critical times when it could have the biggest impact.

When Keith Mayoh managed to get a written interview between George and UAPinfo, we were ecstatic. I was going to have the opportunity to ask Mr. Knapp (Skinwalker, Bob Lazar) a question on whatever my little brain could think of. In the end I asked about how Ufology should approach the extreme claims of 'whistle-blowers'. His answer was 'Caveat Emptor'.

Buyer beware (7).

❋ ❋ ❋

Conclusion

When AAWSAP started to investigate Skinwalker Ranch it posed a problem. It legitimised the stories for researchers without having hard data and evidence to assess. Currently, the government study of Skinwalker Ranch is either classified or highly sensitive and for whatever reason has not been opened up for the scientific community.

If they accounts are true, and various types of UAP are frequently spotted across the ranch, it also means that we have to consider the associated paranormal phenomena. And for the 'nuts and bolts' researchers, who categorically state that UFOs are extra-terrestrial in origin, it also poses a problem - why would aliens frequently fly across the universe to visit a ranch in northern Utah? (Although, you can probably make this argument about the entire extra-terrestrial hypothesis).

What is an interesting point about Skinwalker, is the correlation of UAP to paranormal phenomena. Apparently, they are linked, although we might struggle to prove this.

The stories (and that's all we have, *stories*), tell us that a wide variety of bizarre and illogical phenomena seemingly appear on this property. Although paranormal events occur worldwide, for some reason the intensity and frequency are increased within the small geographical area. Again, my thinking is that something within, o, above or under that ranch holds one of the keys to this puzzle. We also need a full in-depth analysis of whether there are significant uranium deposits/radioactivity under the property and in the northern Utah area. I mention uranium, as this might potentially be another potential avenue of interest for UAP, although in no way should we currently conclude a significant correlation. Interestingly, the activity at Skinwalker goes back decades, as do the reports of UAP in the area, however we again are stuck with the themed problem this book raises.

We can't verify any of this to a high degree of certainty, and certainly not to an acceptable scientific standard.

References

(1). Vallee, J. (1969). 'Passport to Magonia: from folklore to flying saucers.'
Daily Grail Publishing.

(2). 'Blumenthal, R., Cooper, H. and Kean, L. (16th of December, 2017). 'Glowing Auras and 'Black Money': The Pentagon's Mysterious U.F.O. Program'.
The New York Times.
https://www.nytimes.com/2017/12/16/us/politics/pentagon-program-ufo-harry-reid.amp.html

(3). Kelleher, C. & Knapp, G. (2006). 'Hunt for the Skinwalker: Science confronts the unexplained at a remote ranch in Utah.'
Paraview Pocket Books.

(4). Murgia, J. (2020). 'Speigel Skinwalker Ranch Show Transcript: Knapp/Corbell – Paranormal Hitchhiker Phenomenon Followed Bigelow Home And Played A Role In His Selling Ranch.'
UFOJoe.
https://www.ufojoe.net/knapp-corbell/

(5). Basterfield, K. (2018). 'Dr James T Lacatski,
AAWSAP Program Manager's career "ruined"'
Unidentified Aerial Phenomenon – Scientific Research.
https://ufos-scientificresearch.blogspot.com/2018/11/dr-james-t-lacatski-aawsap-program.html?m=1

(6). Elizondo, L. (2018). 'What We Know And What We Believe Are Not Always The Same Thing. Here's How Our Perception Of Fact Influences Our Worldview.'

Medium.
https://medium.com/the-ascent/what-we-know-and-what-we-believe-are-not-always-the-same-thing-d77d3c8019a7

(7). Silva, D. (28th of October, 2018). 'Interview with George Knapp.'
SilvaRecord.
https://silvarecord.com/2018/10/29/interview-with-george-knapp/

CHAPTER FIFTEEN: UAP
AND THE NUCLEAR AGE

❈ ❈ ❈

There is a direct correlation between genuine Unidentified Aerial Phenomena and our use of nuclear power. They are engaged with strike groups and nuclear powered facilities, nuclear weapon storages and missiles going far back into the 20th century. Many of the 'old guard' Ufologists believe that the modern era of UFOs (1947-2017) began seemingly due to humans use of nuclear weapons. Some also believe that the extraterrestrials have come to save us from annihilation. Although, this perspective has also been challenged from a national security point of view in that nuclear tampering, by anyone, can be seen as a direct threat. Nuclear war might have accidentally been started in such occurrences. We must also consider that UAP actions of tampering with nukes could be intention-less, beyond what we understand and attribute to an 'Alien consciousness'. When all is said and done, we do not know what UAP are, where they come from and what their intentions are with regards to nuclear facilities and weapons. And finally, we must consider the history and makeup of our atomic technology, the plutonium and uranium, the influence on reality and human consciousness (if any).

Something tells me we are missing big pieces of this puzzle.

***

WEDNESDAY

15th of August, 2018
'...correlations are not causations'

That humid Wednesday afternoon, I found myself in Middlesbrough Central Library in search of hardback copies of the Manhattan Project. The upstairs department was emptied of sunstroke readers who might have been looking to escape the extreme heat of the mid-week heat wave. Whilst they sunbathed in the August air, I was dealing with a problem. A pointy nosed librarian looked down her glasses at my request for assistance. All she offered was judgemental looks as I panted in the breeze of their electric fan. She didn't like that, or me for that matter. Nevertheless, I was a law-abiding member of the Cleveland library service and free to stand in front of the cool fan as I asked for the history section. A quick search across the old leather-bound books brought me to what I'd come for.

The Manhattan Project.

The data told me a story as I found my seat. The history was rich, vibrant with details that jumped from the page. This was a time that was unlike any other, the birthplace of the ultimate mass destructive weapon, of a genuine evil that threatened all life as we know it.

"Now I have become Death, destroyer of worlds."
- 	Robert Oppenheimer.

The two nuclear Atomic bombs that levelled Hiroshima and Nagasaki in the August of 1945 are nothing in comparison to the TSAR H-bomb detonated by Russia on the 30th of October, 1961 (1). Or there was America's own attempt at something rather silly with Operation Starfish Prime that obliterated the O-Zone layer on the 09th of July in 1962 with a thermonuclear warhead (2). Not exactly our finest moment.

And from the 1940s to present day there was some 2000 nuclear bombs exploded on Earth (3), the results and fallout of which are still not fully understood less than a century later. Currently, we have about 13'400 nuclear weapons (that countries admit to processing) all facing at each other, just in case we need to ensure they don't survive as well.

Somehow, us humans had stumbled upon a power we were not yet ready to wield, and it changed everything about us. Never before had a human generation lived under the threat of complete planetary annihilation, with world leaders using the threat as a chess piece in their economically driven war game strategy. The manic 'who blinks-first' approach to wiping out an entire species is ridiculous. Some herald President Kennedy as a hero, others as reckless, and for myself, I see him as a part of the evolving global conscious system that must learn how to cope with extreme pressures of possessing extreme technology.

Nuclear technology was always going to be part of our complex human existence in this universe, or at least we can say it was always going to be part of our historical past. Possibly, gaining nuclear status was a benchmark which we must reach and conquer, absorb and evolve past. In the end, the button wasn't ever pushed on both sides as we approached midnight on the Doomsday Clock and maybe that was our test, and maybe we passed? You might argue the introduction of the UAP was our way of waking up to the possibilities of other realities, that we as humans aren't the heliocentric masters of the universe and that there might be others.

THURSDAY
16th of August, 2018
'Where it all began.'

My second day back in the old town library was different. Not that the physical place, with bricks, cement, shelves and books were any different, but I was. My perspective had changed. After my research showed just what us humans had done to this planet with our atomic testing over the 20th century my mind considered the implications.

Hundreds upon thousands of cubic radioactive particles and nitric tons of oxide have been dumped into the Earth's atmosphere. The research states that when a nuclear weapon is detonated in the atmosphere, the immediate air is significantly heated before experiencing dramatic cooling. This process produces a significant amount of nitric oxide which are carried up into the upper atmosphere and effect the Ozone layer. It is theorised that almost five thousand tons of nitric oxide is created for each megaton of nuclear detonation (4).

The general consensus is that nuclear testing had no significant effect upon the O-Zone depletion, although for me there is still no credible data to directly suggest what specific effects the early nuclear testing had upon Earth's upper atmospheric at that time, mainly because, putting it mildly, they weren't actually testing or looking for effects in the 1940s/50s/60s.

Similarly, following the 1945 Trinity detonation, scientists had no concept that the radioactive fallout would spread so far on the winds which then poisoned Americans, and increased infant mortality rates, and cancer rates. After a nearly half a century of denial and pushback, the US Department of Energy concluded in 2006, *'the Trinity test also posed the most significant hazard of the entire Manhattan Project.'* (5).

Scientists in recent years have theorised that Operation Starfish Prime – a high altitude nuclear detonation – punched a hole in the O-Zone layer in 1968 (6).

This is not to state that nuclear testing might only account for the O-Zone depletion across those 50 years, after all, there are many other scientifically credible attributable factors which have been proved to affect the chemical balance of the upper atmosphere. It's interesting that of the thousands of global nuclear detonations over the last 50 years, there has never been the in-depth scientific investigations and precursors into their harmful effects upon our planet. But I guess this is national security we are dealing with, which comes with its own funding, agenda and political pressures.

And don't forget. Even the very obvious UAP issue still isn't recognised by government or scientific community, so it wouldn't be surprising to learn one day that Operation Starfish Prime was responsible for significantly impacting the O-Zone layer and possibly climate change.

The other more speculative part of Starfish Prime was the hushed conspiracy whispers that the military were actually hunting UAP. It is sometimes theorised in some dark corners of 'UFOTwitter' that EMP weapons (that activate with nuclear detonations), target UAP and bring them down.

Obviously, none of this is verifiable and I would take issue with how an EMP device would bring down a highly advanced UAP in the 1940s/50s and 60s.

How it started, how it's going.

According to the Los Alamos National Laboratory, German chemist Martin Klaproth was credited with the official discovery of Uranium, which, he named the new element after the recently discovered planet Uranus – ironically named after the Greek god of the sky, which some Ancient Astronaut Ufologists believe was termed due to Greek philosophers seeing aliens in the ancient skies. Synchronicity for some, a complete stretch of imagination for others.

But it was *Uranium* was found to be the key – an Earthly element found underground and mined since the 1890s.

Eugène-Melchior Péligot, a French chemist, isolated pure uranium in 1841 by heating uranium tetrachloride with potassium (7).

Then in 1896 Antoine Henri Becquerel discovered that uranium exhibited invisible light or rays - this was radioactivity (8). In 1934 research by Enrico Fermi and others eventually led to the use of uranium fission in the first nuclear weapon used in war and later in the peaceful use of uranium as fuel in nuclear power production (9).

The start of the nuclear age had begun, and the secret

to winning a war which hadn't even started was being worked upon in secrecy.

There are many good factual accounts of the Manhattan Project. In her book *'The Manhattan Project'* (2009), Cynthia Kelly, makes a great case for historical accuracy and details a fascinating time in history. Her book is a recommended read for those interested.

The details surrounding the Manhattan Project began in 1938, when German scientists Otto Hahn and Fritz Strassmann inadvertently discovered nuclear fission (10). Nuclear fission is the splitting of a large atomic nucleus into smaller nuclei, what is produced are gamma photons and large amounts of energy and radioactive decay.

This sparked imagination and creative discovery as the world raced to gain the war-ending technology. The Hahn-Strassmann bombardment of Uranium with neutrons showed that the core of the Uranium 'breaks up,' which was a significant step forward towards harnessing nuclear power (11).

A few months later, Leo Szilard along with Albert Einstein, sent a letter to President Roosevelt warning him that Germany might try to build an atomic bomb (12). In response, the President established the creation of a 'Uranium Committee' which was a group of top military and scientific experts to determine the feasibility of a nuclear chain reaction that could be used for the purpose of war. By the end of the war, the United States had won the atomic race and the very first nuclear testing at White Sands was launched. The first ever nuclear explosion was detonated on the 16th of July, 1945, on the dry desert sands of the Alamogordo range, also known as Jornada del Mureto.

Robert Oppenheimer code-named the test, Trinity (13).

The radioactivity spread across the testing range and to this day still holds radioactive waste across the surface of the desert to this day. Those who lived downwind suffered an increase in cancer rates and infant mortality rates. Those residents were neither evacuated prior, during or after the Trinity test (5).

Atmospheric nuclear explosions were officially banned by the 1963 Partial Test Ban Treaty, following international concerns and outcry over the radioactive fallout. Underground testing began, as did, underwater tests within the Pacific proving grounds in the Marshall Islands and off the Kiritimati island.

Within those years a significant amount of nuclear material was dumped into the atmosphere and oceans, and with it came something else. It is only now, that we are starting to realise just how important the nuclear testing was to the frequency of these strange aerial anomalies. Remarkably, if you look through the history books there is no mention or correlation between these two historical phenomena. It was only the 'fringe' researchers who correlated the data from within Ufology that first associated the link. As much as I've been critical of Ufology, it was in fact those researchers who discovered the link between UAP and nukes.

The emergence of the nuclear anomalies

'In many instances, there seems to be a direct correlation the phenomena exhibits with respect to our nuclear and military capabilities.'
-        Luis Elizondo, *Director of AATIP, Resignation Letter (2017).* (14)

Our combined UAP research within the community has historically and currently lead us all to the same unified point, that nuclear activity and the anomalous phenomena are significantly linked in proximity. As America stockpiled Uranium, detonated nuclear weapons and spread radioactivity across the dry southern deserts, the emergence of black-eyed alien monsters suddenly appeared on Earth in high volume.

The waves, spikes and reports of various UAP within the years from 1940s to the 1960s can be statistically paralleled against the nuclear tests in frequency and proximity. But this doesn't necessarily mean a direct causation correlation. We can argue that 'Foo-Fighters' and 'Mysterious Airships' all were present and operating before nuclear testing, however, we must also in fairness consider that these may not be the same phenomena.

We are at the very beginning of UAP research and may not have the theoretical frameworks to currently understand why nuclear technology and radioactive substances are of proximal concern to the anomalous phenomena. But it doesn't stop us asking questions. What is it about nuclear technology and UAPs? Why do these bizarrely shaped objects engage nuclear powered strike groups such as the Nimitz (2004)? Why have they hovered over nuclear facilities in America, Russia, China and the U.K.? Is there an intention?

'UFOs and Nukes' (15) by Robert Hastings was an unfortunately titled book that is quite unique and quite brilliant. Hastings managed to document and catalogue genuine encounters of strange aerial vehicles which have consistently and deliberately engaged nuclear sites across America since the 1950s. Whether that is to state the increased use of nuclear activity has caused UAP to appear and engage us is another matter for debate. What we can look towards is a positive correlation. Hastings is probably one the most profound researcher in this specific area over the past 70 years and has managed to bring together the most substantial body of evidence from government witnesses, the most famous of which was Robert Sallas, whose testimony at the Citizen Hearing on Disclosure in 2013 reported that a large red UFO had shut down nuclear missile silos. One of the better-known cases that was at Maelstrom Airforce base, 1967, had a red glowing object hovering over the base that displayed advanced propulsion abilities. Apparently, 10 nuclear missiles were shut offline at the same time their particular UAP appeared. However, we might pose the question of direct intention or indirect interference.

My research in 2018 took me to some strange concepts, non-more so than the nuclear connection. We have learned from some well-placed sources, that the anomalous are often reported in the vicinity of nuclear strike groups, nuclear reactors, nuclear power plants, at storage facilities for *Uranium* that includes mines.

And the activity is increasing.

A question of radioactivity?

Uranium was itself discovered in 1871 when prospectors dug for gold in deep underground mines in Colorado. The area produced around 50 tons of high-grade ore between the years of 1871 and 1895, with most coming from the Colorado Plateau of Utah and Colorado.

Uranium has been around for all of human history and emits radioactivity. I wonder what the effects of this are on human consciousness?

What is it about nuclear activity and radioactive substances that draws in the anomalous phenomena? I believe that it must be at the quantum level, something chemical, something atomic, some consequential factor that we have yet to uncover.

To me, this is why their interest in nuclear activity is so perplexing. The anomalous display a very human trait when they seek out and interact with nuclear activity/radioactivity. When you think about it, what point is there in monitoring/observing/being in proximity to such human activity '*if*' they are completely self-actualised? (With no desires, wishes, needs, etc).

Point being, there must be something relevant for the UAP in that specific interaction for it to engage time and time again. They must be gaining something from the repeated behaviour (whether that is psychological or physical). Which suggests to me that 'they' aren't self-actualised, or at least they are pretending to us that they need such an interaction?

If they are observing our activities then why not do it covertly, cloak and become invisible (low observability – five AATIP observables). Why then does their engagement/appearance increase with the increased levels of nuclear/radioactivity? Could they be making a statement to humans? Or are they completely intention-less, unwittingly interfering with nuclear weapons. Regardless, one thing is for certain.

They are like moths to a flame.

New age liberal perspective

Some argue that UAP want to warn humanity about the issues of harnessing nuclear weapons, others have argued they want to trick us into nuclear war. But the truth is probably much stranger and much more complex than we could anticipate, and we should be careful against advocating any situation that humanises the anomalous psychology. We don't know the intentions behind their behaviours.

Military perspective

The 'threat narrative' has been pushed to gain further military funding - at least that is the claim of some conspiracy theorists. In truth, the military would and should see unidentified aerial vehicles as a threat to national security. After all, it's their job to protect people. The military see UAP as observing the capacity and capabilities of their arsenal, because, well that's what they would do in their shoes. The truth is we don't know their intentions, and therefore we cannot fully attribute their behaviours as an overt threat to our nuclear weapons.

Interjectionist perspective

When we consider the Nimitz encounter, we must consider that the nuclear strike group was buzzed by a 'fleet' of white oblong shaped objects that dropped down from the stratosphere (and above) within 0.78 seconds before instantaneously shooting back up. The interventionist might consider that the anomalous are intending to deceive humans into thinking they are extra-terrestrials, or maybe they are imprinting human expectations into themselves and creating very real vehicles as part of this deception. However, we again don't know their intentions (if they even have intentions like we understand) and therefore should be careful about assigning motives and agendas to the anomalous phenomena.

✳ ✳ ✳

Conclusions

There's something about UAP and the nuclear process, maybe it's fission, fusion, radioactivity or none of the above. Maybe it's the Uranium that is used. Maybe it's something to do with Gama-radiation, the electromagnetic radiation arising from the radioactive decay of atomic nuclei. Maybe the anomalous study it, quarantine it, control how we manage it, drink it in, or maybe it's none of the above. Maybe this possible anomalous energy-based life form feeds on electromagnetic radiation, absorbs it, digests it as an energy fuel source. What if the anomalous actually are attracted to the decay of radioactivity?

Does this explain why they use the world's heavily radioactive oceans?

We simply don't know at this point.

Our only lead is that UAP display proximity to radioactivity. Which would indicate that they are not fully 'self-actualised' under the Maslow hierarchy, meaning the anomalous continue to repeat this nuclear proximity pattern because they *need* or *want* something from that interaction.

They are predictable.

Little did I know at the time of researching in 2018, that less than a year later in the July of 2019, would an intentional coming together of nuclear strike groups on the west coast of America bring about a swarm of UAP.

Almost like it was intentional.

References

(1). Downing, S. (16th of August, 2017). 'The monster atomic bomb that was too big to use.'
BBC.
https://www.bbc.com/future/article/20170816-the-monster-atomic-bomb-that-was-too-big-to-use

(2). Gutierrez, B. (15th of July, 2021). 'Why the U.S. once set off a nuclear bomb in space.'
National Geographic.
https://api.nationalgeographic.com/distribution/public/amp/science/article/why-the-us-once-set-off-a-nuclear-bomb-in-space-called-starfish-prime

(3). United Nations. 'Nuclear Weapons.'
https://www.un.org/disarmament/wmd/nuclear/

(4). Atomic Archive.
AromicArchive.com.
https://www.atomicarchive.com/science/effects/ozone-depletion.html

(5). Alvarez, R., and Tucker, K. (2019). 'Trinity: "The most significant hazard of the entire Manhattan Project"'
TheBulletin.org.
https://thebulletin.org/2019/07/trinity-the-most-significant-hazard-of-the-entire-manhattan-project/amp/

(6). Westport News. (20th of September, 2012). 'Explosive new theory on O-Zone hole.'
NZHerlad.co.nz.
https://www.nzherald.co.nz/nz/explosive-new-theory-on-ozone-hole/6HXJPDFCMK3BELB67JSRUO26DA/

(7). World of Chemicals. 'Eugene Melchior Peligot – isolated uranium metal.'
World of Chemicals.
https://www.worldofchemicals.com/183/chemistry-articles/
eugene-melchior-peligot-isolated-uranium-metal.html

(8). APS News. (2008). 'This Month in Physics History March 1, 1896: Henri Becquerel Discovers Radioactivity.'
APS Physics.
https://www.aps.org/publications/apsnews/200803/physicshistory.cfm

(9). APS News. (2007). 'This Month in Physics History December 1938: Discovery of Nuclear Fission.'
APS Physics.
https://www.aps.org/publications/apsnews/200712/physicshistory.cfm

(10). Kelly, C. (2009). 'The Manhattan Project: The Birth of the Atomic Bomb by Its Creators, Eyewitnesses and Historians: The Birth of the Atomic Bomb in the Words of Its Creators, Eyewitnesses, and Historians.'
Black Dog and Leventhal.

(11). Atomic Heritage Foundation. (04th of June, 2014). 'Nuclear Fission.'
Atomic Heritage Foundation.
https://www.atomicheritage.org/history/nuclear-fission

(12). Lipscombe, T. (02nd of August, 2019). 'Einstein Feared a Nazi Atom Bomb—But Immigrants Made Sure the U.S. Got There First.'
TIME.com.
https://time.com/5641891/einstein-szilard-letter/

(13). Office of Legacy Management. 'Work Trinity Site - World's First Nuclear Explosion.'
Energy.Gov

https://www.energy.gov/lm/doe-history/manhattan-project-background-information-and-preservation-work/manhattan-project-1

(14). Stahl, F, A. (2018). 'Letter of Resignation.'
The Unidentified.
https://www.the-unidentified.net/aatip-files-luis-elizondo-resignation-letter-from-ousdi/

CHAPTER SIXTEEN: THE UNIDENTIFIED

✻ ✻ ✻

When the end came for the organisation UAPinfo (due to artistic differences), it also signalled the end of the very first UAP research initiative. UAP was our rebranding and repackaging the UFO phenomena into absorbable, bite sized mouthfuls that the public could consume one spoonful at a time. UAP would be presented in a way which represented the anomalous (non-human technology and intelligence), but in a way that wasn't stigmatised and wasn't ridiculed on the back pages of tabloid newspapers. Yes, this took strategic planning, most of which hasn't been revealed, and most probably never will be. We created a platform in 2018 that housed not only UAPinfo, but the UAP conversation with its boundaries and parameters that kept mainstream Ufology at bay. At the same time, we couldn't simply block out Ufology, we needed the vast numbers that followed the UFO subject closely, but who were rational and logical and understood why strategy was important. UFOTwitter, although originally termed 'TwitterUFO' by Keith (UAPinfo) and Danny Silva, was the foundation of the UAP revolution across Ufology. The platform was created and termed in 2019 by TTSA supporters who would later become UAP Activists, this was the very beginning of the Golden Age, the birth of the Unidentified Anomalous Phenomenon initiative.

But is this campaign any different?

Well, up until 2017, Ufology produced thousands upon

thousands of 'UFO' based websites and research groups. And by UFO based, I mean a paradigm that assumed all unidentified aerial vehicles were 'nuts and bolts' extra-terrestrials - if they weren't human. The paradigm also maintained that the governments were holding and developing alien spacecraft in hangers and studying UFOs behind the scenes in classified special access programs. Personally, I could not deduce how much of this was fiction, disinformation or exhausting speculation mixed with half-truths, but in the end in didn't matter. What was important was that we couldn't use any of the 'UFO stuff', real or not, it was simply too unbelievable for the public to accept and without government verification it worked against efforts to have the mainstream accept the UAP reality. We recognised this and consequently adopted UAP over UFO and everything that went with it, and it worked. As UAPinfo ended, other - AATIP based - UAP themed initiatives took its place, each focusing on credible UAP military encounters that could be verified, including our own new website, 'The Unidentified'.

Bringing in new ideas of research into a field that is heavily against new ideas will leave you being labelled a disinformation agent. Daring to change a 70-year paradigm is the fastest way to get yourself exiled from mainstream Ufology, not that I or we in 'UAPinfo' or 'The Unidentified' were ever 'in' Ufology, but we still provided a threat. The UAP concept and terminology of focusing on military cases was not acceptable to many in the field.

But we didn't care.

***

MONDAY
10th of September, 2018
"A new beginning…again."

'Unidentified Aerial Phenomenon Information' (UAPinfo) ended whilst I was away in the Lake District with my family. That week at the end of summer, in 2018 was spent in a log cabin, surrounded by trees and barely enough Wi-Fi signal to muster two bars. On an evening, I lit the fire and cooked with the barbecue grill. We sat with our drinks, ate our beef burgers and looked up to the clear star lit sky through the treetops that surrounded us.

My mind would ask questions about our place in this vast universe or even a multiverse, and wonder if we are here by design, or if we are all a complex result of random chaos.

Those few years spent in the log cabin at the end of each summer, were some of my favourite times when my daughter was young. She was a bright little girl, happy and cheeky as the energy of life resonated through her every smile. As I sat watching the night sky, I knew it was my responsibility to make this world a better place for her.

The days in the park were spent with long walks through the woods, occasionally we would go swimming in the pool. It was perfect, a chance to let the world wash away for a few days a year. But even then, the UAP reality was always there on my mind. As much as I tried to push the anomalous away, I knew I had to be a part of what was coming.

And it was coming.

TUESDAY
11th of September, 2018
"Never forget."

The next day was overcast as light rain fell through the treetops. Pulling on my trainers, I took the rubbish down to the bins some fifty metres down the dark forest path. As I walked back up to the cabin I remember looking up and seeing an old Spitfire type of aircraft as it flew very low to the tree line above me. It wasn't flying relatively fast, and you could see it intricate details of the underneath, the silver colours and delves, rivets and what have you. I remember stopping to consider how someone must have felt to have seen a genuine 'Flying Disc' or 'Tic-Tac' at such close range. What it must have felt like to experience something you knew was genuinely anomalous, and how it must have affected people, or do I say the phenomenon *infected* people. Questions over a change in DNA are often discussed, and the concept of post-traumatic stress is often associated. When you see something that is unidentifiable, something truly anomalous that society is telling you doesn't exist, well that's when your world changes forever. There is no going back. Even worse, you can't tell anyone.

Unless you want to be called crazy.

WEDNESDAY
12th of September, 2018
"The owner and the campfire."

After a few hours walk, myself, my wife and my daughter came home to the log cabin to relax for the afternoon. Having recently read George Knapp's 'Hunt for the Skinwalker,' (1), I was particularly looking forward to watching Jeremy Corbell's documentary 'Hunt for the Skinwalker' (2), which had just been released. I watched it on my phone in a cabin located within the woods of Cumbria. It covered the events of the book and took us through the Uinta Basin history of sightings. The documentary followed the Sherman's struggle with the phenomenon and then the introduction of NIDS. Famous English singer Robbie Williams made a surprise appearance, as did the current ranch owner, Brandon Fugal (although we didn't know this at the time). It was a good documentary.

THURSDAY
13th of September, 2018
"Every silver lining."

UAPinfo was over. The UAPinfo adventure had lasted 8 months, March to September. As I was told happened with most efforts in Ufology, the arguments and counter arguments of that week unfortunately hindered the progression, and the group would split but remain friends. Our unofficial slogan was '*no one ever really quits*,' but sadly, we did quit, and we did split. The team of UAPinfo was no longer together, the seven of us broke into separate groups. I kept in touch with Danny Silva, who would go on to become an important blogger and UAP commentator that would more than rival my own efforts. It was a friendly rivalry, but one which pushed us both forward to do better.

Ultimately, we would spend the next few years working apart, he created 'SilvaRecord' (3) and gained the attention of some important people and contacts whilst I would co-create a UAP blog and research site called 'The Unidentified' (4) with Keith, Sven, Jason and Christian.

Was it ego that ended UAPinfo? Or was it incompatible differences? At the time, my entire focus was on trying to uncover the origins of UAP. In a way it consumed me to the point of obsession. Part of wished I could go back and forget about UAP, but you can't. Once the anomalous has you, and once you believe, you can never not believe. The infection model is very real.

It was the end of UAPinfo, and the start of The Unidentified. A new chapter had begun, and I was on this carousel until the very end.

TUESDAY
25th of September, 2018
"Infinite cosmic powers, tiny little living space."

I was fortunate to speak via social media with various people close to the UFO issue, one such person was Doctor Garry Nolan. Nolan was a professor and scientist at Stanford University in America, and one of the origin members of TTSA. Doctor Nolan also worked closely with Doctor Hal Puthoff, Doctors Eric Davis, Colm Kelleher and Jacques Vallee, who were basically the scientific minds that held security clearances and were working as contractors to AATIP with both BAASS and before that NIDS.

I'd asked a million silly questions. The most important of which was about ultra-terrestrials on that Thursday I believe.

I asked what data or literature was available. 'John Keel' was the answer I got, who along with Jacques Vallee covered the inter-dimensional concept from as early as the 1960s. Doctor Nolan was highly intelligent (obviously), and I honestly couldn't match his insight, knowledge or critical thinking into UAP, so unfortunately, I didn't have much to offer.

Although I'm sure he appreciated me asking a thousand random questions about R.E.M. sleep cycles and the 'anomalous antenna'.

✳ ✳ ✳

Conclusions

The UAPinfo initiative was historical, and full of 'firsts. At least for me it allows will be. This was the first time I fully considered myself a researcher of UAP, it was also the very first groups which applied 'UAP' in the title and adopted UAP terminology towards research. The whole team at UAPinfo was supported by a wider team (Akam, Aida, Andy, Dan, Dave, Chris, Graeme, Kik Plenty, Paul, Stephen and many others – see acknowledgment chapter). These were the people who would go on to create and influence early #UFOTwitter, and I am thankful for the opportunities that came. In its prime, The Unidentified hosted many guest writers such as Deep Prasad and Jamie Keyworth whilst interviewing famous Ufology people such as Ryan (Post Disclosure World), Richard Doty and Nick Pope. We even got a blog comment from Luis Elizondo, and he would answer questions about TTSA's ADAM project in 2019.

Above all, it was the start of a research and activism

website that would go on to be read by people such as Doctor Hal Puthoff, Luis Elizondo and even Christopher Mellon, and would run for years after. Although a different time period from UAPinfo, The Unidentified was still just as relevant to me personally.

References

(1). Knapp, G., & Keller, C. (2006). 'Hunt for the Skinwalker.' Paraview Pocket Books.

(2). Corbell, J. (2018). 'Hunt for the Skinwalker.' JKLC Productions.

(3). Silva, D. (2018).
SilvaRecord.
https://silvarecord.com/

(4). Stahl, A, F. (2018).
The Unidentified.
https://www.the-unidentified.net

CHAPTER EIGHTEEN: HIGH STRANGENESS

* * *

The absolute brilliance of the anomalous phenomena is that whatever these things are, whatever part of existence they come from, *whoever* they might be, they are undoubtedly something we simply didn't understand in the year 2018. The December 2017 articles that had disclosed the Advanced Aerospace Threat Identification Program (AATIP) to the world were profound in many ways, and no more important than the fact the Pentagon UAP program started the ball rolling for the disclosure process, it was a massive first step for the world's understanding in a post Project Bluebook era that had lasted for over 50 years. However, despite AATIP's significance upon early UAP activism efforts, it was actually the Advanced Aerospace Weapons System Application Program (AAWSAP) which was the more important program. For whilst AATIP focused solely on military engagement cases of aerial phenomena, AAWSAP looked behind the anomalous mask, how it was operating and why.

If we simply stick with AATIP and military UAP cases, we would be limiting ourselves, unable to discover the true origin of the phenomena. The people behind AAWSAP knew that something strange was occurring, something that couldn't be explained logically or rationally. The concept of portals to other times and dimensions was considered to explain the 'high strangeness' of UAP cases.

Seemingly, the anomalous phenomena are incredibly

complex, beyond simple lights in the sky. We can assume that this extreme technology is controlled by non-human intelligences, but we simply cannot clarify the reality of such things. The consciousness of such phenomena cannot easily be categorised, classified and easily referenced.

And after all, we are here to ask the question, *'What are UAP?'*

Even if we struggle to answer that question.

***

MONDAY
08th of October, 2018
'Ultra-Terrestrials.'

I n early October I had finished reading the book *'Trojan Horse,'* by American author and researcher John Keel (1) – same person who wrote the Mothman Prophecies. Very interestingly, Keel advocated against the theory that UFOs were extra-terrestrial in origin (the popular opinion in the 50s and 60s), and instead, promoted the literature of that time that these objects were *'para-physical'* in nature, that they push through the visible light spectrum and vibrate at a higher frequency. His work in parts was very thought provoking, however in no means does he approach with a sceptical methodology. Additionally, I didn't care too much for his overly certain conclusions based on data that wasn't repeatable and from a dataset which was highly questionable. Having said that, I did find his theories fascinating as a hypothetical argument. It was Keel who introduced the ultra-terrestrials (UFOs are intelligences from Earth) as a mainstream concept, as most famously suggested that the case reports followed a subtle sequential pattern, and that pattern didn't advocate extra-terrestrials coming from another planet. Apparently, there is a research paper by Doctor Hal Puthoff on ultra-terrestrials, but finding it has been almost impossible.

Keel promotes the concept of complexity, that UFOs are

only the tip of the iceberg, and we can see that through the patterns within case data. For example, what was being reported in the UFO-waves (or Flaps – e.g., 1896/87, 1909, 1913, 1934) were simply too complex for any basic extra-terrestrial conclusions (1), and more often than not, didn't make logical sense from the reported observations.

Both Keel and Vallee both make use of the late 19th century UFO wave to point to the 'high strangeness' that is associated with the phenomena. Theories of 'high strangeness' incorporate all of the weird and illogical paranormal incidents and associated phenomena that is tied to UFOs.

For instance, the UFO phenomenon changes through time, moves itself historically and matches up with the cultural quantum subconscious. The anomalous present us with a world view that we can understand, absorb, accept and most importantly, *believe*.

Keel reports that flap/wave areas contained not just a specific type of airship or vehicle, but a rich variation of advanced aerospace vehicle that often-defied logic when unpicked and analysed, most often, these were a technology we didn't have at the time. Vallee and Keel both reported on the sightings from civilians with close encounters, meetings with these strange people who often offer their guest a ride before dropping them back where they found them. The reported strange aerial vehicles were often displaying advanced propulsion abilities and had taken to engaging the America heartlands, almost as if a portal to someplace else was opened and these things were sailing right through.

From 1896-1897 the wave of airships intensified with reports coming across various states. The mysterious airship wave of the late 19th century acted very similar to a typical 'UFO' wave, albeit instead of silver metallic discs there were clunky wooden blimp type airships.

Most strange, was the encounters were with all manner of differing people/beings, some human, some looking less than human (some claiming to be from Mars and other places), and all traveling in ships that the experiencer has no accounting for. The technology and vehicles reported were a bizarre mix of crude blimp like airships that had the ability to accelerate and move beyond what was understandable at that time. Keep in mind, that in 1896-97 the American people had no functional working airships, let alone ones that could perform what was being reported. We would not take to the skies in planes for another decade.

Despite this, the cases did follow a pattern, Keel and Vallee report that the airships are often on the ground in need of *repair* when the experiencer engages them - the occupants themselves telling wild stories about their origins and destinations which don't make sense.

And then there is the pattern of reports, the airship wave followed the same pattern of the UFO waves of 1947 and 1952 etc, they generally stick to clustered geographical areas across the country (with outliers). Also, Keel reports that he found the UFOs appear more often on a Wednesday, and that they appear between the hours of 8pm and 11pm. Again, whilst we have no reason to doubt his research conclusion with the dataset available to him, we must also be aware that there is a lack of significant quantitative data to further give such research credit. A greater and wider dataset will potentially impact the sample being studied, and to this we can argue that more data is required. Much, much more.

If we are to speculate on such conclusions, we may end up drawing wild parallels between the anomalous and the human world. For example, for the phenomena to appear mostly on a Wednesday is highly indicative of how human beings organise their world (and also with the timeframes of 8pm and 11pm). Keel, et al, argue that this ensures intention is displayed by the 'alien intelligence', as part of a covert focus of intention, mostly to deceive mankind. To me this should be taken into consideration, however, we must also consider that this doesn't necessarily mean an 'alien' intention like we humans understand it. The patterned behaviours from within

UFO-waves might be without intention (sinister or not), they might be displaying a level of consciousness we simply do not understand – a concept I will discuss under the 'Interjection Theory' later in this book.

***

The psychology of anthropocentric intention

Intention is very much a characteristic of psychology (some argue consciousness), a dog can intend to bite you, a cat can intend to scratch you, a fish can intend to evade you, but a plant cannot intend to do you harm (that we know of), it cannot do anything other than to be a plant. We attribute intention to others through our own agreed upon observations.

But what can we agree upon about the anomalous phenomena? Can we truly assign intention to *them/it* through our observations? The problem is our observations are influenced by the very measurement of measuring - being human. We as humans, are flawed in our logic in one very critical way, we attribute a final conclusion by what we personally experience. When we assess UAP, we subconsciously influence our own decision process, we look for a desired outcome rather than a true objective one.

Consequently, I started to consider that the 'high strangeness' is a mirrored (physical) representation of the human subconscious. Historical UFO cases often act and behave like things we see in our dreams. But we aren't dreaming.

Are we?

***

We humanise our observations and our observed target. This is particularly evident when UFO believers advocate those extra-terrestrials are here to save us against nuclear weapons or debunkers advocate a mass sighting are military flares.

Applying anthropocentric intention to the anomalous phenomena is dangerously speculative. Researchers Keel, Harpur and even Jacque Vallee's *'control system hypothesis'* all discuss the possibilities of how other alternative dimensional beings are influencing human history for some unknown reason. This may indeed be a plausible explanation; however, we need to ensure we consider such theories without conclusively subscribing to them. We simply cannot infer the mindset of an anomalous phenomena by which we still do not have a complete dataset for.

Historical problems with cold cases

Sceptically, we must be open to all possibilities and be careful not to set about debunking concepts as terrestrially trivial - simply because we do not understand them or because our *favourite-debunker* has a new book to sell and clicks for their website. We are not the masters of the scientific universe, and we don't know everything there is to know. In fact, in the early 21st century we probably know as much as those living in 500 B.C., contrasted against a futurist 31st or 41st century human civilisation. I can imagine they are laughing at me and my attempt to understand.

Consider the reports from history, we shouldn't assume that similar behaviour or similar technological abilities mean a direct correlation of origin or causal linkage. As good researchers and scientists, we must try to disprove our own theories. Also, we must be sceptical, not as a tool to dismiss a phenomena, but as a means to open up more questions.

Take for example the 'Mysterious Airships' - unlike the majority of 'Flying Disc' reports and historical waves - the airships would often land, and their occupants engage and speak fluently with the locals openly about knowledge they had of America. The 'Flying Discs', however, would sporadically land, but would more often than not take off when discovered by locals and act more elusive. The interactions were very different, the engagement was different, the length of time on the ground was different – although in truth, there are reported cases in which 'aliens' that were out fixing their ships (similar to the airships).

Also, we must consider that the 1896/97 wave of unknown airships almost matched the intensity of the 1947 and 1952 waves, which were scattered and focused in different geographical location areas across America. If you were to look at a map of the United States head on, and then draw a straight line down the middle of the country, the 'Mysterious Airships' predominantly appear to the right of that line and as far towards the east coast as Illinois, Indiana, Ohio and Kentucky and clustering around Lake Michigan, as shown by Vallee (1). This discrepancy in geographical reports sightings, may, however be simply explained due to more densely populated urban and rural areas will statistically equal more reports.

There are simply too many confounding variables we can't consider because we don't have the data from those timeframes.

In fact, the same problematic principles can be applied to any historical case report, plus the further back we travel the more this problem exists. Take for example, two mass sightings from the Renaissance era are notable for the appearance of multiple 'Orbs'. On the 14th of April, 1561, Nuremberg, a broadsheet news article documented a mass sighting/aerial battle occurred in skies above the town. Hundreds of 'Spheres', 'Crosses,' 'Cylinders,' 'Lunar Crescents,' and other odd, shaped objects that moved overhead. Apparently a large 'Black Triangle,' then appeared and a crash proceeded to occur outside of the city, although details are limited with the medieval German article. This is an interesting case for sure, not only do we have an array of better well know UAP battling each other/putting on a display, we also have the appearance of a large black triangle (that would become infamous in 2021 and beyond). The problem is that due to the age of the case, we can't verify the data presented or evaluate what was seen and reported and by who. Some debunkers have tried to explain the Nuremberg case with illusions of the sun; however, the reported data, movement and shape of multiple objects don't fit the attributed explanations.

The problem is we can't correlate such data or verify each case appropriately on their own merit and therefore shouldn't conclude on limited data or assign faulty assumptions based on our own psychological needs and pre-existing narratives.

Another case we can look at from that era was the 'Basil mass sighting' in Switzerland. The 26th and 27th of July, 1566, and again we see another article that documents strange aerial phenomena that included unusual celestial bodies and reported 'Black Spheres'. Can we draw parallels between the cases? It is a difficult issue to consider.

However, we again must be careful with historical cases when considering any correlation. Each case must be treated on its own merit, even if that case is flawed by a lack of corresponding information. Simply to assume that Basil (1566) or Nuremberg (1561) are the same anomalous phenomenon (non-human intelligence) is intellectually negligent, or even that either of those cases are true anomalies. We can't evaluate and provide an assessment of the five AATIP observables in such cases.

How can we trust the assessment ability of people living 500 years ago to accurately depict celestial bodies? We can't. And yet at the same time, we cannot dismiss such cases either. Providing inadequate explanations as conclusive fact would leave us no better than a pseudo-sceptic or debunker with a pre-determined narrative to uphold. Our assessment methodology and data collection are not good enough to conclude in these very old cases.

TUESDAY
09th of October, 2018
'Intentions.'

"For them, reality is negotiable."

The unbelievable words of Jacques Vallee, confirmed to me by a scientist in 2018 over social media. Those words opened my eyes to just how 'god-like' this anomalous technology actually might be. This unidentifiable anomalous *'thing'* is almost unimaginable, it is incredibly complex in scope and practice and not part of this subjective reality. If the *phenomenon* can control the quantum particles at the atomic level, it is infinite, it is eternal, it is beyond us in every way humanly conceivable. And yet, we still don't understand it.

Why don't understand why UAP puts on needless light displays, buzzes nuclear strike groups and crashes into the New Mexico desert? Hypothetically, these non-sensical god-like anomalies have been here engaging us for all of human history, but in different ways and different forms.

Jacques Vallee documents a 'Century of UFO Landings' from 1868-1968, a snapshot of history, in his iconic book *'Passport to Magonia.'* Although limited in reference due to the lack of additional sensory data from historical cases - the 923 cases Vallee presents show a reality which isn't compatible with our own. Instead, we see brief glimpses into other possible realities as they occasionally bleed into our own. I would argue that the 'Many Worlds/Multi-Verse' theory fits perfectly, and this is a case of 'portals' opening and anomalies flying back and forth.

But my feeling is that something isn't quite right with that hypothesis. There is more to this due to the fact there are similar patterns within the displayed psychology of the anomalous in ways which shouldn't make sense (paranormal, high strangeness). The sheer amount, and distinct variation, within these reported craft over the last century would mean that at some point, one of these objects would land and stay landed in this reality. Surely, the beings would step out of their vehicles and be greeted with flowers and commemorative tributes, the President would welcome them to Earth, and they would be a permanent fixture here. Humans would then accept them as real, seeing is believing.

But they don't land and stay landed.

For all of the thousands and thousands of reported sightings of different UFOs and different beings that are supposedly witnessed across the 20th century, we don't see them here for long. They are almost in a superposition of states between real and not real, here and not here.

It doesn't make sense.

The debunkers would say that all of these witnesses are wrong, with either hoaxes or misidentifications. This is scientifically poor and an easy way out of a difficult, complex problem that needs to be evaluated fully and eventually solved.

So, for me, this is why 'high strangeness' is so important, it changes the dynamic of the origin mystery.

***

Ufology would have you believe that these 'alien beings' think like we do, that they are influenced by what we experience to be human emotions and human thinking. Allegedly, they *care* about our nuclear weapons destroying the planet (there is a concrete link between the anomalous others and nuclear weapons and facilities), but this is not evidence of intention. These are human concepts of intention and human behaviours, wishes, goals and ideologies. We are imprinting ourselves onto them, assigning them what we believe they should do because that's how we interpret the world and out reality.

The most bizarre part is that the anomalous are seemingly acting on those human assigned agendas and expectations. Amazingly, it would appear that humans are subconsciously assigning them a role to play and then they are physically and psychologically becoming that role.

Hypothetically (of course), their interest in nuclear activity is a result of our own projection, that the aliens are here to (insert agenda) save us, monitor us or eat us. Obviously, any aliens would be very interested in our capabilities and how we are managing the planet. Possibly the anomalous intelligence itself, isn't intelligent, or at least no more than we attribute it to be.

We can also consider that the anomalous phenomenon might be a quantum wave – some yet to be discovered array of various signals that make up human reality. What if the true nature of the anomalous phenomenon is so *unrecognisable* that we see 'Tic-Tacs' and 'Flying Discs' because that is what makes sense to us and that is what it makes us see as part of a symbiotic relationship. A continuous 'Möbius loop.'

Or maybe as Keel proposes, the phenomena (ultra-terrestrials as he called them) do have an agenda, to trick us into accepting and believing. Either way, it seems plausible to suggest that the anomalous have a deep underlying connection and their interest/intentions are directed towards human consciousness.

Again, these are simply unverifiable hypothetical ideas which cannot be tested, sourced or analysed.

The neurological anomalous phenomena

Here is where this gets really strange. Along this bizarre journey, we learn that some individuals have a bio-genetic trait that some others do not.

This trait is apparently linked to, *experiencers*. Experiencers are individuals who have claimed to have been in contact with extra-terrestrials, but let's just call them the *anomalous*, aka, non-human.

We must also the question, how much of this anomalous phenomena impacts humans at a neurological level? *If* a genuine encounter has occurred between humans and the anomalous, as with all these crazy theories, how much of that is because of a bio-genetic difference within the brain?

The work of Stanford Professor Garry Nolan spearheaded the work into what he refers to as the 'Antenna' –

a part of the human brain which houses the anomalous signal. Naturally, working within clinical neuro-rehabilitation, I was very interested to know how, why and where within the brain structure that this anomalous 'signal' was originating. As usual, I got myself in there to ask questions and found myself puzzled at the answers.

Doctor Nolan's work had revealed (2) that experiencers (of the phenomenon) had an increased activity within a specific part of the brain. The Basal Ganglia, and more precisely, the Caudata Nucleus and the Putamen that makeup the *'brain within the brain'*. Nolan gave a talk in 2018 that explored his upcoming research paper.

'The leading reason for the talk is questioning whether there is evidence for biological indicators that identifies people with unique forms of intuition and the two subtexts being the intuition itself with related information on what's known as "experiencers" – more on those later'.

- Twitter User Jay (@jay09784691), Silva Record. (2)

Essentially, when shown on a CT scan, the Basal Ganglia is highly excitable in experiencers, more so than in non-experiencers (control group). This is not evidence that such people are telling the objective truth about 'aliens' etc, as we should consider a neurological abnormality that makes individuals more susceptible to hallucinations or even psychic projections. Again, much more data is needed to fully interpret such genetic considerations when applying to the anomalous phenomena.

Having said that, I really would love to see the CT results of certain navy pilots who encountered the 'Tic-Tac'.

WEDNESDAY
10th of October, 2018
"Fourth Gear."

F ollowing Skinwalker Ranch and cases of high strangeness, my focus had changed fairly quickly from the 'nuts and bolts' physical craft to something exceptionally complex. A paper wrote by Vallee and Davis (3), refers to the high strangeness of the anomalous phenomena and how we should apply a more robust methodology when considering not only UAP, but also other harder to explain phenomenon such as the Marian apparitions. Vallee in his work, has stated that the UFO/UAP should be considered from the position of six layers of anomalous events.

'*(1) physical manifestations, (2) anti-physical effects, (3) psychological factors, (4) physiological factors, (5) psychic effects, and (6) cultural effects*'
- Davis & Vallee, (2006). (3)

The six layers that are introduced serve as a good measure to capture the traits of anomalous phenomena, but for me they do not explain the origin. As I've stated previously, linking any number of Marian apparitions to UAP is problematic. Unfortunately, and as an example, we do not have access to hard materials from the cases of Fatima or Lourdes to test or evaluate, additionally, we do not have videos, credible photos to truly examine the apparition figure. We have *testimony*, which is not enough to conclude.

Similar problem with Skinwalker Ranch, we do not have the hard materials of some of the physical crypto-terrestrial figures that were reported. How can we scientifically compare the atomic structure of say a *Grey Alien*, *Bigfoot* and the *Lady of Lourdes*?

We honestly cannot prove that the anomalous is one thing pretending to be lots of things.

Additionally, if we are to propose that this 'high strangeness' is a phenomenon (single) rather than a phenomena (plural), we would need to somehow show a link beyond observations of cold cases. Which we cannot do for reasons we have discussed earlier in this book.

In their paper, Vallee and Davis make references to what they see as the possible nature of UAP technology. They assume that the six layers are a direct product of UAP technology that integrates *'physical and psychic phenomena and primarily affects cultural variables in our society through manipulation of physiological and psychological parameters in the witnesses,'* (3).

Vallee and Davis make the following accretions in their 2006 research paper: That the phenomena are a product of a technology that manipulates the laws of physics. This unique technology can bring about 'psychic' effects as either being intended or side effects. They assert a very 'intention based' thesis, that the technology could be manipulating human-culture (3).

Whereas the Vallee and Davis hypothesis suggest that the phenomenon is the product of UAP technology, we could propose - through a theory of *interjection* - that the UAP technology itself could be a direct product and consequence of the anomalous phenomenon (or phenomena). That is, the reported aerial machines of *'Saucers'*, *'Tic-Tacs'*, *'Foo-Fighters'*, etc, are created by or through the phenomena (for whatever reason) and by definition of such ability has complete control over physical space-time at the localised quantum/atomic level. Potentially, we might have to consider 'trans-morphia' the ability to control and manipulate subatomic particles and layer them to form whatever craft or being they desire.

All possible at the quantum level.

The issue of UAP origin, therefore, might come down to intention, and more specifically whether or not what we are observing actually has consciousness and intelligence in the way we would consider. Vallee et al, would draw reference from the encounters with Marian apparitions and from encounters with extra-terrestrials, whose claimants also follow a similar narrative with a specific message or prophecy relevant to that time period and usually one which is understood by the claimant.

As a counter argument, we can point to the one constant throughout the entire history of UAP reports.

Human beings.

I would propose the Jungian subconscious implications of modelling or *imprinting* could account for what is being observed. This means that the phenomena models expected behaviours and appearance of its target and mirrors them back to the host (humans). It becomes what the host expects it to be to reach a desired goal.

Whereas Jung advocates the psychosocial implications upon society as a result of the human mind – that the phenomena isn't real as such. We instead, can use this and go a step further to advocate a hypothetical situation in which the anomalous is tapping into our quantum subconscious and amending itself *without* intentions and not for a 'Trojan Horse' goal. The behaviours, intentions, appearance, colours, shapes, abilities are coming, from us.

'*It, just is.*'

As the famous psychologist Carl Jung stated, the projected image appears as an ostensibly physical spacecraft, independent of the individual's own psyche and mind (4). Basically, '*the mandala becomes a spaceship controlled by an intelligent being.*'

To understand them, we need to understand ourselves

We need to think about ourselves, we need to think about *WHY* we do things in this reality, in our own life. As humans, we do things for a sense of achievement, that feeling of self-worth/self-efficacy, of relevance and of achievement. Humans grade themselves upon a form of 'self-actualisation', a psychological requirement that sits top of the Maslow pyramid – the hierarchy of needs (5).

The psychology of the anomalous phenomena is a continuous theme I have discussed through this book. Does a 'God-like' phenomena have such primitive needs and wishes? What does a phenomenon that has no more goals, wishes or needs really require? Would such a hyper-advanced intelligence share our human need for affection, self-efficacy and appraisal? Does it worry about job interviews, feeding the cat or making sure it eats enough vegetables? Does it pop to Tesco for milk and bread?

Possibly not.

What we are dealing with might not even have intelligence the way we attribute the concept.

Take for example, Cmdr. David Fravor and the 'Tic-Tac' UAP. When you strip away all else and look at the 'Tic-Tac' - what do we see?

A pure white vehicle in the truest sense.

It has no wings, no obvious propulsion, no rotor, and it outmatches the best F-18 fighter jet known to man. If you were to speak to David Fravor's subconscious and ask it directly to create the perfect aerial vessel, that would be it. The anomalous 'Tic-Tac' represents what we want, what we expect to become, it is the next step in our evolution. UAP are almost a by-product of our imagination and logical assumptions, straight from the depths of our very own subconscious.

The human mind is wonderful thing.

"I have no idea what I saw," Commander Fravor replied to the pilot. "It had no plumes, wings or rotors and outran our F-18s." But, he added, "I want to fly one."

- Blumenthal, R., Cooper, H. & Kean, L. *The New York Times.* (6)

❊ ❊ ❊

Conclusions

The cases of high strangeness occur and have been associated with UAP sightings/encounters. Unfortunately, beyond that I'm most other things, not because I don't believe they may not be true, but because we can't adequately prove them with the data available. What I do believe, is that to solve the UAP origin mystery we must look past the 'nuts and bolts' dogma. 'High Strangeness' within cases may prove to be the key to the UAP mystery. My theories about the anomalous phenomena 'modelling', 'imprinting,' and excerpting itself onto humans in an intention-less way may be unique, but not without criticism. We simply do not have the data to verify such radical claims.

References

(1). Keel, J. (1970). 'Operation Trojan Horse.'
Anomalist Books.

(2). Silva, D. and @Jay09784691. (2018). 'Experiencers, Unique Intuition and Biomarkers.'
SilvaRecord.
https://silvarecord.com/2019/01/09/experiencers-unique-intuition-and-biomarkers/amp/

(3). Davis, E. & Vallee, J. (2006). 'Incommensurability, Orthodoxy and the Physics of High Strangeness: A 6-layer Model for Anomalous Phenomena.'
National Institute for Discovery Science.
https://www.researchgate.net/publication/254695883_Incommensurability_Orthodoxy_and_the_Physics_of_High_Strangeness_A_6-layer_Model_for_Anomalous_Phenomena

(4). Jung, C. (1961). 'Flying Saucers: A Modern
Myth of Things Seen in the Sky
Routledge.

(5). Maslow, R. (2017). 'A theory of human motivation.'
www.bnpublising.com

(6). Blumenthal, R., Cooper, H. & Kean, L. (16th of December, 2017)

The New York Times.

CHAPTER NINETEEN: THE ANOMALOUS MARIAN APPARITIONS

* * *

T he most important part of trying to understand the intentions and behaviours of the anomalous phenomena have so far been based around a very humanistic psychological traits of wishes and needs. Naturally, as humans we attribute the world to how we see it, we subjectively *humanise* this shared reality in a way which prevents us from seeing objective truth (remember how we fooled ourselves into thinking UAP weren't real for over 70 years?).

We believe (rightly or wrongly) that everything in this reality follows the rational logic of a human thinking. So naturally, as we have engaged and been engaged by the anomalous, we in turn attribute our humanity upon them. Simply put, we think that the behaviour of 'aliens' can be associated with a binary ideology: 'friend or foe', 'good or evil', 'here or not'. The truth might be that whatever these things are, we simply are misreading them because we tend to see them anthropocentrically.

We do this very famously with religion. Having been brought up Catholic, I am very aware that God and Jesus are human-orientated in nature. The Bible tells us that God made man in his own image, and almost everything in the bible relates back to man. The same can be said of the UFO phenomenon with most aspects of extra-terrestrials relating back to mankind somehow - nuclear weapons, genetic engineering, mutilating livestock, chasing fighter jets, abductions, etc. Simply put, *'dem aliens'* are obsessed with us, almost as much as we are with ourselves.

But as we considered earlier, this is humans trying to humanise reality. Imposing ourselves into what we see and wish to see.

This idea of humanising reality was an important consideration for me, one which I made a part of the 'Interjection Theory'. It was from this perspective that I thought it would be interesting to build on the work of Keel, Vallee and other researchers with regard to historical religious cases in a way that is objective and doesn't humanise the truth. Whereas others attribute a misinterpretation that extra-terrestrials accounted for religious encounters, I looked at how such an *'alien'* consciousness might be a factor in religious orientations and how we formulate ideologies of belief and faith.

Not an easy task.

***

TUESDAY
30th of October, 2018
'All souls and saints.'

Late October, my efforts of rebuilding UAP research for 'The Unidentified' after the closure of 'UAPInfo' continued, but also, I was looking to branch away from the 'nuts and bolts' aspect to UFOs. My influences came from George Knapp and Doctor Garry Nolan, who had taken to the work of Jacques Vallee and John Keel. Knowing that Jacques Vallee had taken an interest in the religious case of Fatima (1917), I wondered myself how many other religious cases *might* be interpreted as something they were not, and to what extent.

How many religious encounters through history were in fact, the anomalous phenomena?

It was in these Autumn days I was told that the Marian apparitions were highly likely to be part of the anomalous phenomena, and yet, I was sceptical. How can proposed historical religious apparitions have any links to extra-terrestrials?

Even *if* these encounters were all real, and all linked as a common phenomenon, how do we advocate them as such to a highly dismissive public? How would we evaluate cold cases without access to testimony and hard evidence? Basically, we cannot draw correlative parallels without issues. We would have to consider some very serious critical flaws within the methodology that would bring us to such wild conclusions.

But that should that stop us evaluating what data is available?

WEDNESDAY
31st of October, 2018
"That's me in the corner."

M aybe it is fitting that the very day that celebrated the paranormal (Halloween), was the same day I received a message from the scientist, advising me to look into religious encounters. What choice did I have?

That Halloween night, after we had been trick-or-treating with my three-year-old daughter, I put her to bed and took some time to research in the old attic. By that, I mean looking for literature on the internet and YouTube videos for religious encounters - as my own dusty bookshelf was limited on paranormal books.

My wife shook her head at me, hopeful that our earlier trip to church that week hadn't sparked some new cult like obsession. It hadn't, I am a lazy catholic at best.

Late into the night my eyebrows were raised at a question. How is it, that so many people believe something so intensely without real proof? Is this what belief really is? Why is belief so important? It's not like human beliefs can change objectivity reality.

What we have are religious stories, much in the same way UFO/UAP experiencers are presented. Many credible people saying incredible things, but with no tangible proof. Take for example the Catholicism apparitions who are better known as the 'Marian apparitions'.

These heavenly apparitions essentially founded and established much religious ideological doctrine these past few hundred years. These encounters are reported as supernatural appearances, such as the Blessed Virgin Mary and other spiritual figures that appear to civilians around the world with a message. That message of the apparitions, when you break it down, is a request for *belief* in whatever they appear to be. *Acceptance* and *belief*.

In the case of heavily religious persons, it becomes about whatever their god expects of them. The encounter itself is very often named after the town or location where it was experienced, Lady of Fatima, Lourdes, etc. Similar to UAP encounters, the place is usually in the title of the case, Roswell, Phoenix Lights, etc. Other similarities extend to the apparitions who are sometimes reported to revisit the same site over an extended period of time, reoccurring again and again to the same person(s).

Famous researchers such as Jacques Vallee have touched upon cases such as Fatima and made reference to the high strangeness cases (1), (2). For me it was interesting, I could look without buying, investigate without subcribing.

In the mind of the Marian apparitions

There seems to be some overlying themes amongst the Marian apparitions, one of which is the request for a message to be given to build a church on the location of the area where the apparition appears. How strange is that? What is the point in doing such a thing? Well, we know that a church brings in people who pray and give thanks to God, and also it reenforces belief systems around Catholicism and religion.

We can ask the question. Why therefore, is it important

for these various apparitions to have strong belief requirements? What exactly drives them? What motivates them at the neurological level?

This got me interested in the ideology that maybe what we were seeing as Christian Marian apparitions were more than simple hoaxes, weird sightings or hallucinations, maybe they were more than what we would have experienced as messengers from God. What if these things are indeed a part of the UAP phenomena like some researchers have proposed?

I started to get the idea that maybe we are looking at a phenomenon that isn't limited to origin of singular form. I needed to find out more and reading the literature in this area was the way forward. Chapters and verses from the bible didn't really help but reading the testimony of the experiences to the events gave me a better understanding.

I speculated; human belief systems are apparently important to these phenomena apparitions.

Why?

Let's consider, the anomalous appeared in front of thousands (Assiut, 2000/2001, Fatima 1917), then they requested churches built to honour them (Lourdes, Walsingham, Pillar, etc), and they appeared as already established Christianity religion figures and requested their message spread.

What do they gain from this?

What is so important about wanting humans to give them devotion and conscious attention? Such egotistical actions are very humanistic, we desire praise and social reward.

We can argue that the anomalous having humans '*believe*' in them was seemingly a goal for 'them'. Is it an intention? Is it a psychological gratification feedback that would be placed under 'self-actualisation' on the Maslow chart of needs?

What does this suggest about human consciousness and beliefs?

What does this suggest about the anomalous consciousness and beliefs?

Is there something about beliefs we are unaware of yet

that interacts with the phenomena. It would seem there is much more to the phenomena/paranormal and supernatural than can be taken at face value. Maybe my own belief structure is somehow integrated within the phenomena itself.

What are the dynamics of human belief, *really?*

However, we need to be careful about going too far. The same issue occurs with the Marian apparitions, we don't have enough historical case data to fully assess and determine their origin, which makes it impossible to adequately attribute a link to other phenomena.

THURSDAY
01st of November, 2018
"Need only look in the mirror."

The following day for whatever reason I sat and watched a film on Netflix called Annihilation. It had the actress Natalie Portman in it from the Thor films, well, the first two, and apparently, she going to be the new Thor? Anyways, the film was a decent film and the concept behind it was really entertaining. An alien comet hits Earth, starts changing the DNA molecules of living things, Natalie Portman is sent to find out what happened. By the end of the film, she comes face to face with the alien creature, it then mimics her behaviours. This basic concept was something I had considered prior, that the anomalous phenomenon mimics human subconscious thought. Take for example the Marian apparitions, they interject and model their very appearance and behaviour upon what the individual expects them to be. In the film, the Anomalous are a bio-para-physical-genetic mirror that 'trans-morphs' itself with the humans, animals, plants, and anything that has DNA. Essentially, it replicates when it comes into contact with to create something new, something that doesn't quite make any sense, despite its attempts. Even in its behaviour, the anomalous is mirroring the human (Natalie Portman), reflecting back the intentions and behaviours. My mind wondered - how would one explain that in terms of modern-day quantum physics? Also, it would be interesting to get more perspective on the psychology of the anomalous. If they know everything or can be anything, then what's the point in having intentions?

* * *

Conclusions

If we are to accept and understand the Marian apparitions and all the hypothetical considerations, we must also accept that they potentially are a phenomenon and not a phenomena. That is, that they are one thing pretending to be many things (which is hypothetically just as complex to grasp as the Anomalous being many things).

Consider, one intelligence, one origin with potentially one agenda for humans which arguably would be covert. Possibly, they have been controlling human history for a long time.

However, we must also consider that unlike the anthropocentric ideologies of Keel and Vallee (1), (2), (3), (4), and their evaluations of anomalous intentions towards humans, we must also consider the anomalous phenomenon might have no intentions, desires, behaviours that aren't an extrapolation of our own human consciousness (subconscious).

Also, we must be very careful, ensuring that such theories remain hypothetical and not presented as conclusive given that we simply can't begin to understand an 'Alien' mindset which could be millions of years more advanced. Furthermore, to fully benefit our cause, we must look inwards towards our own illogical human cognition, our interaction with this reality and more specifically, quantum consciousness. Once we grasp the meaning behind humans, we might also grasp the meaning behind the Anomalous.

And again, this is all theory, we must drag ourselves back to the starting line as we simply do not know who or what they are. That is the truth right now.

References

(1). Vallee, J. (1979). 'Messengers of Deception: UFO Contacts and Cults.'
Daily Grail Publishing.

(2). Vallee, J. 'The Invisible College: What a Group of Scientists Has Discovered about UFO Influence on the Human Race.'
Anomalist Books.

(3). Vallee, J. 'The Invisible College: What a Group of Scientists Has Discovered about UFO Influence on the Human Race.'
Anomalist Books.

(4). Keel, J. (1970). 'Operation Trojan Horse: The Classic Breakthrough Study of UFOs.'
Anomalist Books.

CHAPTER TWENTY: ADVOCATING AN APPROPRIATE SCEPTICAL METHODOLOGY FOR UFOLOGY

* * *

A dopting a sceptical approach to research is incredibly important. Whether that's critically assessing a Pentagon UAP video or the testimony of a navy pilot, it is important to objectively evaluate data from a holistic methodological approach. However, it is also imperative to consider that being sceptical must apply to your own thinking, ideologies, hypothesis and conclusions. Essentially, you aren't trying to prove something, you are trying to find objective truth, not your version of it. As my old professor of clinical psychology once told us – *'you should be just as sceptically minded with your own hypothesis, if not more so, than that of others'*.

And she was exactly right. The aim of professional research isn't to start with a conclusion and work backwards to reach a predetermined, desired result, the aim is to not even care what the end result is and let the holistic data lead you wherever it leads you. Your hypothesis comes second.

This is how science works.

If Ufology is to become more than fringe, it needs move past the unscientific processes, the speculation dressed up as factual conclusions, the knee-jerk pre-debunking that instantly dismiss cases with ridiculous explanations, and the conmen believers selling extra-terrestrials for profit. We need to abolish the believer vs debunker ideologies and move into science.

Being sceptical is a representation of that scientific process, not a means to forge subjective narratives. Unfortunately, the field of Ufology (study of UFOs) has been heavily dogmatic in its approach, criticised by the scientific community and labelled as fringe for too long. This is primarily due to the ways in which UFO researchers approach data from the perspective of believing that 'UFOs' by absolute definition are extra-terrestrials. And this critical issue comes through mainstream media and the public sphere itself and is abundantly obvious when the topic comes up in mainstream media.

Believers of the extra-terrestrial hypothesis are a problem to the scientific process. They have already established a conclusion and are working backwards to ensure case data fits their narrative. Sadly, this is not contained to Ufology. The general public believe that UFOs are either 'aliens' or they are terrestrial misidentifications – there is no middle ground and zero appreciation or application of a clinical, holistic approach to analytical data evaluation.

Any introduction of an alternative, more complex theory to explain the anomalous is often neglected in favour of a psychologically accepted explanation that has foundations from within a social community. A social paradigm which holds objective truth second to subjective needs.

Very little of UAP study within Ufology has basis in scientific knowledge or any valid approach that evaluates and critically assesses new data that may challenge the current ideological paradigm.

Now this is not to say that some UAP might indeed be extra-terrestrials and given the extreme (AATIP five observables) abilities displayed by these vehicles, it is not outrageous to consider a non-human origin as a hypothesis (not conclusion). However, to assume because something anomalous might be non-human does not automatically assign the origin as 'aliens' coming from another planet.

Over the last year, the ideologies for UAP explanations have ranged from extra-terrestrials, ultra-terrestrials, inter-dimensional, time-travellers, multi-verse travellers and even a product of human consciousness. Most interesting, is the concept that the anomalous is a quantum anomalous phenomenon, that brings into question the function and origin of such an 'alien' consciousness. None of the above are considered by debunkers or believers. But how do we assess these hypotheses given that the government won't release critical UAP data – add to this that Ufology can't apply an appropriate scientific research methodology and that the biased scientific community refuses to accept that UAP are even real.

What is needed, would be a rigorous scientific methodology that appropriately assesses UAP data and formulates a hypothesis which can be tested and then retested. Should that hypothesis not be testable due to lack of correlating data? Then we shouldn't be afraid to say that is the case, or simply, *'we don't know.'*

For me, this is why scepticism is vitally important.

Just because I consider that UAP might have the potential to be anomalous phenomena - some non-human intelligence/technology that originates from an unidentified origin - doesn't mean we should assume that as fact, and it doesn't mean we should conclude on limited data. The scientific process should welcome a *'we don't know,'* scenario, as opposed to assigning a *'best guess'* and then dismiss approach.

The other unfortunate aspect of UAP research, which is just as problematic, is the pseudo-sceptics or *debunkers*.

You know exactly who these people are. Historically, these are people who hide under the guise of a scientific process but in reality are desperately trying to find ways to explain and dismiss UAP case reports. Such groups have over the years, proposed outlandish conclusions based on little to no data, often taking fractions of a blurry video and building a narrative.

Pseudo-claimants have advocated terrestrial explanations that ignore holistic case data - from system glitches, bokeh, weather balloons, flares, swamp gas, Venus, seagulls and any other explanation that simply dismiss what was reported by multiple military and civilian witnesses. In some unfortunate cases, data has been manipulated by both believers and debunkers to show a specific outcome.

Naturally, this is not acceptable and is opposed to the scientific process for finding objective truth. Such people have no place in UAP research.

Over the past year, one of the worst (almost conspiratorial) YouTube claims came for the 'Go Fast' UAP video. This claim stated that the unidentified object in the military video was a slow-moving balloon – that somehow the United States military can't identify rouge balloons that enter the airspace of nuclear strike groups.

Which is ridiculous.

The conspiracy claim further proposed that somehow, this short, blurry, UAP video (and others) were apparently used to fraudulently convince a naïve congressional oversight committee into establishing a UAP task force.

Which is again, ridiculous.

Similar themes emerged for 'FLIR1' video, that the 'Tic-Tac' UAP was a seagull, and the 'Flying Disc' of 'Gimbal' was a lens glare – despite pilots stating exactly what happened in each case. But still debunkers ignored their testimony in favour of their own narrative.

These are individuals who are similar to believers in approach, they adopt the exact same poorly placed methodological process of attempting to start investigations with an already decided upon conclusion and work backwards. In the case of the debunker or pseudo-sceptic, it's that all UAP have a terrestrial origin, and quite often you will find they will assign any explanation to the case, *so long as it doesn't conclude 'aliens'* and so long as the case is not left unexplained.

Another issue is that the debunkers will also attempt to deviously label 'UFOs' as extra-terrestrials themselves as part of a 'straw man' argument, thus, framing the entire conversation of debate away from the fact *something* is in the skies which needs official investigation. And even worse, believers fall for it every time, they play the debunkers game, a game that's rigged from the start. After all, how does one prove *UFOs* are extra-terrestrial in origin without hard tangible proof? Without an 'alien' on a podium, bodies in pickled jars or keys to the hanger doors buried deep in the desert it becomes a difficult task for even the most well connected member of the Mellon family.

Additionally, what would constitute that proof beyond a reasonable doubt to the world? We don't have deep space tracking on UAP on radar as they leave orbit, and then tracking said vehicles for light years across outer space is surely *impossible*. Even if Roswell wasn't a Mogul balloon, and if the crashed Roswell bodies were non-human, and then even if somehow, we had access to them, that still doesn't equate to them being from another planet. Much more data is needed before we even begin to arrive at such a conclusion.

All of this plays into the debunker and believers' endless cycle of trying to prove and disprove a hypothetical conclusion which ignores the fact that *something* real and unidentified is in our skies. An endless game of cat and mouse.

The third problem group we can identify, is the scientific community – particularly the astronomers. Across 2018, and going back decades, we have very well received voices such as Carl Sagan and others who have been the champion of denouncing 'UFOs' and the associated technology. Take for example, SETI – the Search for Extra-terrestrial Intelligence, who are heralded as pioneers within their field and filled with beautifully brilliant minds. This historically well-funded group of scientists and astronomers have chased down the possibility of life on alien planets by using radar signals and listening to the cosmos, whilst at the same time ignoring witnesses to UFO encounters.

I've found that such individuals within reputable positions uphold a strong subjective position to UAP, automatically assuming (without evidence) that the argument basis is for *extra-terrestrials*, and then look to address the fallacy of that position based on linear-thrust propulsion of chemical rockets for interstellar travel. Distance, mass, energy, time, etc. All valid points to impose on our own 21st century technology, but, who are we to impose our limitations on others, potentially races that are more advanced?

What SETI and others haven't done, unfortunately, is to then provide alternative and better fitting possible hypotheses for 'non-human' intelligences here in our skies.

The theories of anomalous are left to amateurs such as myself and my colleagues at UAPMedia to take wild stabs at. This is a problem.

Modern science, as brilliant as it is, has one major flaw - the fallacy of human's inability to incorporate him/herself into the observer equation. And this is no more evident, than with UAP technology. As a scientific community, they were unable to holistically interpret the 'UFO' data, because they didn't look at it, their clinical judgment critically affected prior to observation, thanks to the psychology of stigma. And it was these self-reflective limitations which prevent the scientist from objectively assessing the information and processing it. Obviously, *not in a way which tries to specifically prove or disprove the extra-terrestrial hypothesis*, but in a way which looks at the radical UAP technology and concludes more data and official investigation is needed.

I've also found that, the higher the public position held, and the higher self-esteem held by the scientist, the more pushback they display against UAP investigations. We found this time and time again across 2018 through speaking to scientists and monitoring their reactions to UAP news and published articles.

For some unknown reason, an astronomer gets quoted in mainstream UAP articles rather than a physicist, or a defense contractor or an aerospace engineer. The astronomer is expected to make comment because the uneducated counter-assumption for UAP is extra-terrestrial, which then needs to be debunked by the astronomer and journalist in an unwitting combined effort.

Consider also, the social attitude towards the scientist is in high regard, whereas the social attitude towards the 'UFO believer' is low. As a 'UFO person' I have first hand experience of this.

Now consider the idea that the 'tin-foil hat' wearing crazy conspiracy theorist was *right* and the high-ranking scientist in the public eye was *wrong*. Wrong about the most important issue in history.

Such a scenario would produce significant cognitive dissonance for the scientist and might therefore explain their strong negative pushback to UAP investigations. Then you might configure into the equation the subconscious foresight of potential issues over reputation and threats to government funding. Not something they would want to advocate.

In light of these problem groups, what we need to do is to stop concluding on limited data. Certainly, hypothesise about UAP origin, but then work forwards in your research, not backwards and most importantly, work to disprove your own conclusions before others do it for you.

We need a better class of believer and sceptic if we are to solve this UAP mystery.

MONDAY
05th of November, 2018
"Remember, Remember."

G rowing up in England, Guy Fawkes night (or Bon-Fire night) was a big deal for us as kids. I remember there was always an air of excitement as me and my sister would watch from the attic window, hoping to see the biggest, loudest and brightest fireworks as they soured over the suburban rooftops in Linthorpe. November 05th was the celebration of the gun powder plot and how it was thwarted in 1605 A.D., but more than that it was a chance to see various explosions in the sky.

By the time we had reached the 05th of November in 2018, my wife, daughter and myself were stood in the front garden looking up to the night sky as the dark was eliminated by explosive light and colour. The atmosphere was saturated with sound and activity, the fireworks lit up the distant skies as far as the horizon. My conscious mind flashed back to those childhood memories, and my mind drew comparisons to those cold dark nights. It was quite beautiful and always sent a chill down my spine, in a good way.

I remember, as we stood watching the skies, and unidentified object came into view from across the bungalows. The strange object was a fiery reddish orange that flickered and slowly drifted across the Teesside skyline. A slight glazed over expression came to my wife's face as she stood motionless, her eyes unable to process the object as it came closer and closer towards us. I wondered if my tales of UFOs had influenced her? Probably not. My wife is as logical as she is pragmatic.

It wasn't long before the combined look of relief and elation became apparent.

"It's just a Chinese lantern!"

A smile came across her face as normality was resumed. Obviously, I hadn't declared anything that resembled a conclusion, but when you are interested in 'UFOs', people assume that you think everything unidentified hovering in the cold night sky is an alien spacecraft. The stigma of being a 'believer' is hard hitting and something I've purposely tried to distance myself from.

The lantern on fireworks night brought a concept to my mind, the concept of how the phenomena is *unidentified*, and how it has remained unidentified for over 70 years. Obviously, the government's closure of Bluebook in 1969 ensured any further investigation was halted, and, in doing so ensured that the entire phenomena remained abstracted from the world's conscious awareness.

At that point it struck me, what if the very nature of the phenomenon itself is hyper-dynamic. What if it does change constantly? What if it deploys a 'trans-morphic' styled ability or injects itself into our reality at will?

What if the scientist and Vallee/Keel are right and the phenomena has hidden itself from us through the untenable nature of its own design?

An interesting concept if not at all probable. Although we can speculate without subscribing.

If true, what impact does that have for a sceptical human understanding and ability to be able to detect such a phenomena? Personally, I believe we would struggle to identify this, even with our advanced scientific processes and such a phenomena would fly under the radar (no pun intended).

If we as humans, have a psychological predisposition to always attempt to label and constructive reality in a way that we can understand it, what does that means if we encounter something that isn't part of our reality?

Consider the Skinwalker Ranch anomalies (or at least the hypothetical implications) or consider the fundamental change of reported UAP appearance over the past 100 + years. Maybe they aren't even linked, but then maybe, just maybe, the anomalous are actually a phenomenon (singular) and not a phenomena (plural)? What if the anomalous are one 'alien' consciousness, interjecting and masking itself as many things? What if all (or at least a large percentage) of UAP are connected to one intelligence? It's almost infinitely complex to decipher. You can see why most Ufologist researchers stick to extra-terrestrials.

I would be willing to claim that the deployed UAP technology is the same, but beyond that, it is difficult to assess fully.

Extraordinary evidence

As thick smoke drifted across the night sky, the words of a scientist rang through my mind without apology. Only the distant sound of fireworks could be faintly heard as they became nothing more than muted background noise. Those words were intriguing.

"It's definitely something not human... And the reason it had remained a mystery for centuries is the untenable nature of its definition."

Without verifiable data, how can we even be sure of such a position? The more I researched the less I knew. My best guess assessment was broadened dramatically to the point I had no data I could trust conclusively. All I could safely say is that the anomalous, by hypothetical definition, was real. Beyond that, I like most people are lost on a sea of uncertainty.

In Ufology however, there was much more certainty about what UAP are. Or *UFOs* as they obsessively refer to them.

For example, there are those who claim themselves to be experiencers of extra-terrestrial contact, and whilst I shouldn't discount unusual things have occurred for such people (myself included) it becomes very problematic to take their word from a scientific perspective without tangible evidence beyond testimony. Sadly, people have a tendency to believe what they want to believe and if something sounds even remotely true, they jump on it.

Assigning an extra-terrestrial origin is problematic and just because something isn't human doesn't mean it's aliens from another planet. And from a true sceptical perspective, we need to accept the experiencer data without dismissing it, ridiculing it, labelling it or subscribing to it. My feeling is that contact cases will prove to be an important part of the mystery. But not yet. Not until we have the focus of the world.

As I've mentioned earlier in this book, there is also a

massive disconnect theme between the scientific process and evaluation of anomalous phenomena and anything remotely associated. Alien abductions/experiencers for example, are highly sensitive and perceived as stigmatised within western society, and consequently have been sidestepped by the TTSA/AATIP/UAP initiative who have aligned themselves with the scientific community. Despite this, the experiencer data and testimony are a massive part of formulating the origin of UAP as we ask the question of who/what they might be. As suggested earlier, we simply cannot factor it into a conclusive UAP model of assessment right now. And this point is valid for most of UFO history, very rarely have we seen a case that exceeds the subjective Carl Sagan benchmark that has put the phenomena beyond us scientifically.

> *"Extraordinary claims require extraordinary evidence."*
> -   *Carl Sagan*

Rather than simply showing that *something* anomalous is in our skies and our oceans, we set the bar to an impossible standard, we set the bar to demanding evidence of extra-terrestrials, which is an almost impossible task. As I've stressed before, Ufologists and UFO researchers were set up to fail by debunkers. The debunkers set the scene and gave the preconceived narrative prior to any investigation. They then requested that believers prove extra-terrestrials with evidence they had no access to. The deck was stacked. And as already stated, the old guard within Ufology fell for it every-time.

Even to this day believers persist in labelling UFOs as extra-terrestrials, and it carries into the mainstream. As do the debunkers who are more than happy to see Ufologists fall for the same trick over and over, arguing a straw man argument decade after decade. Worse still, the world believes that UAP are either extra-terrestrials or Chinese lanterns. There is no scope for any variation. The *sceptical* process is incredibly flawed with regard to UAP.

My personal perspective in research is that we should hold off on concluding about UAP origin, we instead need to find and discuss appropriate hypothetical considerations and provide a critical assessment methodology that works. And that is by no means easy to change a flawed paradigm that spans back decades.

But then, who am I?

FRIDAY
09th of November, 2018
"Ahead of time."

The internet is weird and wonderful place, it allows for strangers to safely and sometimes dangerously interact. For the topic of Ufology, it revolutionised the way in which UAP information was being transferred. No longer were 'UFO conferences' on the circuit the answer for people searching for the truth about the phenomena. People from all over the world could now use social media and find an online research community. UFOTwitter was the very first platform to do so (created by the team at UAPinfo). Although originally called 'TwitterUFO' (In 2019 I would change the name to UFOTwitter as it sounded *cooler*) the concept was revolutionary in allowing non-UFO people of the world to have the conversation.

It was in November that I was able to learn more about the phenomena than I would have in any other forum. For UFOTwitter was UAP orientated, and by that, I mean it held natural sceptics who examined data with a holistic eye. This was a group of researchers who subscribed to science and the process model of data assessment and evaluation.

This was the beginning of a platform that advocated genuine scepticism, holding believers and debunkers accountable.

✻ ✻ ✻

Conclusions

Not following a 'sceptical methodology' had unfortunately led the field of Ufology into the fringed taboo, a second amusing thought to professional scientists and researchers from the mainstream. I personally struggled in the beginning, having come from the professional academic research fields of psychology, criminology, occupational theory and currently (at time of writing) neuro-rehabilitation.

The absence of any credible voice that challenged UAPinfo was more than alarming. The field of Ufology was filled with pseudo-debunkers who apply bottom bargain basement experiments and get away with the most absurd conclusions, simply because they aren't saying it's aliens. Somehow, this process of building a narrative, actively looking to find a conclusion is accepted in Ufology because it isn't concluding on a stigmatised concept. There are as many pseudo-science debunking websites across Ufology as there are pseudo-believer websites, all of which are equally damaging to the scientific process. The worst of these being Youtube UFO channels that shown CGI videos and hoaxed content.

They cheat the truth in favour of imprinting their own narratives and the worst part is that these cult-type groups with their accepting followers are no different on applying predetermined methodology and conclusions than the believers they do vehemently oppose.

Simply put, Ufology needs to move past this ideology of narratives and let the truth have its day. Unfortunately, due to the fact we humans make emotional decisions rather than logical ones, this UAP issue may not free itself of this problem anytime soon.

Also important to note, we must be careful not to conclude on limited data whilst being mindful of assigning an anthropocentric perspective. Imprinting our desires, wishes and ideologies onto the anomalous phenomena will not help us to determine the truth of UAP origin. This is true for both believers and debunkers who must be willing to change their approach to UAP and adopt a genuinely sceptical approach. Unfortunately, Ufology is awash with people who don't understand the professional research process, they have no experience of working towards an appropriate methodology that carries its own credibility.

This will change in time, and once mainstream science finally realises the importance of UAP, it's technology and the revolution of physics.

References

(1). Vallee, J. (1969). 'Passport to Magonia: from folklore to flying saucers.'
Daily Grail Publishing.

(2). Vallee, J. (1979). 'Messengers of Deception: UFO Contacts and Cults.'
Daily Grail Publishing.

(3). Vallee, J. 'The Invisible College: What a Group of Scientists Has Discovered about UFO Influence on the Human Race.'
Anomalist Books.

CHAPTER TWENTY-ONE: THE NEXUS BETWEEN QUANTUM PHYSICS AND CONSCIOUSNESS

W hat extreme and unusual theories can we attribute to the anomalous phenomena? What can we propose, what methodology exists that might help us formulate some kind of working theory to explain what we are dealing with? How might we explain objective reality without the anthropocentric eyes of the subjective human observer? As with previously examined chapters on 'Skinwalker', 'High Strangeness' and the 'Marian Apparitions' we had to consider the human observer and the possibility of how human consciousness impacts the anomalous phenomena. Or is it that the anomalous intelligence(s) influence human consciousness in a symbiotic loop that benefits both species? One of the themes we have looked in this book is whether the anomalous actually have consciousness in the way that we understand it, whether they have a varied 'free will-deterministic' reality, based on physical and psychological needs that drive them forward as they do us, or is the 'Alien' consciousness imprinted completely from our collective subconscious as human beings?

Essentially, we are asking, *'What is Consciousness?'*

***

MONDAY
19th of November
'Schrödinger's Orange Cat'

My first real correspondence with Luis Elizondo was from a reply I had sent him on a medium article entitled, '*Why Unidentified Aerial Phenomena Are A National Security Risk And Also An Opportunity For Progress*' (1). At the time, I had been fed a few research articles of consciousness, quantum physics and UAP. Naturally, my thinking was to ask the Director of AATIP. Obviously, my questions revolved around whether the anomalous phenomena resided within the nexus between consciousness and quantum mechanics. How does one even begin to interpret such a concept? A phrase that had originated via Lue, who was in a position to have a better understanding than most, although would never refer or consider himself an expert. I asked.

'I would love to hear your thinking on advanced quantum physics such as quantum entanglement, superposition and retrocausality with regards to the phenomena. How much will such revelations of correlation then uncover discoveries about the fabric of reality itself?

You may never actually read this, and I may never get an answer.

Thanks, Adam (Andreas)'
- Adam Goldsack (*Aka. Andreas Freeman Stahl*). (2)

The reply I received.

'*As it happens, I do indeed read posts :) Your questions are certainly insightful. As a result, I am drafting another article to address some of the areas of the quantum conundrum we face. Simply put, "yes", the quantum world is truly bizarre in ways we have yet to truly understand but then again, so are things like love, war, and taxes. Thankfully we have friends like Hal, Steve, and Gary to help us sort through the math. :)*

As we continue to peer through the veil of this mystery, we are finding that the universe is full of surprises. Thank you sincerely for your comments!

Stay tuned!'
-   Luis Elizondo.

***

<u>*Why UFOs don't land on the White House Lawn*</u>

'The Anomalous Phenomena resides in the nexus between consciousness and quantum mechanics'
-   An American Patriot.

There you have it, your answer to the UFO mystery, that somewhere between the quantum mind and quantum physics lay these bizarre phenomena. Ok, so maybe not. The truth is that the complexity of whatever UFOs/UAP actually are, probably means we won't have the scientific understanding for a long time to accurately state what the anomalous origin and nature really is. As the Fmr. Director of AATIP told me in a written interview not long ago, the mystery of UAP will probably need a multitude of disciplines working together to apply research. And this is currently a problem. The lack of theoretical physicists who look into UAP, for example, is a massive issue and instead, we are left with UAP researchers such as myself who have backgrounds in criminology, psychology and clinical neuro-rehabilitation rather than physics, chemistry and aerospace. I am not qualified to speak about the quantum phenomena, but if people like me don't, who will?

We need to find answers to why there are hundreds of reported variations to differing types of discs, pyramids, cylinder, triangle UAP forms that extend beyond an anthropocentric perspective. We also need to stop *conclusively* applying and imposing our own assumptions onto whatever UAP might be, or what we want them to be, and instead step back and look at the problem objectively.

We can still pose questions that require further official research and find answers as to why *they* don't land on the White House lawn.

Anomalous Quantum Entanglement

In 2017, the U.S.S. Nimitz case was thrust into our awareness on the front page of The New York Times, and with it the 'Tic-Tac' UAP – an anomalous vehicle that was able to display the AATIP five observables. But more interestingly, the UAP displayed some very interesting behaviours, firstly that the Tic-Tac mirrored Cmdr. Fravor's manoeuvres as he circled his target, and then the UAP appeared at the CAP point, some 60 miles away – something it wasn't supposed to know the location of, and it reached the location in seconds.

This is fascinating, and a unique window into possibly the anomalous psychology (should it have conscious intelligence that is) or maybe, we can see this in terms of a 'Quantum Anomalous Phenomena'. As humans, we like to apply an anthropocentric view to that which we study. We simply assume that UAP are extra-terrestrials, and we assume that UAP have beings inside, we assume that the anomalous have consciousness and intelligence just the same way we do – maybe that is all true, but shouldn't we also examine alternative theories to their which have dominated Ufology for 70 years?

Again, crudely put, quantum entanglement and its 'non-locality' within the quantum mind might explain both the mirroring behaviour of the 'Tic-Tac', and the UAP appearing at the CAP point destination. Basically, information was obtained by the UAP in ways we don't yet fully understand.

Going back to 1935, a famous research paper by Einstein (3) proposed how quantum entanglement leads to what's now called 'quantum non-locality', or the 'spooky effect' that appears to exist between entangled particles. If two quantum systems meet and then separate, regardless of distance, even thousands of lightyears, it becomes impossible to measure the features of one system (such as its position, momentum and polarity) without also changing the other system into a correlated, one corresponding state.

The problem is how can particles within specific quantum systems transverse vast distances of space and time without actually traversing it? When examining Einstein's 'spooky effect' most physicists have tested quantum entanglement over space and time. The given assumption is that this non-locality refers to the actual entanglement of given properties across physical space, however, what about if quantum entanglement also shows significant effects across time? Yes, this quantum phenomena occurs at the micro-level, but can this be possible at the macro-level? Can the behaviours of the Anomalous be explained effectively by quantum entanglement? The problem with most of this field is a lack of theoretical or practical research, applying quantum physics to the anomalous is unheard of outside of defense intelligence circles, primarily because the civilian scientific community doesn't acknowledge UAP (beyond *extra-terrestrials*).

Anomalous Quantum Superposition of States

One of the weirdest things we might encounter on the quantum world is the concept of 'collapse of the wave function' - which has most famously been displayed in the double-spilt experiment. Essentially, as I understand it, we have matter and light that can be adopted to both wave and particle form depending on external conditions. Following on from an 1801 experiment by English physicist, Thomas Young, Davisson and Germer then showed in 1927 that the same properties occur in electrons, well before the wave-particle duality of quantum mechanics (4).

As fascinating as this was for the emergence of quantum mechanics, it also brought into play some very serious theoretical frameworks that struggled to be easily explained by classical physics.

What is so bizarre, is that somehow when the particles in the experiment are observed, to see exactly how they change into a wave (or how they at least act like waves), the particles remain as particles when closely observed, and even after the particles have passed through the double slits and then recorded, the particles still remain as particles. Experiments with crystals that split a photon equally, have also shown that observer influence still affects the result, *retrospectively*, which brings up questions of quantum entanglement and quantum eraser theories (5). Also, the double split experiment engages us with the paradox of '*Quantum Superposition*,' which is when a system (object -macro, particle -micro, etc) exists within two states and in the same place.

A commonly held interpretation of this quantum mechanics paradox is that of the Copenhagen interpretation. Essentially, within the Copenhagen interpretation, a system stops being a superposition of states and becomes either one or the other when an *observation* takes place. Essentially, the act of measuring the quantum particle, gives it its position.

Observation collapses the wave function.

From a strict deterministic perspective, any observation that collapses the wave function is basically a paradox, it is impossible. The cause-consequence nature of a determined universe/reality prevents such a scenario, from the '*beginning of time*', (aka, the Big Bang) and therefore certain outcomes have always been fixed to the timeline of this universe. Such deterministic perspectives dictate, there is no equal chance within that moment, there is always one direction that is based on a historical cause-consequence timeline which act as predictors. Basically, reality is a movie and was always destined to play out that way from the beginning no matter how many times it's watched.

However.

Consider, our theory that the anomalous phenomena have no historical timeline as it enters this reality from some-other dimension. The UAP in theory, has *nothing* to determine its future as it has no past in our reality timeline (a fascinating concept I will discuss later in the chapter). In such a scenario, the UAP has no historical predictors within a superposition of state in this timeline and determined universe.

Let's look at Schrödinger's poor cat. A closed metal box contains a cat inside with a poison that has a 50/50 chance of being released, which to the observer, the poison might have an equal chance of being released and not being released. So, from the perspective of the observer outside of the box, the cat itself can be considered to be both dead and alive simultaneously due to the equal probability of the toxin being released or not. Mr. Schrödinger's theory, despite ignoring a very serious ethical and animal cruelty policy, is the first to describe what is hypothetically happening at the macro level what is seen at the micro (quantum) level. Specifically, Schrödinger's experiment can be interpreted to mean that while the box is closed, the system (cat) simultaneously exists in a superposition of the states "dead cat" and "living cat", and that only when the box is opened, and an observation performed does the actual wave function collapse into one of the two states. Then as the box opens, the timeline autocorrects a deterministic history to incorporate a dead cat or an alive cat.

Now in reality, or at least from a deterministic perspective, this is a complete paradox, as the poor cat cannot be both dead and alive in such a state within that un-observed box. There have been many ways to try and resolve this conundrum by theoretical physicists. One, proposed by Hugh Everett in 1957 is referred to as the 'relative state formulation' (6) or more commonly known today as the 'Many Worlds' theory, Bryce DeWitt (7). This is a truly fascinating theoretical proposition to the superposition paradox, in which the wave function doesn't actually collapse and instead an infinite number of possible *worlds* are created to resolve the state of superposition. In such cases, the cat in the box both dies and lives as they split into separate contrasting timelines.

Another explanation for the superposition paradox might be that paradoxes are a natural part of reality (as much as we humans don't like the idea of a real paradox), another explanation could be that such paradoxes are simply our limited understanding of them, and additional data required to resolve them.

Interestingly, this is a fascinating concept and argument for quantum consciousness, that our reality *might* be more interconnected to ourselves, and quantum minds than originally thought. Some have argued that it is indeed human observation which resolves the state of superposition – which again is still very much in the realms of philosophical thinking right now. But it does help us to ask questions of UAP. For example, Just as Schrödinger's cat can exist in a superposition state of both being dead and alive at the same time…. what if the anomalous phenomena also linger in such a superposition state within our reality? What if, *whatever* they are, they are dependent on *observation*, imprinting and by extension, collective human quantum consciousness. What if *they* cannot be *anything* at all without us. An undetermined entity entering a determined system.

Currently, it must be said that in Ufology at least, there is no extensive, credible literature to suggest that human consciousness influences the creation of the anomalous at the quantum level, and understandably, this is very extreme. And yet is very interesting.
For the anomalous to exist in such a state of hypothesised superposition, it would require a lot of complex, difficult to explain, varying scenarios to play out, specifically within our understanding reality itself. And also, it must be considered for the anomalous to be in such a position, there must be 'strict 50/50 probability' outcome measure that are dependent on removing historical cause-consequence predictors - as with Schrödinger's cat, the paradox occurs through a non-agreed upon reality, a lack of observation which represents a collapse of that specific wave function. It might also suggest that reality itself is dependent on human consciousness to some extent – maybe this physical reality itself is created

by a general, agreed upon consensus, of human consciousness (the total number of minds in the universe is one, etc.) that is created 'moment to moment', but then collapses into a deterministic timeframe upon our agreed upon observation, and the collapse of the wave function. Now in terms of probability of the Anomalous' appearance and behaviours, we might argue that the phenomena/phenomenon could be coming from an entirely different dimension, meaning it has no historical markers of prediction, no previous quantum wave function, and nothing to determine anything about it. Bizarrely, UAP might have no desires, needs, wishes, attitudes or behaviours. This hypothetically, might then suggest that when something anomalous interjects into our reality at whatever point in history/future/present, it remains in a quantum superposition until an external point of influence, in this case the collective human (sub) consciousness, imprints upon it and collapses the wave form and it becomes what it is to us.

We might also argue that the limited exposure of UAP (why they don't land on the White House lawn) and interaction with humans is a by-product of this continuously unresolved quantum state.

We, in our collective quantum conscious reality, simply haven't agreed upon *what* they are.

Do we determine them? Do we give them the appearance and behaviours? This is a theme which we have discussed previously within this book. A theme which seemingly has no way of being answered.

Additionally, if this shared collective human reality is made up of 'moment to moment' instances, meaning we all experience the 'here and now' which is generated from elsewhere, and possibly perceived by our quantum minds in this 3D space-time - then we would need to accept that a cause-consequence linear reality or specifically a deterministic reality is a masked illusion. If the 'moment to moment' reality exists and determinism doesn't (or some mixed variation), then can we truly accept a compatible reality in which the poor cat is both dead and alive and that UAP are both real and not real simultaneously. Maybe, we haven't all agreed that UAP are real in any specific given form, from the 'Mysterious Airships' of the 19th century, to the 'Flying Discs' of the mid-20th century - hence the proposed state of superposition which we associate with this constant game of hide and seek. Is the UAP, both here and not here?

Or potentially, the other theories would say that human 'non-quantum consciousness' may not be influential on the argued state of superposition that UAP might experience – it could however be argued that UAP are regulated in two paralleled states as a consequence of their technology, that transverses dimensions or alternative multi-universes.

The difficult question would be, what variables from within human collective consciousness then determines what they are, and how/why the Anomalous behave in the ways they do?

Or would it be more of an individualistic entanglement between the UAP and the quantum mind?

Is proximity a factor in such imprinting?

Why are there hundreds of reported variations from the similar types of vehicles (discs, triangles, cylinders, etc), and why is there hundreds of variations of weird '*beings*' in contact cases? (Particularly in the 20th century).

There are a lot of problematic questions that arise due to this theory, but that shouldn't stop us from asking extreme questions, after all, the entire issue of UAP is just as extreme. Either way, we need official research to answer fundamental questions about them, us and our shared reality.

So why don't they land on the White House lawn? Maybe it has very little to do with us humans, or maybe it has everything to do with us.

SATURDAY
15th of December, 2018
"A new theory?"

T he nature of reality is one which has been debated amongst scholars for all of human history. Our tepid understanding of the natural physical laws are still heavily promoted by modern day physicists as conclusive without reproach. The attempts to integrate general relativity with quantum mechanics have not as yet been reconciled. String theory, with all its issues, has revolutionised theoretical physics and allowed for the possibility of other dimensions to be considered. In addition to this, the officially accepted intro-duction of quantum consciousness is still not seen as a priority within mainstream science, it is fringe at best, a passing amus-ing thought and by no means in the same league as string the-ory. To add to this, science does not recognise the 'phenomena/phenomenon' of UAP and its severe implications and this leads us to a major problem.

The anomalous phenomena are most famously known for their association with Unidentified Flying Objects (UFOs) from as far back to the 1940s 1950s and through to the present day. However, some former/inner defense intelligence circles are reportedly whispering of the phenomena equating to that of 'quantum physics' and others, specifically whisper quietly, 'quantum consciousness'.

When one researches the closely correlated patterns within the data, it becomes clear that there is more to these phenomena than can be taken at face value. At a base line it would appear the phenomena is of non-human intelligence and is heavily orchestrated (directly/indirectly) within the se-crecy of its very own nature. One famous theory, this that the sequential patterns within data suggest that the phenomenon take on various forms (either at entry to this universe or once here). It could be one phenomenon pretending to be many things – which might account for why there are hundreds of reported UAP vehicles of the similar appearance – but different in shape, colour, size and design. Can we tie in 'trans-morphic' UAP ability?

Could we now see a culture change, a moving away from the traditional physical 'nuts and bolts' approach to UAP (that are solely extra-terrestrial from another planet) and more towards a framework in which the phenomena has inter-dimensional properties. After all, research tells us that UAP are disappearing and reappearing at will, changing shape, size and colour, and changing their contextual form with the changing of human psycho-social cultures from year to year, decade to decade. Such a concept would be something completely unthinkable. This hypothetically could however, explain why we as humans have historically struggled to define and accept UAP.

In late 19th century it was 'Mysterious Airships', in early 20th century it was 'Ghost Rockets' and 'Ghost Planes' followed by 'Foo-Fighters', then 'Flying Discs' of the 40s and 50s America, then 'Black Triangles' in the 60s onwards and today there are 'Tic-Tacs' and 'Cubes' reported by military pilots. The contact cases have changed over time in conjunction with the change in reported vehicles.

How might we explain this? How much is based on the makeup of reality and how we understand it? And most importantly, how careful should we be with such extreme, unverifiable ideologies.

Current understanding of physics

String theory was one of the revolutionary and most controversial concepts of the late 20th century. Within current theoretical physics it purposely aims to unify all particles and fundamental forces of nature into one single theory. The 'String Theory' supports the idea that as a baseline there are at least 10 dimensions in this universal existence (8). From our human conscious perspective, we can identify the first *three* which extend indefinitely into outer/inner space (that we assume currently) and are physical and observable to us from a certain point.

So, in principle, *where* are the other spatial dimensions leading up to the 10th dimension?

Theoretical physics apparently tells us that they are right here with us.... but curled up snug and cosy upon themselves, that is, they are 'compactified'. (The extra-dimensions are just compact manifold which is too small to be detected by us). To go further down this road, we could even have look at the Kaluza-Klein idea of compactification and a possible unified electromagnetic and gravitation theory. But I am a one-time qualified psychologist and not a theoretical physicist.

Anyways.

Here is a generic definition of a manifold anyways (if it helps?).

Calabi-Yau manifolds, studied prior to their application in string theory, are the 6-dimensional manifolds that are the compacted dimensions of the theory. So, in string theory manifolds are a high mathematical probability, and also it means that 'other dimensions' are also a high probability. Which very crudely sets us up nicely for the next segment.

Reality Interjection Theory

Jacques Vallee once pointed to the work of a French scientist from the Middle Ages, Facius Cardanus. Cardanus managed to summon from the air seven Sylphs (Elementals) to his laboratory, he was able to ask them about the nature of God and the universe. Vallee stated that two of the Sylphs disagreed with one another - the first said that that God created the universe from the beginning and here we are today as a consequence. This is the cause-consequence 'physical model' of reality we are all aquatinted with and accept as the 'Big Bang' theory. The second Sylph said, no - God creates the universe from moment to moment, should he stop, the universe will end - Quantum Mechanics. To go further it can also bring up opposing questions on reality, determinism vs freewill. The argument posed by the first Sylph suggests the 'physical model' ensures the universe is determined via cause-consequence variables and therefore it is deterministic in nature. The argument posed by the second Sylph suggests that a 'moment to moment model' would allow for freewill and that the universe isn't solely determined. Also, it can be said that human consciousness isn't determined. (But with this thinking, how can there exist freewill if we do not have all the available consequential knowledge of our actions?).

If our universe is being generated via a higher plane of existence as suggested by Vallee, and others, would this suggest that reality is being created moment to moment, everything that exists...does so at this very moment, no past and no future.

On this basis, the case can be made for a 'Reality Interjection Theory'. Let us look at how the two above approaches then fit in with considerations of the anomalous phenomena;

a) 'the universe **was** deterministically created'
b) 'the universe **is** created moment to moment'

So, let's start with, **a)**

Deterministic anomalous phenomena

Our universe was created from the Big Bang some 13 billion years ago and is ever expanding. Everything within this '3-Dimensional' reality is governed by time and space, it follows a strict cause-consequence, deterministic sequence of events. As an example of such a set universal timeline, we can think about watching the film 'Forrest Gump'. We press play on our DVD player and watch as Tom Hanks makes his way on an adventure through life. No matter how many times you watch the movie, Forrest Gump's mother always dies in the film at an exact point in the later stages. This is determinism and can be likened to our own lives – whatever happens was always meant to happen and cannot be altered.

So, in this example, a 'Gray Alien' turns up in your bedroom and is ready to probe you at a certain point on your life timeline. Not cool.

Everything in such a deterministic universe follows a path, you are there in your bedroom because of what has gone before, you simply cannot just come into existence one day. Under a cause-consequence deterministic universe, that 'Space Alien' in your bedroom must have been the consequential result of the initial Big Bang - following '13 billion' years of evolution - and now is there with you in the dark and ready to do whatever it is going to do with its probes. It has a history and a future the same as yourself. It has followed a path and arrived.

So now let's consider, **b)**

Freewill anomalous phenomena

'The universe is being generated moment to moment', our quantum conscious minds are perceiving these *signals* and interpreting them in this reality. An example might be, like watching Forrest Gump again, but this time the movie may be able to be edited on your computer with the right software and may even be streamed from someplace else other than your DVD player. In this example, Forrest Gump's mother might not die because you, the observer, can edit out her death scenes from the start, or maybe even edit her out completely. The entire film can be altered and swapped around if you have the technological instruments and software to do so. This is genuine 'free-will' as you have all possible options open to you and you are living 'moment to moment'.

In contrast, no-one in the movie example has any idea of the edits and alterations that have taken place and the movie plays out regardless. Those poor souls are trapped in their determinisitc reality.

In reality for us humans, we cannot edit reality and thus we have no foresight of future events and therefore we have no true free-will.

If we further apply this concept to our own 3-dimensional reality, we can ask if the anomalous phenomena has the *technological software* to do this? Can they interject a foreign anomaly into our universe (*Flying Discs, Tic-Tacs, Cubes*) in such a way that it will alter the deterministic timeline of this universe to their own desires? What direction would the human race have taken without the secret history of UFOs? Would we have annihilated ourselves through nuclear war without their silent influence and hidden presence?

We need to be careful here as we simply don't know.

These hypothetical interpretations suggest a deterministic universe may not be the only definable factor within the laws of reality, particularly when we consider interjecting anomalies from other dimensions or universes that were not part of that initial system.

So, you once again wake up in the middle of the night and a 'Gray Alien' has come into your bedroom with that probing look in its eyes. The phenomena has manifested/created that being from what we understand as the quantum *nothingness*, it has no history and no future, it is only present in that instance, moment to moment. From our perspective, the UAP appear, linger in this reality for a period of time and then they disappear completely. Theoretically, UAP are not governed by the laws of our deterministic reality.

When the anomalous leave they possibly transverse into some other unknown dimension and have no trace of it ever being here (sometimes). Remember, it does occasionally crash into the New Mexico desert, leaving parts of it behind. We can call this the 'shedding skin theory' (credit: Doctor Nolan, 2018). When the phenomena vanishes as suddenly as they appeared, the UAP disappear from sight and from radar to wherever or whenever they go to. The 'Space Alien' in your bedroom is edited out of your own personal movie as though it was never even there.

The anomalous phenomena only exist in that moment.

Determinism or freewill?

Both. In all probability, I would guesstimate it is both a) and b) simultaneously. This physical world appears to be deterministic with cause-consequence effects, but could be overlaid by a moment-to-moment creation at the quantum level. Maybe we have an element of free-will that effect the deterministic timeline of this universe. It does make you think about the free-will of the anomalous phenomena and how much insight into the deterministic future these beings have.

If you have complete knowledge of every future event and outcome, does that allow you absolute choice over the future?

Definition of a 'Phenomenon Interjection Theory'

The basis for the 'Interjection Theory' revolves around the theoretical notion that our consciously perceived quantum reality is being uploaded and 'transmitted' from another dimension (or universe) before being downloaded by our quantum minds and then perceived as 3-dimensional space-time. One might consider the quantum consciousness theories that allow for the understanding that the human brain is a neural transmitter and not the creator of our consciousness.

Any foreign concepts interjected into our deterministic timeline reality - such as UAP - must be retroactively auto-corrected backwards *and* forewords into that deterministic compatible timeline by the conscious 'universe'. It must fit the equation of this reality, it must flow smoothly, or it will create extreme paradoxical events that would 'crash' the universal simulation.

Non-determined retro-consciousness could be used as phrase of definition. It would imply that your consciousness is here and now, moment to moment. It suggests that reality is a dynamic fabric which changes, amends and autocorrects with consciousness.

The future is not set, and neither is the past, what is generated here and now filters back to the 'beginning' of time to allow a deterministic, cause-consequence sequence of events to unfold leading to a path to which you currently find yourself. The same of the future, what happens now with your choices, freewill, impacts your 'determined' future and past. So essentially Forest Gump would be right, freewill and determinism are paradoxically entangled right now, moment to moment created that autocorrects on the deterministic timeline.

Let me stress that this is all pure hypothetical considerations, an exercise in philosopy and nothing more.

Anomalous quantum consciousness

Hypothetically speaking, the anomalous might be something we simply cannot understand with our limited human brains. They might be something that is beyond us. Something that isn't limited by the constraints of human psychological and physiological needs. Possibly, human and anomalous consciousness exists separately from the physical brain.

Perhaps the anomalous are an amalgamation of human consciousness of the conscious universe?

They might not be a 'they' at all. As humans, we have a big problem with objectivity. Essentially, we can never achieve a true sense of objective truth because we are highly subjective creatures, we see the world through human eyes, we are motivated by social emotions, our actions and thoughts governed by the culture by which we live in. This means that we create our own collective subjective reality and often assume (wrongly) that we are seeing an objective reality. (This is based upon my assumption that there is an objective reality, one which would remain in place if all humans died tomorrow). We imprint into everything with our human perceptions. So, when we consider the anomalous, we are seeing them as we expect to see them. We are seeing ourselves.

Are they us?

Do we imprint our consciousness into them through processes such as quantum entanglement?

If 'they' are truly something unknown and separate from ourselves, perhaps coming from the multiverse or another dimension or wherever (maybe not even a *place* as we understand it), then it might be that they have no consciousness like we recognise or can understand. What if when they enter our universe/reality an *empty vessel*, they are an uncharted void, a form which hasn't been assigned a form like a piece of clay that has yet to be carved. And yet, this spooky anomalous collection of entangled quantum particles somehow has the ability to instantly change its shape, to transmorph, to build itself into any known form or substance, to create itself at the atomic layer, to breathe life into human looking Marian figures like the Blessed Lady of Lourdes or the grey space aliens, or into 'Tic-Tacs', 'Saucers', 'Cubes', 'Pyramids', 'Triangles', 'Flying Airships', 'Foo-Fighters' or 'Ghost Soldiers' in the sky.

Such things we cannot even imagine.

What if it has no message, what if it isn't interested in whether we look after our planet, or whatever use nuclear weapons? What if it is displaying psychological intentions, behaviours and physical form because it is coming into contact with the collective human consciousness. Is it modelling and imprinting itself onto us?Or then, maybe this isn't even remotely accurate at all. And here we have the start of a hundred-year-problem, possibly longer.

❄ ❄ ❄

Conclusions

Under this quantum paradigm, there are two competing theories of the anomalous origin. One is that of the 'Many Worlds' concept, that the wave function doesn't collapse and that an infinite number of worlds are created alongside our own at any instant. The 'Multi-Verse' (Many Worlds) explanation of UAP fits what we are seeing and explains why there are so many variations of 'close encounter' contact beings and different looking vehicles. In the case of multiple UAP coming from the 'Multi-Verse' under the 'Many Worlds' theory, the phenomena (plural) are real and have a history from another place. These UAP are simply coming through 'portals' or 'wormholes' into our world and timeline, somehow, and for some reason.

The second theory, is the one we have discussed at length in this chapter, is that the anomalous may possess an inter/extra dimensional element. In this theory the wave function does collapse and UAP are caught in a state of superposition, either dependant on human consciousness or their dual position between two realities/dimensions is a by-product of their technology being deployed.

Again, we can speculated about the 'empty vessel' UAP theory as it enters our universe, that it shapes itself upon entry or during its stay it can 'trans-morph'.

We also looked at the anomalous consciousness and if they have the ability to alter the human history timeline by interjecting anomalies with the foresight of changing future events.

Both theories have their possible pros and cons and unfortunately lack credible historical UAP data to fully substantiate the concepts.

The extent by which consciousness and quantum mechanics is relevant to the Anomalous, humans and our collective reality is yet to be understood. Currently, there are more theoretical hypothesis which are based on very sketchy, limited phenomena data, than hard science. As we humans, in 2018, still don't universally accept UAP as Anomalous in nature, and therefore we struggle to apply any credible unified theory which might explain the origin and nature of 'Unidentified Anomalous Phenomenon' within the quantum world. And as for quantum consciousness, that is yet another step too far for mainstream science who still are unwilling to move past the pseudo-scientific fringe element, that the body, and more specifically the brain, could be an antenna of consciousness, rather than the other way around. Possibly, quantum consciousness is the key to unlocking the Anomalous phenomena.

Consider that the modern era UAP/UFOs have both, existed and not existed, in this reality since 1942 and beyond. They don't exist because humans haven't accepted them on a global level into our reality, we haven't decided upon what they are collectively as a species. But then how can we? If the phenomena are a *phenomenon*, and the Marian apparitions, paranormal creatures of Skinwalker Ranch, 'Foo-Fighters', 'Flying Discs' are all one thing - then it is almost impossible to agree collectively when they refuse/are unable to settle on one form.

Also, can we ask, do they exist because certain individuals under certain conditions fleetingly witness them. This statement is actually true of physical (exist) and socially/psychologically (don't exist) perspectives under a deterministic approach.

Rather than a collective human influence over the phenomena which might determine their intentions, behaviours, shapes and size, perhaps it is very much under the influence of the individual in such encounters. Aka, a 'Flying Disc' appears to a specific person in a certain way, solely because of varying neurological characteristics of the person it has appeared and engaged with. Interestingly, we can ask what happens when when multiple people witness a UAP? Under such a theory, who then determined that the 'Phoenix Lights' would be a huge triangle shape? Does one initial person subconsciously determine the anomalous' holistic form, the UAP then projects/manifests itself into reality only to appear in that final form to multiple other people? We don't know as we don't have radar data to confirm origin or destination. Other considerations have been discussed. For example, what about asking a question of a universe in which a UAP can physically exist and not exist simultaneously as a result of the deployed technology. Also, we might hypothetically ask if the human collective mind might act as the observer, whilst the UAP would be 'Schrödinger's cat', and that we simply haven't opened the box to collapse the wave function.

Obviously, this is all highly theoretical and speculative. We must be very careful not to let unverifiable theory lead us down a wrong path. The vast complexity of trying to evaluate and understand the technology and consciousness of the phenomena will always leave us guessing. We simply cannot link various historical phenomenon as one deceitful intelligence – which Keel and Vallee have suggested as a hypothetical consideration.

We don't know that Marian apparitions, Bigfoot or Aliens have any basis in this reality, let alone a casual inter-dimensional link. Additionally, we might struggle to even begin to consider how the anomalous phenomena interacts with human consciousness or vice-versa, and we would struggle assign any origin based upon human interaction. On this basis we must be careful not hold to much sway within the quantum anomalous state of superposition, as intriguing as it might be. We also do not know enough about the quantum world and its incompatible relationship with classical physics and the macro world, and until we do, it becomes incredibly difficult to introduce UAP into the mix – a phenomena/phenomenon which is happy to transcend both with ease. What we need is for theoretical physicists to openly accept that UAP is a real phenomenon and should be worthy of their time and funding.

References

(1). Elizondo, L. (2018). 'Why Unidentified Aerial Phenomena Are A National Security Risk And Also An Opportunity For Progress.'
Medium.
https://medium.com/hackernoon/why-unidentified-aerial-phenomena-are-a-national-security-risk-and-also-an-opportunity-for-progress-5f219768fa8f

(2). Goldsack, A. (2018).
Medium.
https://medium.com/@adamgoldsack/i-would-love-to-hear-your-thinking-on-advanced-quantum-physics-such-as-quantum-entanglement-d75585159527

(3). Einstein, A. (1935). 'Can Quantum-Mechanical Description of Physical Reality Be Considered Complete?'
APS. Physics Journal.
https://journals.aps.org/pr/abstract/10.1103/PhysRev.47.777

(4). Davisson, C.J., and Germer, L.H. (1928). 'Reflections of Electrons by a Crystal of Nickel.'
https://www.ncbi.nlm.nih.gov/pmc/articles/PMC1085484/

(5). Kim, Y-H, Yu, R, Kulik, S, Shih, Y, and Scully, M. (2000). 'Delayed 'Choice' Quantum Erasor.'
APS.Physics Journal.
https://journals.aps.org/prl/abstract/10.1103/PhysRevLett.84.1

(6). Everett, H. (1957). 'The Many-Worlds Interpretation of Quantum Mechanics'.
https://www.pbs.org/wgbh/nova/manyworlds/pdf/disserta-

tion.pdf

(7). DeWitt. (1970). 'Could the solution to the dilemma of inde-
terminism be a universe in which all possible outcomes of an
experiment actually occur?'
https://physicstoday.scitation.org/doi/10.1063/1.3022331

(8). Williams, M. (2014). 'A universe of 10 dimensions.'
Phys.Org.
https://phys.org/news/2014-12-universe-dimensions.amp

CHAPTER TWENTY-THREE: THE ANOMALOUS PHENOMENA

* * *

In recent years, the United States government have used the term 'Unidentified Aerial Phenomena' as a wide sweeping term that could include anything from balloons, drones, planes or the less favourable terminology of 'alien spacecraft'. The problem of attempting to classify the anomalous phenomena as something 'non-human' is in itself a continuous battle. I already knew the issues going into this field of research, but never initially considered the answer to the mystery was *unanswerable* beyond labelling UAP as non-human. Which let's be honest, the anomalous phenomena are highly likely to be 'non-human' on the basis of the extreme technology displayed.

I say this because my conclusions only lead to more questions, which lead to even more questions and those pointed in one difficult direction. A direction we don't have the correct signposts for.

Simply put, I do not believe we have enough tangible evidence to say that the anomalous are an 'alien' phenomenon (single entity of one origin). I do believe however, that the anomalous *might* be a phenomena (multiple entities of multiple origins). Although, we can't prove that either, which is a huge problem.

No matter which direction you turn in UAP research, no matter if you try to link the work of Keel/Vallee to Skinwalker Ranch to the Marian apparitions or to Roswell or even the 'Foo-

Fighters', we are let down by our *Ufological* dataset that has no hard radar data (to pinpoint origin of UAP), sensory data, videos, photos or official government verification. The people within DoD who hold all the sensitive anomalous information don't want to let it out into the public.

The current scientific community will not accept the current data available. Most people in Ufology don't care either way, but the truth is we need the scientific community.

Scientists operate in a nicely defined box that makes sense to them, venture too far and you find yourself, and your funding, cut short pretty sharply. Not far enough and you are protecting a conventional narrative in the name of self-preservation.

Take Oumuamua (1), the thinly shaped 'extra-terrestrial' object that was first tracked in 2017. Commonly assumed to be a rock that expelled gas to change its direction and explained its abnormal movements. Astronomers at the time were quick to clamp down on radical thinkers such as scientist Avi Loeb who suggested the various explanations should be considered (2). Loeb has famously noted in recent years the possibility that Oumuamua might even be an interstellar probe from some extra-terrestrial civilianisation (3). This is a big no-no in academic world, historically you simply don't ask the non-human intelligence question, at least not seriously.

In recent years, the scientific community however has very slowly started to explore the hypothetical idea that some extra-terrestrial vehicles/probes are reaching our solar system, although very few academics will cross that sacred line into the world of UAP.

For most respected scientists, the standards of 'UAP research' are too low to engage, particularly those that point to the possible non-human anomalous phenomena. It is far below them and without any form of government investigation and acknowledgment, they dismiss all data instantly. Try having a conversation on social media with some of these types of people and you soon find emotional decisions are rife.

Their absence is telling.

Consequently, we are left drawing amateur hypotheticals in an amateur field with no agreed upon methodological parameters, funding or professional direction. The anomalous phenomena's untenable nature is due to human's inability to detect them.

To me, the anomalous are still a mystery of our own making, the secrecy born of an unidentified threat from the skies, a threat we had to bury for 70 plus years until we were ready to face the terrifying and exhilarating truth that we may not be alone on the planet.

Possibly, we never were alone.

***

SUNDAY
16th of December. 2018
"A year in the life."

It had been a full year since the New York Times story that started the beginning of UAP research. A year in which the mainstream media were forced to change their approach to how they reported UFOs. From 2017-2018 we saw a paradigm shift in attitude and opinion and for the first time we saw people speak about the phenomenon in a rational, objective and scientific manner. I remember spending the late Sunday evening considering the achievements of 2018, the rise and fall of UAPinfo, my own research into the UFO/UAP topic and the first established 'UFOTwitter' community (or TwitterUFO as it was first known) that wasn't based in conspiracy and silliness. What was needed, was a revolution, to consider the past respectfully, but to rewrite the future under a new paradigm.

The modern UFO era can be classed as going from the 'Flying Saucer' wave of 1947 and Roswell, then through the rest of the 20th century. The era spans right into the 2017 AATIP revelations, TTSA, Elizondo, and the 'Tic-Tac'. Whilst the modern UFO era was about government secrecy, denials and conspiracy, the 'UAP revolution' (that began 2017), is about opening up the secrecy, government transparency and regaining trust.

Throughout 2018, a small faction within DoD had been fighting to bring about 'disclosure' of the UAP reality. However, the question was whether they had enough firepower to be able to influence those in key strategic positions of power to act, and, if they had enough momentum. Additionally, as the end of year came into sight it was clear to me that no genuine answers to the UAP issue would be gained through mainstream Ufology, no matter how well meaning, or how good the set of researchers were. Without the acknowledgment of government there would be no long-term answers to the mystery.

SUNDAY
30th of December, 2018
"And the horse you rode in on."

B y the end of the first year the scene was set. The path was clearly marked, the signpost indicated why needed to happen. We needed to *kill Ufology*, well, we needed something that would drastically amend it at the very least. We needed to end both 'believers' and 'debunkers' and replace them with something within the centralist middle, something better, something that was purely devoid of researcher bias. Maybe a sceptic who considers the concept that UAP is equal to something anomalous, or a believer who critically questions every case report through a sceptic's eye. Possibly, someone who can look into the complex issues involved without subscribing to them. We can dream right?

Not only did we need to remove the hallmarks of credulity, but we also needed to ensure it was replaced by something else, something that would allow the general public to become a part of and openly discuss UAP. However, in the first year proceeding the AATIP revelations there was not much hope of anything happening soon. At the time, there was a handful of passionate bloggers and twitter users talking openly about the phenomena, different to the usual old school ufologists.

But it was a start. These people would tune into the UAP research community-based form within UFOTwitter and eventually would become UAP activists. We needed to create a platform which would turn people into centralists, who could understand how professional research was applied and in a way that used credible holistic methodology.

MONDAY
31st of December, 2018
'What are UAP?'

O ver 2018, I managed to look into the biggest cases and the most credible aspects of the UFO/UAP issue whilst delving back through some of the massive amounts of literature. Admittedly, taking into consideration 70 years of history in a way which condensed the data into a single book format was not enough. There was simply no way to incorporate everything that has happened and certainly no way to then appropriately conclude as to the origin with the data. And then I must consider that the UAPdata available is in no way accurate enough to draw conclusions to a satisfactory level. I would have loved to look in-depth at the nuclear aspect to the Rendlesham Forrest case (1980) or the Belgium flying triangle wave of the 1990s. Then there is Cash-Landrum (1980), the crash retrieval cases of Trinity- New Mexico (1945), Aurora-Texas (1897), Kecksburg – Pennsylvania (1965) or Height 611 – Soviet Union (1986). All important pieces of the puzzle.

Other questions pertain to the nature of the phenomenon which I haven't been able to answer satisfactory: why for example, has the frequency and *physical* dynamic of various reported shaped vehicles seemingly changed over the decades? Why were 'Mysterious Airships' seen in the late 19th century then 'Foo-Fighter' spheres of light reported in World War 2, then 'Flying Discs' in the 1940s and 50s, 'Triangles' in the 1960s onwards?

Where did they all go to when the respected waves needed?

Why are there so many different reported objects of size, colour and shape? And most importantly, why (with respect to a few outliers) did the previous format of wave vehicles, reduce in frequency in place of other strange craft?

The sheer volume of different reported anomalous vehicles is staggering. It's not that we have one type of 'Flying Disc' or 'Triangle', we have hundreds of variations of each type within that framework. Yes, much of this can surely be attributed to misidentification by witnesses, memory can be faulty, individual projection and interviewer bias undoubtedly play a part. However, the witness descriptions often detail very specific vehicles that are backed up by multiple witnesses to the event. The result of this, is that we are dealing with either multiple variations of UAP objects that are traveling here from somewhere else, maybe they are hiding in the oceans, or we are dealing with a something more complex that can trans-morph itself into anything it wishes, which might explain the change of craft type, decade on decade and the slight variations in description.

But we don't know that.

To say the phenomenon is extra-terrestrial is mainly based on the premise that the displayed technology is not human made. We simply didn't have human made 'Flying Discs' in the 1940s, we don't have them today in our defence capabilities, at least not ones that can display the five AATIP observables. We didn't have 'mile wide' sized triangles like that which silently hoovered over Arizona in 1997. We don't have 'Foo-Fighters' or 40ft long white 'Tic-Tacs' that can drop down from space or shoot across the horizon in a split second. For this isn't a technology that applies to the laws of physics as we understand them, this is a technology that is radically extreme as it was in the 1940s through every reported decade to the current day reports of Navy fighter pilots. We don't even know that this is a 'technology', they could be living entities we don't understand.

This is potentially, something else entirely.

However, with this in mind, to state *conclusively* that UAP are extra-terrestrial (or anything else) is false. It is false because we don't have the data to confirm this, at least not in the public sector. We don't have radar sensory data that tracks the upper/lower atmosphere, we don't have satellite data which shows objects leaving Earth's atmosphere and heading for deep space and most importantly we don't have open access to bodies and crashed material (if there are any). Then there is the question of how do you track them beyond our own solar system? But this is not to say that UFOs/UAPs aren't human, from what I have learned these past few years that is a very real possibility.

The concept of something 'Inter-dimensional' or ultra-terrestrial must also be taken into consideration as part of the origin thesis. The strange religious Marian apparitions hold similarities to the 'High Strangeness' of UAP cases, but are in themselves separate instances, and proof of a solid link almost impossible.

The activity at Skinwalker Ranch and other places suggest we are looking at a strange assortment of paranormal incidents that may be the result of *portals*. As far-fetched as such an idea might be to people, we must consider that certain conditions at the quantum level as a result of Earth's magnetic field and nuclear effects might be creating the conditions. Would that explain what is happening? Does that explain why a dense concentration of various anomalous objects alongside weird crypto-terrestrial figures and non-sensical events are occurring in certain geographical areas of the world.

We simply don't know.

Again, we are left without hard data, empirical research isn't available to be peer reviewed. Instead, we have questions that might be relevant but ultimately redundant.

And then what about human consciousness and UAP?

Why does the phenomenon hide on the edge of our conscious reality? Why don't the hundreds and thousands of different phenomena reported around the world simply get caught wondering into a shopping mall, or hovering above a football stadium for a day, or why don't they land on the White House lawn? Why do they make *contact* in remote areas? Why does it engage people late at night or in the dusty old attic or basement? Why do they crash in the desert? Why have UAP become strongly attached to the nuclear activity? Why are there so many reports of UAP engaging nuclear strike groups and nuclear facilities?

If the anomalous have been here throughout history as ultra-terrestrials, then why do they change their appearance? If we are to understand the phenomenon as we would understand ourselves, we would imply that *they* are doing this for their own benefit. Our relationship with the phenomenon must be symbiotic, otherwise, they would not put on a show for us, essentially, they have something to gain from us. However, this brings us back to the question of them, what needs do they have for self-actualisation?

There is so much of this that doesn't make any logical sense. And maybe that's the point. Possibly, it doesn't make sense because it something that can't be explained by human intelligence and cognitive thinking right now. Perhaps an 'alien' consciousness that comes into our dimension/reality/consciousness and is fragmented. It doesn't even know what it is because it is not conscious as we understand consciousness. What if UAP are a blank clean slate without input, without intention or behaviour, and what if it is something truly anomalous that has complete control over the quantum level? Maybe, it arranges itself physically at the atomic level to represent whatever the laws of our universe require of it. Maybe it moulds itself, it bends itself, it trans-morphs and becomes what it is exposed to, using the atomic makeup of this world to do so. What if it draws from human subconsciousness and becomes the aliens and 'Flying Saucers' because it is imprinted upon? It's what it thinks we expect it to be, it mirrors us, presents us with a reality we can understand, that makes sense to us.

But why?

Why is it important that it makes sense to us? What does '*it*' care whether we humans understand it or more to the point, accept it and believe in it? What is so important about having us humans accept UAP? And whilst we are at it, what is the significance of the phenomena and its interest in humans accepting a collective objective reality?

Are they us?

I just don't know the answers. I also don't see how it matters. We can theorise and project our thoughts, but when all is done, we are still human, and we are still subjectively imprinting what we believe based upon our own needs and wishes. We are filling in the blanks, we are filling in the missing data with subjective realty, and the phenomenon is responding to us as we do so.

We are linked. We just don't understand why.

Anomalous Theoretical Implications: Origin of Species

The sheer complexity of Unidentified Aerial Phenomena (UAP) is undeniable. It is almost impossible to conclusively determine the origin of UAP right now in the year 2018. As stressed throughout this book as a major theme, we have poorly sourced data which is the biggest hindering factor to understanding UAPinfo in a way which can be appropriately concluded upon. Personally, my year of investigation throughout 2018 had left me with various potential hypothetical considerations, however this all that they are, hypothetical considerations. Yes, I was fortunate to speak to various individuals (Scientists, Directors, Researchers, Ufologists) who would be in a position to know what possibilities might account for what is being reported, but my conclusions are that there are no conclusive answers. The biggest, most significant problem is that despite 70 years' worth of data within Ufology, the data is essentially meaningless by official scientific practices. How can we infer that an event is *anomalous* when no official body of investigation has concluded it as such? How then can we incorporate that specific case and its data set into official research when we haven't even officially verified the dynamics of the case?

The truth is we can't, and this is the heart of the UFO/UAP problem.

It is because the governments of the world have acted negligently to this issue that we are left in the dark. Their collective apathy to such a serious issue has meant that from the closure of Project Bluebook in 1969, 50 years' worth of data has been lost. Civilian and military encounters were still unofficially reported in these decades, and some really interesting cases have been documented within Ufology, however, ultimately this is unverifiable data. Lost data. Data we cannot use beyond gaining a limited sense of misunderstandings and placed into inaccurate platforms. But that is not to say Ufology hasn't done its best with what it has, an amateur field that by enlarge has showed the phenomena is prevalent in our skies, and seemingly displays a radical technology akin to AATIP's five observables. And it is through Ufology research and data collection that we can make crude estimations, hypothetical implications as to the origin of UAPs.

1) *Extra-terrestrials*

Extra-terrestrials would be classified as non-human, intelligent beings or craft, travelling to Earth from another planet, potentially from somewhere in another solar system using a technology that isn't linear thrust propulsion and primarily based on chemical reactionary rockets. At least, if they are coming here from there, then they (who or whatever they are) are much more advanced than we are in the 21st century.

Currently, extra-terrestrials are the front runner in this UAP race.

But the question is, *are*, these anomalous vehicles really from another planet? Is it really that simple? Or is the UAP issue much more complex? To have a better understanding of the extra-terrestrial concept, we must travel back and wade, feet first, through the murky, credulity swamp that is main-stream Ufology. An almost impossible place to navigate, where the real treasures are buried deep beneath the mud and thick wet soil, a place where you are much more likely to become bogged down and sink than to come away with the answers of a lifetime. However, the truth is out there, buried beneath.

Most notably, within Ufology, the earliest commonly known definition of UAP and UFOs was attributed to the wave of 'Flying Saucers/Discs'. These potential anomalous vehicles are notoriously considered to be associated with the Holly-wood depictions of 'little grey men.' It is these semi-fictional life forms that are alleged to be engaging humanity in a cov-ert capacity. They are ash-grey in skin colour, have big heads, large black almond eyes, standing at only 4ft tall and they are said to have telepathic abilities. These 'bugs' come for you in your nightmares, occasionally abduct you and experiment upon you. They are allegedly a hive mind of advanced artificial intelligence.

The 'Greys' have a long association with Ufology stories going back as far as Roswell in 1947, and then beyond. They are often noted as being part of the much contentious and stigmatised abduction phenomena. Some cases (Bob Lazar, Betty and Barney Hill) have indicated the *Greys* made claims that they come from the Zeta Reticular star system. These stories are fantastic and should be highly scrutinised, we must question the validity of such claims on a case-by-case basis without losing our objectivity, whilst still not dismissing them completely. Doesn't mean they are lying, but we should still consider all options.

Data is still data.

Another problem is that these claims are incredibly difficult to validate, particularly without access to the original source, and by that, I mean we don't have anything to study, no 'Extra-terrestrial Biological Entity' (EBE) to cross examine, question or to put on a lie detector machine.

And then we also have the problem - that even if the EBE 'Grey Alien' was indeed actually real, and genuinely telling the experiencer or government personnel, etc, they are from another planet, can we actually trust what we are being told?

Would they lie to us?

Even *if* the Greys are real, and flying around in anti-gravity discs, and then abducting humans under certain circumstances – can we trust if they are being truthful with us?

What if they are projecting what humans expect to be told for some unknown obscure reason?

Again, we simply cannot trust the data as verified facts for many differing reasons. You might understand why the scientific community has stood-off such claims for 70 years.

For me, we need to thoroughly strip back our assumptions about UAP being extra-terrestrials. Until we have access to extensive radar data which spans out into deep space and tracks potential UAP-spacecraft entering Earth's atmosphere, extra-terrestrials therefore cannot be ruled out as a possible explanation for UAP/UFOs, otherwise, how can we confirm they are from someplace else in the solar system or galaxy. The evidence is circumstantial.

I hold judgment about the reality of the 'Grey Alien', and although the consensus in mainstream Ufology is that there are dead creatures taken from crashed UAP retrieval operations that span back to the 1940s, I am reluctant to conclusively accept this as fact without further data or the acknowledgement of government.

***

Another issue I found with the extra-terrestrial hypothesis, and a very important question that should be asked is, '*why don't astronomers see UAP in space*'?

After all, astronomers and astrophysicists can track and scientifically observe celestial bodies as they enter our solar system. Take the much publicised 'Oumuamua' (3) we discussed earlier, the unidentified object that passed through our solar system in 2017 - becoming the subject of much *safe* scientific debate due to its slightly unusual dynamics. This interstellar object was tracked as it came into our solar system and did a 'drive-by'.

Consider the scrutiny this was given as it was tracked closely.

My question is, '*where are all the astronomer reports of extra-terrestrial-UAP as they travel back or forward through our solar-system*'?

Consider, for the hundreds and thousands of NUFORC and MUFON annually reported cases worldwide, we don't see the equivalent reporting from astronomers and various space surveying organisations. If there really were all these objects consistently visiting Earth, the UAP leaving and entering Earth's orbit would fill the skies and thus be tracked by our scientists doing all these amazing technological feats. But we don't see that.

The numbers don't add up.

To answer this, we can assume that the UAP reports made within MUFON aren't genuinely anomalous, and are misidentified terrestrial objects, thus reducing the amount of exposure for observations in Earth's orbit by astronomers. Or, as some have theorised, maybe the UAP are there in numbers but there is a *conspiracy* by NASA, the European Space Agency and the extensive civilian world surveillance system companies. This seems unlikely, even though there are some interesting occasions where NASA have cut the feed to the space station cameras as *something* appears in orbit. However, these could have been ice particles, satellites, space dust or space debris – we simply can't conclude and certainly don't know why the feed was cut, if intentionally at all. To me, it seems highly unlikely that scientists would all be in on the 'cover-up.'

What other alternatives might explain this problem? Well, another alternative, is that all the hundreds and thousands of UAP reported objects are accurate and indeed anomalous, however they are mistakenly recorded by astronomers, scientists, etc, as meteorological phenomena, space junk, satellites, the space station and/or classified military technology (Space Force vehicles). However, that would also mean that such professionals couldn't appropriately track or identify something unusual in the night skies, and this would have had to have occurred multiple times. Let's consider the 1997 Phoenix Lights triangle craft or Stephenville 2008 case (4) in which multiple reports stated that the object(s) in question was over a *mile wide* - how does that massive vehicle go untracked by the world's military and civilian scientists as it *enters* and *leaves* Earth's atmosphere? Also, keep in mind that we were able to track the Hale-Bopp comet months in advance of it entering our solar system.

You might argue the military would keep radar data and satellite data classified/quiet, and certainly not run to the press. I fail to believe that the quantity of UAP within Earth's atmosphere wouldn't also be seen by civilian astronomers and hobbyists as they hypothetically travel outside of Earth's atmosphere.

One more logical hypothesis is based around the assumption of UAP technology itself. Should UAP be extra-terrestrial, it would mean that *they* aren't using rocket propulsion technology, it would mean that they are using a form of advanced physics that we don't understand. Potentially, it might also mean that this UAP propulsion technology is so *quick* and undetectable that they are evading tracking? Maybe they use another form of alternative *dimensional* travel that means we don't see them on our deep space radar or via satellites, or by the world's most sophisticated planetariums and observatories as they enter and leave for deep space.

***

From a psychological intention perspective, the question of *why* they haven't landed on the White House lawn remains a big question in answering this contradictory UAP mystery. Firstly, you might argue they haven't openly landed because the extra-terrestrials are our enemy, they have intentions of hostility toward humans. That might include a covert operation, using stealthy tactics in some probing mission that we have no idea about. Possibly, the UAP vehicles that we are seeing are scout ships, sent to scope out and map Earth prior to either an invasion or annihilation process. Secondly, we must consider they are here to make peaceful contact with us at the right time, and their intentions towards us are protective in the same way we protect certain vulnerable lesser creatures here on Earth. The 'prime directive' from Star Trek comes to mind.

Potentially, you might explain this constant observation behaviour as part of a 'Zoo Hypothesis', that *they* are keeping us in check, monitoring our technological, spiritual and biological development, ensuring we don't annihilate the planet with our nuclear weapons - which might explain why they turned up in numbers after the first atomic detonation in July 1945.

Possibly, the extra-terrestrials may have some unknown bases on the moon or within the oceans, some type of outpost they can check in and out from. Again, this ventures into some hard conspiracies. Any such extra-terrestrial base would have been detected by the world's militaries long ago (and then kept secret).

Additionally, however, if they were like us, and had come here in exploration and peace, they would potentially have landed and made contact, openly talked to us and said to us what we need to be doing about nuclear proliferation or climate change. At least, that's a very human expectation of what we think they would do, providing that we didn't view our hosts as a threat.

But then, is that true?

Maybe we, as exploring humans (as the extra-terrestrials) would step back from our unwitting hosts in the same way we do on an African safari, or with a lost indigenous tribe, maybe we know that our direct exposure would completely change them, and their way of life. Would we want to leave them alone?

When the Europeans and Conquistadors landed in South America in the 16th century, it was the viral infections which wiped out the native Aztec and Inca people, for which they had no immune defence. Should there be biological entities piloting UAP vehicles, what advanced bacteria and diseases do they carry? If any? What devastating impact might such infectious viruses do to our race of primitive humans in the 21st century.

Consequently, this brings up a whole range of questions.

Should UAP be of extra-terrestrial origin, how would they consider us? Maybe not as intelligent creatures, but a biological specimen limited by understanding and imagination. Maybe they are simply apathetic to us. After all, despite us being intelligently more advanced than an ant, we might not even be considered any more advanced to the extra-terrestrials who might be millions or billions of years more advanced. What could we possibly offer them?

We can ask, what else might explain the strange elusive behaviour of the UAP?

***

Historically, extra-terrestrials are the most thought of explanation for 'UFOs.' Consequently, the ideology of 'aliens' within Western society has become unfortunately stigmatised in a way which prevents serious conversation. Scientists have become so intoxicated by the negative connotations of extra-terrestrials being here on Earth as UFOs, that the topic is ridiculed very quickly. Additionally, we at the UAPMedia team have found that a certain astronomy demographic within a well-known organisation that searches for intelligent life has become almost religious in its dismissal of anything to do with the anomalous phenomena. Then there is the question of reputations and funding, '*if*' it comes to light that UAP are a form of extra-terrestrial intelligence, it would mean an incredible humiliation for the scientific community who received millions and millions in their research whilst the field of 'Ufology' was left to fester and decay under the influence of hoaxes, conmen and well-meaning semi-professional researchers. And then, there is the extremely subjective shock-factor involved with the extra-terrestrial hypothesis that has proved to be grounds for completely dismissing the phenomena, aka, '*it can't be, therefore it isn't*'. Such a shock factor hasn't been helped by the mainstream.

After 70 + years of the mainstream media and Hollywood exploiting extra-terrestrials as the evil unknown that wants to annihilate and eat the human race, we are left with a form of negative conditioning that has created the conditions for psychological barriers. Barriers which impact rational thought and logical decision making on such an important issue. The extra-terrestrial hypothesis for explaining Unidentified Anomalous Phenomenon has for too long been significantly tainted by factors unrelated to appropriate scientific methodology. The will to believe and disbelieve has clouded research to the point it becomes meaningless. Researcher bias has resulted in critical errors and flaws within mainstream Ufology that includes both 'believers' and 'debunkers'.

Ufology of course is a problem. Extra-terrestrials are rife across 'trash-TV', too easy to accept and dismiss, too easy to project one's own wishes and needs onto, too easy to maintain a paradigm of ridicule and stereotypes. And most importantly, it's too easy to assume UFOs are extra-terrestrials without scientific evidence. From the understanding of humans in the 1940s, the extra-terrestrial hypothesis makes sense from the perspective of those understanding UFOs at that time. H.G. Wells had populated the early 20th century with the idea that 'men from Mars' had come to destroy us in their metallic machines. Fiction and facts intertwined in the quantum collective conscious mind of humans.

Although the planetary origin of UAP changed with time and increased knowledge, the basic concept of UAP origin remained. Even today, most mainstream people who haven't researched the topic believe that if UFOs/UAP are real, then they must be aliens coming from another planet. Additionally, the extra-terrestrial hypothesis is still the most quoted ideology throughout mainstream Ufology, from Steven Greer to Stephen Bassett. They possibly might be right; however, we can't say that with any confidence right now, even with the acknowledgment that anomalous technology is real and possibly non-human.

Then there is the consideration that UAP aren't extraterrestrials at all, that they are originating from someplace else, inner Earth, the oceans, Antarctica or even some other form of dimensional existence or another universe. The possibilities are endless and need scientific investigation.

However, this is an unfortunate pre-conclusion that doesn't have all the information to hand. Essentially, we do not have the radar data which would show where these UAP are coming from and where they go to once the encounters have been reported. For the extra-terrestrial hypothesis to be a consideration, we need to see UAP tracked from deep space as it enters our solar system and then into our atmosphere. Even then, how do we check the craft/beings are specifically from another planet? Do we check their passports? Do we believe them at their word that they are from Zeta-Reticulum? For me, the 'ETH' is too simplistic to explain all of the phenomena.

Again, possibly some are craft from another planet, but I reserve judgement at this point. We will still need to seriously consider the extra-terrestrial hypothesis until we can rule it out, but it comes down to data. Data which we don't have right now.

2) *Multi-Verse / Many Worlds theory*

Possibly, UAP are multiple phenomena that are coming from multiple universes and multiple worlds, maybe even multiple versions of our own planet Earth from different time periods and alternate timelines. (This doesn't mean from 'another dimension', this is alternative timelines and versions of our 3-D world).

If we consider the 'Many Worlds' theory of quantum mechanics, we might be able to apply a the 'Torero' algorithm framework for such concepts. This might explain why we see so many different shapes and sizes being reported. Take the traditional 'Flying Disc' for example, there are hundreds and hundreds of different reported variations over the past 70 years from various countries, most prominently was the United States waves in 1947 and 1952. Potentially, we can say that human memory for specific detail isn't always the best source of determining what occurred, and that the variations are a result of human interpretations and faulty memory reporting. However, in a lot of cases, the reports are of extremely (unmistakably) different 'Flying Disc' shapes taken from multiple witnesses. Different colours and sizes are reported across cases, some have been reported to be as large as a football field, whilst others are only 8-10 feet across. Initially, the first reported case came from pilot Kenneth Arnold, who stated he saw 9 *'crescent shaped'* objects that moved like saucers skipping over the water - not that they looked like the 'Flying Saucers' - that we are accustomed to seeing in science fiction and historical UFO reports. Poor debunking explanations often show this as 'proof' that the change of UAP shape is simply down to human error through cultural hysteria. Hence, they fail to explore any other possibilities.

Consequently, the vast difference in the appearance of multiple UAP objects can be explained by a *'Multi-Verse'* or *'Many Worlds'* hypothesis.

Can the 'Multi-Verse' hypothesis also explain the 'High-Strangeness' cases that occur on locations such as the Skinwalker Ranch or even explain religious encounters such as the religious Marian apparition cases?

Should different phenomena be entering our reality and populating a specific geographic area from an infinite possible universes and worlds with endless timelines, we then *might* understand why we are seeing such a variation of 'paranormal' occurrences, creatures and differing vehicles.

An issue with such a theory is that if this was true, and all these different phenomena were entering our world via 'portals' or 'wormholes', we would expect to see more independent, varied UAP behaviour, separate from human imprinting and expectations.

We might expect that hundreds of differing, separate entities and craft would act.... *significantly different,* and not follow the standard semi-covert operating manual that UAP have displayed for the past 70 years consistently.

We might expect some of the phenomena to land in a shopping mall or on a football field and maybe start shooting people with a laser gun (like in the film Mars Attacks) or blow us up (like in the film Independence Day), maybe some variation of species would overtly try to melt us in the streets. We might expect some of the 'good aliens' to forcefully take all our nuclear weapons from us and start a new religion.

We might expect to see something we have never seen before as humans, or some creature or shape or colour variation we have never even considered.

But we don't see that. In all the bizarre historical reports shown by Keel, Vallee and others, the craft and 'aliens' present in a way which we understand on some level.

We see clunky metallic variations of what we already imagine to exist, we see a mismatch of Earthly molecules, clumped together to present something almost human. We see shaped vehicles that we recognise, made from materials we would expect. We see creatures that make sense to us (even if they are an evolutionary conceptual idea of the future).

The whole UAP phenomena is a physically manifested assortment of human cultural, psycho-social reality, taken from a specific historical timeframe.

***

The psychological behaviour of the *'phenomena'* is mostly constant at baseline. They are semi-covertly indifferent to us, for the most part, they stand off us, *observing* mostly. They are hiding on the edge of our consciousness, and when they do expose themselves to us, it's almost as though our every encounter together is the very first time they have ever come across us. When the contact cases with humans occur historically, they are non-sensical with weird confusing information mixed with half-truths. We see a wide range of 'alien' type beings claiming to be from various planets, even Mars and Venus (not true in this reality), which seemed plausible in the 1950s when we didn't know Mars and Venus had no life.

The UAP vehicles themselves act like tentative probes, the same way us humans would do upon finding a new species on a foreign planet for the first time. And they do it repetitively, consistently and meticulously. Essentially, they act like we would expect 'alien probes' to act like, constantly exploring and scanning, trying to gather information prior to whatever they decide comes next. But whatever comes next, never comes.

This is what the psychology seems to tell us - that they don't learn, they don't change widespread behavioural patterns within interactions, as if they are restricted to task, bound by rules of engagement. They are always just out of reach. Which after 70 years of exposure, doesn't make much sense to us as humans, almost as if they exist in both our jumbled dream-state subconscious and our physical reality simultaneously.

However, if they were from our chaotic subconscious, would we not see some weird 'Flying Spaghetti Monster' type creature or some other abstract shape that we cannot even comprehend? But we don't, UAP research tells us we see structured simple geometric shapes over and over;

Triangles,
Cubes,
Ovals,
Discs,
Pyramids,
Spheres,
Cuboids,
Octahedrons,
Translucent shapes.

All reported to perform the AATIP five observables. What does that then tell us?

To me it tells us there is a primal link between them and us, or within this 3D reality/universe at least. *Something* decided that the shapes, we see reported by the military, are the way they appear to be. Something conceptualised them, designed them and made them with whatever they are made from.

Are they created on some factory on another planet, in some other solar system? If so, why make so many different variations of the same types of craft? How, when, where and why are important questions.

Maybe we are seeing multiple species?

The data from UFO waves such as 1947 and 1952 for example tell us a story. *They* have a limited window of exposure and engagement with us. *They* show no interest in allowing us to view them long enough to accept their presence or to get an understanding of them. It almost feels as though they either don't want to…*or*…that they *can't* be here in our reality, for whatever reason. This would make sense if it was a few 'Flying Disc' type of craft, or a 'Foo-Fighters' or the 'Triangles', but this behaviour is displayed by all of the phenomena. And this is the main problem for the 'Many Worlds' hypothesis.

We should consider the 'Many Worlds' concept for UAP, but more understanding is needed of how and why their behaviours are so in synch. Arguably, the thousands of potentially different beings and vehicles would act and look significantly different, far beyond what has been reported. We need to find a way to explain this issue.

3)   *Inter-Dimensional*

Potentially, under the 'Inter/Extra- dimensional' concept, UAP can possibly be *one* singular phenomenon (intelligence) coming from a place that has higher dimensional qualities we simply cannot comprehend in our own 3D reality. Or possibly, multiple UAP can be coming from multiple dimensions.

Coming from another dimension, in theory, is not akin to saying something is coming from another place like with the extra-terrestrial hypothesis or even to some degree, the 'Multi-Verse' hypothesis – both of which must have grounds within a three-dimensional reality, aka, our universe or variations of it.

Hypothetically, coming from another higher dimension is coming from a concept that we don't have words or thoughts for, it might be timeless, without boundaries, without defined shapes, or even inclusive of experiences that have no meaning to us, much like an ant has no understanding of a television as it walks across it. Possibly, some higher dimensions might be something that human consciousness cannot even exist in or understand in this reality.

Basically, we consider entities coming from such places (of places is even the right terminology), could be intelligences unrecognisable to us in their true form, which also spans to their intelligence and psychology. However, if the anomalous phenomena are *here*, then we as humans must comprehend them in some way.

The theory by Keel and Vallee back in the early 70s was that UFOs/UAP were coming from another spatial dimension, that this alien consciousness was entering our world and taking the form of whatever, it wished for its own agenda. There is scope for understanding the phenomena from an 'Inter-dimensional' quality, however we should be careful not to assign such an origin of UAP on the basis that we simply do not fully understand the *dimensions* of a higher-dimension.

Most commonly, it is understood in popular culture that another dimension would be very similar to our own reality, but with only cosmetic differences, often science fiction infers that coming from another dimension is coming from an alternative Earthly timeline. We can point to overlay and misconceptions between the hypothetical considerations of the 'Multi-Verse' theory, these are two different theories, and two differing concepts of UAP origin.

As with the 'Multi-Verse/Many Worlds' theory, the 'Inter-Dimensional' theory again could explain the high-strangeness/paranormal phenomena associated with UAP cases. Additionally, this theory might also explain the reported psychology of the anomalous phenomena, *'should'*, they be directly *imprinting* consciousness from humans (rather than playing out an 'evil or good' agenda).

As the 'interjection theory' stimulates – the anomalous' intentions, behaviours and appearance are the result of human quantum subconsciousness.

The monsters of our own making.

4) *Ultra-Terrestrials*

Since 2017, the John Keel ultra-terrestrial hypothesis has become increasingly popular. Unidentified Anomalous Phenomenon *could* be ultra-terrestrials - some intelligent life form that have been here longer than humans, hidden from deep within inner Earth or within the oceans. They have been here long before us, probably long after us also the way we are going.

Possibly such intelligent entities have higher/inter-dimensional qualities, existing around us on another plane of consciousness. Maybe they are beings, life forms that have developed and become so beyond us, that their technology is hyper-advanced. They are the Gods of the ancient Greek world, protecting their anonymity from us by intention or lack of intention, manipulating human history, present and future. Leading us down certain paths with minor guidance.

Whoever or whatever they are, might be interested in our spiritual development, guiding us forward through the perils of a nuclear Holocaust. Or possibly not, maybe they are looking to ensure the best DNA samples emerge from consistent wars, or that genetic manipulation ensures we are primed for their benefit. Whatever that might be. But this is all speculation and devoid of hard data we can use in the media. We are guessing.

What do we know to bolster the ultra-terrestrial hypothesis?

We know that 'Unidentified Submerged Objects' (USOs), are UAP that are witnessed to have a strong association to large bodies of water, however little is known of USOs in relation to UFOs. Some theories say the USOs derive energy from the high radioactive particles in the ocean, others state that *they* are hiding from us humans down there. We simply don't know the psychology of the anomalous phenomena.

Some have argued that USOs are based somewhere in

the vast oceans that lead down into deep trenches that allow access to inner Earth. However, we have no concrete evidence to support this claim, and again, we don't have access to radar data that specifically states where these objects come from and go to. Currently, we don't have enough data to conclude on this hypothesis.

5) *Consciousness*

Consciousness and the UAP reality are unbelievably complex, particularly with regard to what is reported by the witnesses of such encounters that extended to associated UAP activities. Most sceptics will correctly point to the fallacy of the human mind as a device of recording information, faulty memories which reduce in accuracy over time. When a vast array of differing shaped UAP is reported (thousands of variations since 1942 and beyond), we automatically suggest this is human error within their reporting. And this is without doubt an important point to remember, again, highlighting the much-discussed data collection/verification problem with UAP research. The conscious mind is fallible to misinterpreting visual information, particularly at long distances, we deploy 'scotomisation' – which is the psychological tendency to block out harmful unwanted concepts. Essentially, people see what they want to see. Humans see what makes sense to us, what reduces anxiety.

Reality must flow smoothly.

Additionally, we may face a bigger problem than data verification when we assume that, for the most part, the witnesses are telling the complete truth in what they are seeing. Should we assume that witnesses are reporting accurately, thousands and thousands of various shaped craft across the 20th and 21st centuries, we must then face a very difficult examination of how human consciousness might be impacting upon the physical appearance and behaviour of such phenomena.

How can we see what we expect to see (scotomisation), and then for the phenomena to adopt that human interpretation and amend its own appearance to fit what we expect to see?

One might argue that the anomalous exhibit an unknown *inter-dimensional* quality. Essentially, we might argue such versions of the UAP cannot be both a physically formed vehicle from another world, multi-verse, or extra-terrestrial from another planet, or from another physical place in existence, and instead are a product of a *place* that words and thought cannot even describe.

The argument would be that UAP are under intelligent control, but do not have consciousness in the way that human beings display consciousness. Under the much debated 'Interjection theory', the anomalous phenomena have no self-awareness or intentions beyond those which humans attribute to them on the subconscious level through mirroring and imprinting.

This ideology builds on Jacques Vallee, John Keel and Gustav Jung, it proposes that the anomalous phenomenon creates the advanced technologies such as 'Flying Saucers,' 'Foo-Fighters,' 'Mysterious Airships,' and 'Tic-Tacs,' from the individual and collective societal quantum subconscious expectations of human beings. This theory might explain why the phenomenon changes constantly, person to person, year upon year, decade upon decade and wave after wave.

Could this explain the multiple phenomena variations, as they align with the variation possibilities within the millions of human minds that have existed?

Arguably, the anomalous phenomenon changes because humans change, *they* feed back to us what we expect/need, sometimes acting as a control measure for nuclear weapons or religious movements, other times intervening on individual persons with outrageous behaviours, actions, characteristics because they are being directly imprinted upon, and feeding back to us what our subconscious expects. Our collect-ive mind might use the anomalous to ensure our evolution and survival.

Again, we have no solid evidence for this. We can impose the same questions of why the phenomena behaves similarly across timeframes, cultures and appearance? Human subconscious imprinting would provide a huge deviation in anomalous psychological behaviours, and for example, the UAP would land, and stay landed in some cases – which never happens. There are big problems when associating human consciousness to the UAP origins.

We have stories of Marian apparitions, weird people in advanced airships, stories of alien encounters, all of which may be true, but meaningless. I say *meaningless* because we cannot verify the encounters with a degree of confidence, and we can't verify any correlation between these multiple phe-nomena, at least not with any degree of confidence. We are left scurrying in the dark for a match, but the truth is we might not obtain credibly sourced and accepted data for years and dec-ades. Only then can we fully assess the situation appropriately.

The other concept is that *they* are an unknown and poorly understood makeup of our collectively projected human psyche. Maybe we struggle to define them, just as we struggle to define ourselves through our consciousness. We are at the very beginnings of physics being able to define the con-cept of consciousness – as initially proposed by the Penrose-Hameroff model in 1998 (5). And yet twenty years later, we still don't have a good grasp, we are still not yet able to measure the behaviour of quantum fractals in the brain for example – if they exist at all (6).

Maybe, this shared human experienced reality isn't what we believe it to be, that it can be influenced by our col-lective subconscious, that subjective reality impact's objective reality. That the very fabric of reality is entangled within our own perceptions.

6) *Quantum Anomalous Nexus*

Can we consider that the anomalous are a quantum anomaly, a 'life form' or form of life that exists intelligently within the vacuum, but not as an intelligence we understand? Simply put, they may be a part of the natural quantum world, just something we have yet to fully detect, much the same way sailors couldn't identify the giant squid for centuries.

Possibly they are indigenous to this planet, possibly not, possibly existing in the quantum world that we little understand. Possibly in a state of superposition, awaiting human consciousness to project, manifest and feed, morph and then swarm in numbers, attracting to radioactivity like moths to a flame.

Create the right quantum conditions, and they will come. Feeding on unknown energies.

Maybe it is a phenomenon that has been here forever and exists within various dimensional spectrums. Potentially, we might need to look at *'frequency and duality theory,'* and maybe various historical timelines are existing at one moment in the same location. Places such as Skinwalker Ranch might be more correlated to such quantum conditions?

Possibly the anomalous exist within areas where there is an abundance of radioactive signatures, the ocean (7), the stratosphere (8), which would explain the UAP interest in nuclear facilities. Even the human body holds a limited amount of radioactivity (9). Possibly the phenomena are in a state of superposition, that it is reliant on human consciousness. Quantum entanglement is hypothetically deployed in UAP cases when it mirrors behaviour and reacts to systems completely separate and without any obvious correlation. What are we in this reality, if not a collection of atomic layering and susceptible to such conditions?

The problem is that we are guessing and can only pose questions right now.

* * *

<u>Conclusions of Origin</u>

After a full year of researching the anomalous phenomena, my conclusion, as best I could imply at that moment in late 2018, was one of apprehension. Then, like today at the time of writing, we still cannot state what the UAP/UFO is or where it is from, primarily due to a lack of radar data that tracks origin - we should not conclude on limited data. If you were to ask me what my best guess would be, I would say we are dealing with a phenomena (plural), with multiple sources of origin - but even that comes with contradictions.

Potentially, the phenomena are all of what we have discussed, maybe it is made up of extra-terrestrials and ultra-terrestrials, all coming from another universe or another world, galaxy or dimension across varying timelines.

What I would hypotheses, is that the anomalous is a multitude of possibilities and crossovers from;

1) Extra-Terrestrials
2) Multi-Verse
3) Inter-Dimensional
4) Ultra-Terrestrials
5) Consciousness
6) Quantum Anomalous Nexus

We need to be careful not to adopt a binary position to UAP origin and consider that multiple things might be happening at the same time. Just because UAP could be coming from deep space doesn't mean that *all* UAP are extra-terrestrials. Additionally, just because some UAP are coming from the oceans doesn't mean that all UAP are all ultra-terrestrials. We must accept that there are overlapping phenomena with varying origins.

We simply do not know, and it is here that we find ourselves we at the very beginning of the exciting adventure into the unknown that will involve multiple disciplines, most of which we haven't even considered yet.

But to get there we need to force the governments of the world to accept and acknowledge the anomalous, we need them to tell the people that it is ok to investigate this seriously.

Until we somehow encourage this new paradigm of accountability from government, we will continue to suffer from bad data, incomplete data from us amateurs within Ufology.

I don't mean to be harsh to the entire Ufology field, some are excellent researchers and some great sceptical minds, however most are not. Ufology is a platform which drowns out the credible signal that is hidden away within conspiracy, that turns away mainstream scientific inquiry and professional mainstream coverage.

Ultimately, we are limited by our place in time, limited by our understanding and lack of data, limited by the refusal to accept and acknowledge the phenomena. People fear what UAP might mean for us as a species on this Earth and therefore instead of applying logic, we apply the psychology of deflection and distraction.

However, I am cautiously optimistic, and I'm hopeful that the restraints of our time will be lifted someday and somehow by someone who is a genuine hero. I hope future generations will be free to study this amazing, brilliantly anomalous phenomena and the prosperous technologies that might one day evolve who we are. I hope that you, my two beautiful children, might one day get to research the phenomena openly for the benefit of all living things without fear of reprisal. I hope we can all have an open conversation about *them*.

No matter *where* they come from.

References

(1) NASA. 'Solar system exploration: Oumuamua,'

NASA.
https://solarsystem.nasa.gov/asteroids-comets-and-meteors/
comets/oumuamua/in-depth.amp

(2). Bialy, S. and Loeb, A. (08ᵗʰ of November, 2018). 'COULD
SOLAR RADIATION PRESSURE EXPLAIN 'OUMUAMUA'S PECU-
LIAR ACCELERATION?'
Astrophysical Journal Letters
https://arxiv.org/pdf/1810.11490.pdf

(3). Dorminey, B. (2021). 'Harvard's Avi Loeb Argues That
'Oumuamua' Was Really An Interstellar Alien Probe.'
Forbes.
https://www.forbes.com/sites/brucedorminey/2021/02/11/
harvard-astronomer-views-interstellar-interloper-as-human-
itys-wake-up-call/amp/

(4). Vom Fremd, M. (09ᵗʰ of February, 2009). 'UFO investigators
flock to Stephenville, Texas.'
ABCNews
https://abcnews.go.com/GMA/story?id=4142232&page=1

(5). Hameroff, S. (1998). 'Quantum computation
in brain microtubules? The Penrose–Hameroff
'Orch OR' model of consciousness.'
The Royal Publishing.
https://royalsocietypublishing.org/doi/10.1098/
rsta.1998.0254

(6). Smith, C. (2021). 'Can consciousness be
explained by quantum physics? My research
takes us a step closer to finding out.'
The Conversation.
https://theconversation.com/can-consciousness-be-ex-
plained-by-quantum-physics-my-research-takes-us-a-step-
closer-to-finding-out-164582

(7). Schmidt Ocean Institute. (2019). 'The Ocean is radioactive.'

https://schmidtocean.org/cruise-log-post/the-ocean-is-radio-active/

(8). NASA Science. 'Earth Space. Explore Earth and Space.' https://spaceplace.nasa.gov/stratosphere/en/

(9). HSP. 'Are our bodies radioactive?' https://hps.org/publicinformation/ate/faqs/faqradbods.html

CHAPTER TWENTY-THREE: RECOMMENDATIONS

* * *

The December 2017 revelations of the Advanced Aerospace Threat Identification Program (AATIP) revolutionised Ufology and the research/activism efforts towards UAP. Luis Elizondo, Christopher Mellon and everyone else who never get the credit they deserve (even Tom Delonge and TTSA) for changing how the public sphere understand and appreciate 'Unidentified Aerial Phenomena', (UAP). This was an historic time for the secluded fringe community of 'UFO' types, but also for myself, who somehow became embroiled in the entire saga. Whilst research into UAP is in its professional infancy, we must still be willing to acknowledge the historical cases despite their lack of substantive data that would fully identify the anomalous as something truly unidentifiable.

Conclusions

My research across 2018 sought to answer the question of UAP and more specifically, *what is the nature of the truly anomalous?*

What I found was that the complexity and vast phenomena associated with UAP is impossible to categorise, clarify and successfully evaluate with any confidence. Everything historical, from 'Roswell' to the 'Washington Incursions', 'Foo-Fighters' to civilian based cases such as the 'Phoenix Lights' cannot be taken as 100% credible because, primarily, they were investigated by amateur civilians (with the exception of AAWSAP and Skinwalker Ranch, whose *classified data* is unavailable). This conclusion may upset mainstream Ufology, but the fact remains, we cannot recommend UAP information to the highest peer reviewed research standard without the input of both official government investigations and academic research. This is no different to, for example, the field of clinical neuro-psychology, whose peer reviewed research is provided in official journals and whose findings are taken through White-Papers and intervened upon by government executive/legislative branches. Now consider 'Ufology' in contrast, whose research (as good and well-meaning as they are), are not at the same academic standards. When we refer to 'Ufology', we not only include the poorly un-objective 'believer' syndrome, but also the equally poor 'debunkers', who make similarly unscientific claims of conclusions that simply lack holistic data. As with Ufology believers, the debunkers work backwards from a predetermined conclusion (UAP being extra-terrestrials or not being extra-terrestrials) and apply their methodology in accordance with their own expectations.

From a professional research perspective, this is criminal and needs to change.

It is the fringe of Ufology which is a problem and comes via poorly applied measures from within research. Data and hypothetical considerations should never be stigmatised or ridiculed as fringe, so long as they follow a scientific process. By that thinking, we should not dismiss witness testimony out of hand because the data doesn't fit with one's predetermined narrative. If witness testimony is valid enough to find a person guilty in a court of law, it is also good enough to be considered as part of a holistic UAP case.

Looking to the future

The AATIP and AAWSAP revelations were just the start of a larger plan for the United States government to become more transparent about UAP. That being said, the social stigma and ridicule must be lifted so that the public sphere (academic institutions) can start to research and then be funded by official government initiatives. Ufology needs to disband and drop the unprofessional methodological approach applied by amateur debunkers and avid believers of extra-terrestrials. Essentially, we first need to develop a social media platform which proactively reduces the public's stigma and stereotyping of UAP researchers. This can be done through the introduction of 'UAP Activism' with various initiatives such as UAPinfo that look to deploy a credible form of investigation, free from the 1990's 'X-Files' themed conspiracies.

My recommendation is to support those individuals such as the former Director of the Advanced Aerospace Threat Identification Program (AATIP), Luis Elizondo as he engages government and pushes for UAP transparency.

At that point in 2018, I felt as though UAP research can go no further as no incoming data will ever be good enough. The 'Debunkers' and 'Believers' will go back and forward with endless counter points, nothing will be agreed upon, and ultimately, we cannot use the data to formulate any credible theory of origin.

We need to access the data from a holistic perspective, pushing peer reviewed, professional research to unlock this mystery. We need to overlay graphs and maps of a whole host of historical geographic data such as Uranium mining, Earth's electromagnetic field anomalies, gravitational anomalies and correlate them against UAP reports.

The answer is in that untapped data.

In summary, my conclusions on UAP are that we need more data that can be acknowledged as 'Anomalous' and verified officially by government. Only then can we use that data to formulate a true representation of UAP and what it means for us as humans.

The next step: UAP Activism

Developing a social media platform that has defined UAP-terminology parameters is essential. This allows media organisations and journalists to become involved and hopefully will change the stigmatised paradigm that currently exists around UAP/UFOs. Developing UAP initiatives based around *activism* should now replace most efforts to research. Creating new and engaging ways to advocate the credibility of UAPinfo to young people across social media platforms is also important.

What is badly needed is professional, intelligent, enthusiastic youth who want true change from government and from Ufology itself. The days of the avid believer and pseudo-debunker are coming to an end. Within the next few years, we expect to see more credible researchers and professional institutions start taking the lead on UAP.

We are on the verge of a scientific revolution, but to get there, we need to address the social image of the field, pushing the UAP reality into the political system and reversing the disastrous Condon report conclusions of 1968. We need a complete change of attitude by the scientific community, government, and the *believers* and *debunkers* in Ufology.

And it all starts with asking questions from a fresh perspective which isn't predetermined.

As my wife once said to me, '*you don't know.*'

She was absolutely right.

I don't know.

CHAPTER TWENTY-FOUR: UFOTWITTER ACKNOWLEDGEMENTS

* * *

T here are so many people who I wish to thank that it is impossible to get to everyone. Firstly, my beautiful wife for being the sceptic to my believer. The infamous team of UAPinfo deserve a special mention - Keith, Sven, Danny, Tim, Jason and Christian - who passionately debated and created the early UAP revolution. Without UAPInfo there would be no modern day 'UFOTwitter' or UAP research community. A massive thank you goes to the entire UAP activism and research community team that make up UFOTwitter. UFOTwitter was born from a few random Twitter accounts in October 2017 that wanted to know more about TTSA and the strange things that Tom Delonge was saying. The platform grew from a handful of people to hundreds by the end of 2018, and now we see thousands of differing subcultures within UFOTwitter itself, a platform created to branch away from mainstream Ufology and inject credibility into a new field of UAP research and activism. It wasn't easy. The attacks were hard to take from conspiracy theorists and others who didn't like the idea of Ufology changing. But people held firm and demanded something better from Ufology, a better standard of *believer* and *debunker*. Without the conversations across social media that accompanied the research and activism of those very first people to develop UFOTwitter, we wouldn't have got as far as we have. These were the people who took a risk, dared to be different and challenged the dogmatic scientific community, the mainstream Ufology community and the political system.

These are the researchers, the activists, the pioneers, the young guns, the fanboys, the people who dared to be different. Thank you to everyone who was involved in those early years following the AATIP disclosures. This was all because of you.

Best wishes,

Adam.

* * *

UFOTwitter were:

Akam, Bryce Z, Crew-cut, Julie F, Carl A, James L, TwitterUser J, Jamie K, Baptiste, Jon, Steven O, Jon H, Montana, Mothman2020, Luis E, George K, Garry N, Dan S, Jazz S, Tim Mc, Susan G, Alejandro, Nick, Jay, Michael M, Luis A, Kik P, Chase, Danny, Keith, Sven, Christopher, Tim, Jason, Jamie, Deep, Dreggs, Aida, Mike B, Joyce, Chris W, Paul Re, Ed R, Stephen, Ivan, J-Raza, Lynn M R, Jake, Jerry, Sean Ca, Scott, Christoph, Dan, Dave, Graeme, Andy, Mike (from Germany), Giuliano, Matt M, Kim R, Ryan, Joe, Daniel M, Paul J, Franc, Jeff S, 509th, Luis E A, Christopher P, UKUAP, Will P, AlienBabble (come explore the enigma), Ryan Ha, Nikki N, Jenna, Summoning the Shift, Undead Gaucho, UFOJane, John G, Ryan Sp, Susan F, uapTO, Paul S A, Thomas W, Karen M Y, Dave Sc, Barry 2.0, 40Eridani, Montana, F, Bob P, UFOSatan, Scott M, UFOB, Katie F, Anthony R K, Brendon C, Straiph W, Britt, Nathan, Michael, Ben, Pillars of Creation, Vmotion, EclecticMethod, Witness Citizen UAP, Paul Bu, Corbell, J, Mark, Zac, Steven G, Christopher M, Aethereal, Dave B, Greg, Paco, Dennis, Gurrlly007, Galanvazquez, Mark T, James F, Mikael, Lisa, DisclosureTeam Liverpool, Steve N, RedBlueBlackSilver, Craftmeatl, Luis J,

Mitch, Stephen B, Vern, Stina, Jake S, Tommy Z, VictoriaZ, Brandon F, Cynthia B, Chris Sp, MusicandTruth,

ABOUT THE AUTHOR

Adam Stephen Goldsack

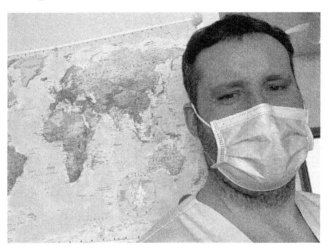

Adam is a UAP researcher, author and activist who writes for the organisation UAPMediaUK.

In his early academic career, Adam gained a Diploma in Health and Social Care, a Graduate Diploma in Psychology, a Bachelor of Science Degree in Psychology with Criminology and then finally a Master of Science Degree in Health Psychology. Using his qualifications, Adam worked professionally across the Tees Valley and North Yorkshire as a clinical assistant within neurological rehabilitation from early 2014, and in 2020/21 would go on to work within a COVID-19 ward during lockdown.

In his mid to late thirties, Adam retrained as an Occupational

Therapist and continued his passion of professional research whilst working closely with patients.

However, it wasn't until late 2017 that Adam took a real interest in writing about UAP technology and hypothetically intelligences. Initially, he started ghost/alias writing articles and blog posts under the pseudonym 'Andreas Freeman Stahl', mainly for the websites 'UAPInfo' and 'The Unidentified' which covered Unidentified Aerial Phenomena (UAP) and the associated technology.

Adam would later go on to become one of the first ever 'UAP Activists' and is credited with co-creating various social media campaigns (UFOTwitter, EndUAPSecrecy and Outreach Program) which all have engaged the American and British governments to declassify and release unclassified data relating to UAP technology under the organisation UAPMedia. It was in these years that Adam found his passion for writing both fiction and non-fiction. His areas of interest include historical UAP case reports, quantum consciousness, the psychology of an anomalous phenomenon and current disclosure initiatives. Adam also has written fictional science fiction and horror books which are released under the publisher 'Sekrecy Books'.

Adam lives in Middlesbrough with his wife and two young children.

Printed in Great Britain
by Amazon